A PERILOUS PLAYGROUND

Misadventures in Snowdonia
and the development of
the Mountain Rescue Service
1805 to the 1990s.

by

Bob Maslen-Jones

A Perilous Playground
Published in Wales by
BRIDGE BOOKS
61 Park Avenue
Wrexham
LL12 7AW

© 1998 Bob Maslen Jones
© 2004 Typesetting and design Bridge Books

Re-printed 2004

Cover illustration: *Cwm Glas Mawr*, © Carl Rogers.

CIP data for this book is available from the British Library

For

Anne

ISBN 1-872424-65-1

Printed and bound by
Cromwell Press
Trowbridge

Foreword

It is a pleasure to contribute this Foreword to *A Perilous Playground*. I wish the book had been available to temper my burning ambition to start climbing back in 1946. I was soloing up the Idwal Slabs in winter. My friends had the discretion to turn back but, not wishing to climb down, I pushed on up into the mist and snow. Not surprisingly I came down on the opposite side of the Glyders to *Pen-y-gwryd*. I had to trudge back via Capel Curig in the starlight to the youth hostel at Idwal where I was staying, just in time to intercept the warden as he was walking to the telephone kiosk to alert the Mountain Rescue Services.

In those days the British Mountaineering Council had only just been created and there were no outdoor pursuit centres such as Plas-y-Brenin, the National Mountain Centre, to teach one to climb safely and competently. One just had to start in one's own haphazard way, hoping to meet up with some kindly and more experienced soul who was prepared to proffer the end of a rope to tie on.

Fortunately, I survived, but mountain climbing is always risky, and falls by mountaineers are never foreseeable. It is a challenging vocation, and this anthology of misadventures involving climbers and walkers, which covers almost two centuries, is an interesting and absorbing narrative for everyone, even those who are not mountaineering-inclined, and although the incidents occurred in Snowdonia, the message is the same for other mountain regions in Britain and, indeed, world-wide.

As the story unfolds, the evolution of the Mountain Rescue service becomes interwoven with the many different types of incidents which are so vividly described. At the end of it all one is left with the compelling conviction that even those who have spent a lifetime mountain-climbing can fall prey to some misadventure, perhaps because of a momentary lapse in concentration, but equally through no fault of their own. Minimising the risks in climbing is all about personal judgement and experience, not rules. Decision-making in the mountains is a complex balance of variables, and at times security must be sacrificed for speed. Because an accident has occurred, it does not mean that an individual is at fault. Risk is inherent in mountaineering; it cannot be eliminated, only reduced.

It is the purpose of this book to bring to everyone venturing on the mountains a better understanding of the dangers always present not only in rock climbing but equally in walking or scrambling on steep, rough ground, in order to reduce the risks involved. Bob Maslen-Jones is to be congratulated on producing this fascinating series of cautionary tales. I hope you will enjoy and learn from them so that your future excursions in the hills may be successful and wholly satisfying, and not be unfortunate to justify inclusion in future editions.

George Band, President, British Mountaineering Council

Acknowledgements

Many people have given me much help in writing this book, and I am greatly indebted to them all. In particular I wish to record the contribution made by the late Jack Baines who spent so much time and effort during the last two years of his life, when he was housebound and racked with the pain and suffering of arthritis, advising me on technical detail and checking historical facts; sadly he did not live to see the work finished, but without his enthusiasm and encouragement, perhaps *A Perilous Playground* might never have seen the light of day.

I also wish to express my great appreciation to Dr Tony Jones MBE for once again preparing all the map diagrams and for allowing me to research the records of the NWMRA and the OVMRO, and much more besides; Peter Hodgkiss and Margot Blyth for their helpful advice and editing the manuscript; John Ellis Roberts MBE for access to his records and for photographs; Harvey Lloyd (Warden of Pen-y-pass Youth Hostel); Mrs Jane Pullee (*Pen-y-gwryd Hotel*); Derek Mayes (Plas-y-Brenin); David Archer, Hugh Roberts and Barbara Jones (Snowdonia National Park); John A Jackson; Dr Ieuan Jones; Ken Jones; Clive Evan Evans; Peter Holloway (The National Trust); Dr Rees Pritchard; Clive Swombow (North Wales Police); Gwynedd Archives; Jesse James; Peter Howells; Dewi Pritchard Jones; Mick Randall; Ron James; Barbara James; the late Tony Bennett; Mrs Lewte; Has Oldham; Alastair Haveron; Neil and Maggie Adam; John Buchanan; Frank Card; Ken McCoy. If I have inadvertently failed to include any one, I can only ask their forgiveness.

An Explanation

For many centuries 'Snowdonia' has been understood to include Yr Wyddfa, (Snowdon, at 3,560 feet above sea level, the highest peak in the British Isles south of the Scottish Highlands), and those mountains immediately adjacent to it — the Glyderiau (commonly called 'the Glyders') and Carneddau (Carnedds) to the north, the Moelwynion (Moelwyns) to the south-east, and the Moel Hebog and Nantlle ridges to the west. In 1951, however, the Snowdonia National Park was established, and the designated area now includes 838 square miles of countryside within a diamond-shaped perimeter running clockwise from Conwy through Llanrwst to Bala, southwards to the east of the Aran Mountains and Cader Idris, then westwards to Aberdyfi. The western boundary of the Park follows the coast line northwards through Barmouth and Harlech on the western flank of the Rhinog Mountains, to Porthmadog. To complete the diamond, the perimeter skirts to the west of the Nantlle Hills as far as Llanberis, and round the western and northern flanks of the Carneddau to Conwy. The area measures roughly fifty miles from north to south and thirty-five miles from east to west, with a population of 25,761 in 1981, and is made up of blocks of high mountains and moorland, intersected by deep valleys. The mountains are for the most part rugged and, because of the narrowness of the dividing valleys, there can be an exaggerated impression of their height. With its variety of scenery and extensive range of habitats it has always been a special haven for botanists, geologists, historians and for those who come just for the pleasure and challenge of walking or climbing.

Abbreviations

ARCCK	Air Rescue Co-ordination Centre, Kinloss.
asl	above sea level.
BMC	British Mountaineering Council
CCJ	Climbers Club Journal
CCPR	Central Council for Physical Recreation
MIC	Mountain Instructors Certificate
MLC	Mountain Leadership Certificate
MLTB	Mountain Leadership Training Board
MR	Mountain Rescue
MRC	Mountain Rescue Committee (from 1993, Mountain Rescue Council)
MRT	Mountain Rescue Team
NWMRA	North Wales Mountain Rescue Association
OAC	Outdoor Activity Centre
OBS	Outward Bound School
OPC	Outdoor Pursuits Centre
OVMRO	Ogwen Valley Mountain Rescue Organisation
SAR	Search and Rescue
SARDA	Search and Rescue Dog Association
SMO	Station Medical Officer

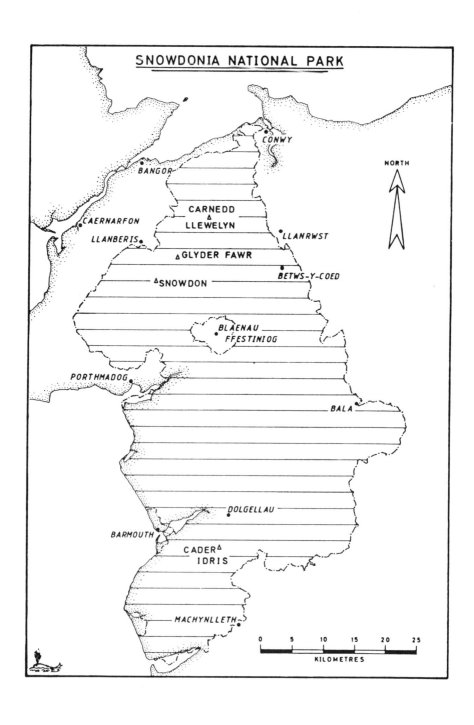

SNOWDONIA NATIONAL PARK

NORTH

CONWY

BANGOR

CARNEDD
△ LLEWELYN

CAERNARFON

LLANBERIS

LLANRWST

△GLYDER FAWR

△SNOWDON

BETWS-Y-COED

BLAENAU
FFESTINIOG

PORTHMADOG

BALA

DOLGELLAU

BARMOUTH

CADER△
IDRIS

MACHYNLLETH

0   5   10   15   20   25
KILOMETRES

Contents

Maps & Diagrams

Photographs

Introduction

When the story begins soon after the start of the 19th century, Snowdonia had long been regarded as a place to be visited in spite of poor communications, and there are records of ascents of Snowdon as far back as the 17th century. For generations before this, however, hill farmers must have toiled in the mountains of Snowdonia and passed on, father to son, the mountaineering skills acquired whilst shepherding flocks high on the wild and inhospitable hills. Early visitors who came to walk in the mountains of Snowdonia knew little about the vagaries and uncertainties of the weather and other dangers to be faced. Many were professional men who worked indoors, but climbed mountains to pursue their various interests, such as the botanist who looked for rare plants hidden in remote crevices in the crags, or the geologist who studied rock formations or the effects of the Ice Age. Others came to make maps, to study weather patterns, or to seek evidence about the existence of prehistoric inhabitants.

The first written record of a mountain guide being hired in Snowdonia dates back to 1639 when a local well-known botanist — Thomas Gwynne MP, the squire of Glynllifon — and Thomas Johnson, [1] an apothecary and keen botanist from London, hired a guide to escort them on Snowdon. He was not a professional guide, but a hill-farmer's son who knew his way around the mountains in all weathers. Although to begin with guiding was only a part-time occupation, we shall see that by the 19th century mountain-guiding had become a fairly substantial source of income for the local inhabitants.

1. Thomas Johnson, *The Itinerary of a Botanist* (1908) — Translation from Johnson's original Latin version dated 1641.

On their return home, visitors would sometimes write accounts of their adventures which were read by a new breed of tourist which, inspired by the often glowing descriptions of the mountain scene, steadily grew. In the late 19th century the popularity of mountaineering in Britain increased, especially amongst the wealthier members of society. Snowdon became a magnet, attracting people from far and wide and, as the communication network was improved and developed, the tourist industry began to play an important part in the local economy.

It is impossible to say exactly when ascending the hills in Snowdonia started to become popular. It was a progressive process but it is known that enthusiasts climbed to the summit of Snowdon to see the sun-rise as far back as the 17th century. Today, people still make the effort and, weather permitting, some youngsters observe the local custom of walking to the summit in the early autumn to welcome the Harvest Moon, or on 31 December to see in the New Year. In recent years, it has become common for parties to climb to the summit of Snowdon to raise money for charitable causes, and the path from Llanberis to the summit is now the venue for an annual International Fell Race which attracts some 600 runners from many different countries. The record winning time from Llanberis to the summit and back is 1 hour 2 minutes 29 seconds!

1: Little Boy Lost

From earliest times there has been a heavy penalty for those not respecting the dangers of Britain's high mountains. The suddenness with which a fine day can give rise to a raging storm is well enough known by mountaineers, but unfortunately the mountains do not discriminate between people who understand the dangers and those who do not.

The first recorded death on Snowdon occurred in 1805, when today's network of roads did not exist. Main carriageways were only just being developed, and many of the present-day minor roads linking them existed only as footpaths. Communication between villages was usually by very rough tracks over the mountains. The lower slopes were covered with forests of mainly sisal oak, most of which would disappear at the hands of charcoal burners by the end of the century. Until hill-walking for pleasure became popular, the mountains were very lonely places.

The story of seven-year-old John Closs is chronicled in the history of the *Pen-y-Gwryd Hotel*, one of today's landmarks for everyone who comes to walk or climb in Snowdonia. The inn was founded at the start of the 19th century by John Roberts from Pen-y-bryn, Llanberis, to coincide with the opening of the road from Capel Curig over the Llanberis Pass to the slate-mining village of Llanberis. Nothing more than a rough cart track at that time, it was several years before the road was up-graded to a turnpike road able to take stage coaches. John Roberts had married a sister of the little boy John, and he recorded the story in his diary.

The lad had been sent from his home in Llanberis to live with his maternal uncle near Betws Garmon in the next valley — Nant-y-betws. Clearly he was still much loved by his parents and his being 'farmed out' may well indicate the difficulties of raising a large family in those distant days. His mother often walked from Llanberis to Nant-y-betws to spend time with her son, and on one occasion John pleaded with her to let him go back home. She refused, said a tearful good-bye to her son, and set off in the gathering autumnal gloom. After she had gone, John turned his pleadings to his uncle, but like John's mother he would not be persuaded. The boy was not to be deterred, however, and soon afterwards he slipped away unnoticed and hastened after his mother.

John knew the area well and was fit and sturdy for his age. He probably expected to overtake his mother, but some time after he set off there was a prolonged heavy snow storm. In spite of this his mother eventually arrived safely at her home in Llanberis, completely unaware that her son had been following her. Meantime John had lost his way in the blizzard as the track quickly disappeared under the snow and he wandered about until, exhausted and demoralised, he lay down to sleep. But the cold and his exhaustion quickly developed into what today would be called hypothermia, and he died as he slept.

As soon as John's uncle found that his nephew was missing, he guessed that in spite of his refusal to let him go after his mother, that is exactly what he had done. There was nothing to be done until daylight, and he could only hope that John had caught up with his mother, and that they had reached Llanberis safely. When his uncle walked over to Llanberis next morning and found that John had not arrived, all he could do was to ask local shepherds to help him to look for the lad. It was an extensive area to search with so few men, and the slopes leading up to Moel Eilió are steep. It is not surprising, therefore, that it took them a week to find John's body, lying by a rock where he had lain down to rest. Subsequently a local shepherd, who had been out on the mountain when the blizzard struck, confessed that he had heard the little boy crying but, not believing that there could be anyone out on the hill at that time, he thought it must be the voice of a fairy, and in blind panic he fled off the mountain.

John's body was taken back to his home in Llanberis, and he was buried in the old churchyard in Nant Peris.

2: Mountain Industries and Tourism

In the 19th century, tourism developed in parallel with local industries such as slate quarrying and mineral mining. Many of these mines were relatively low in the valley, but some, such as the copper mine between Glaslyn and the Bwlch Glas ridge, are of particular interest since they were high on the mountain. It is known that the mine was working in 1810, and probably even earlier: also that the nearest carriage-road to the mine was the Caernarfon to Beddgelert road in the valley to the west of Snowdon. The route over the Llanberis Pass was still only a rough track, and it is interesting to note that the copper ore from the mine workings above Glaslyn had to be carried on the miners' backs up the zigzags to the Bwlch Glas ridge — an ascent of over 600 feet. It goes without saying that those miners were a very tough breed of men. On the ridge the ore was loaded on to wooden sledges which were then dragged by ponies down the Snowdon Ranger path to the roadside by Llyn Cwellyn. [1]

The development of the Llanberis Pass road from Capel Curig to Llanberis began early in the 1800s, but it was not until 1832 that it was opened as a trunk road and the copper ore was then brought down to Pen-y-pass by mule-train. Thence it was taken in horse-drawn carts to Llanberis and onwards to the quayside in Caernarfon from where it was shipped to other ports in Britain, or abroad.

There was a second copper mine on the other side of Bwlch Glas and some way down the steep slopes of Cwm Du'r Arddu. It was called the Clogwyn Goch mine and was on the exposed north-west face of the mountain. An entry in the Llanberis Parish Death Register, dated 30 December 1813, refers to Thomas Williams of Llanberis who was a titled worker in this mine. It states, 'He died by an accident having slipped down the rock near to the copper work at Clogwyn Goch as he was crossing some ice to go to his work'.

This and a few other entries in the parish Burial Register are the only mentions of fatal accidents at work in the mountains. They seem not to have been considered news-worthy enough for a mention in the local newspaper, though by the nature of the work in the various mines and quarries, many workers must have been killed or suffered serious injuries. Yet accidents involving tourists to Snowdonia were given the full media treatment, and were nearly always titled with some dramatic heading such as 'Awful Event' or 'Dreadful Tragedy'.

The report of Thomas William's death is of special interest in that it is the first written record indicating the hazardous nature of the slopes above Cwm Du'r Arddu in winter. The next reports of icing up in this area which have come to light refer to the mid-19th century at the time of the *Royal Charter* storm, (see Chapter 4), and after the Snowdon Mountain Railway line had been cut into the hillside across the top of the cliffs. Midway along Clogwyn Coch there is a stretch of the track which is only just wide enough to accommodate the train. Here every year, almost without exception, snow and ice builds up against the back wall of the cutting to form a convex slope which has caused unsuspecting walkers to slip and fall, sometimes with disastrous results, some 700 feet down

1. Cwellyn was spelt Quellyn at this time.

into Cwm Du'r Arddu. This place is often referred to as 'The Killer Convex'.

During the 19th century, large prestigious hotels were opened throughout Snowdonia, the main centres being Betws-y-coed, Capel Curig (including the *Pen-y-gwryd*), Llanberis, Beddgelert and Dolgellau, and they all offered the services of professional guides. As the turnpike roads were improved and developed, so travellers found it much easier and quicker to reach these centres. Tourism flourished, but as the number of people seeking their recreation in the mountains increased, so did the number of accidents, and even the guides themselves were not immune.

During the first half of the 19th century, there are only two recorded incidents involving visitors, and the first of these merited very few lines in the local paper. It reported that in the autumn of 1832 a visitor called Philip Homer had been reported missing overnight on Moel Siabod, that huge almost featureless whale-back mountain dominating Capel Curig to the north-east. A search party had been organised by the well-known guide, Robin Hughes from Capel Curig, and Homer's body was found on the mountain where he had died of exhaustion. It is one of the first mentions of an organised search in Snowdonia and Philip Homer was buried in the churchyard in Capel Curig.

In that same year of 1832 a young lad from Ruthin called William Williams moved to Llanberis where he became the boot-boy at the *Royal Victoria Hotel* — hence his nick-name 'Will Boots'. He was already interested in collecting stones and insects and spent much of his spare time looking for specimens in the mountains. He soon added botany to his interests and found his way about the more inaccessible slopes and crags where the rare plants could be found. Then he took to guiding to implement his meagre wages as a boot-boy, and his fame spread quickly. Before long he had become a much respected and sought-after guide, a career which he pursued for almost 30 years until he slipped and fell to his death whilst colllecting rare plants high on the east face of Snowdon. Before the century reached the halfway mark, a remarkable event occurred on Snowdon and in the drama which was to unfold 'Will Boots' played one of the leading roles.

3: Llanberis Awful Event

In 1846 a bizarre and tragic incident occurred on Snowdon which profoundly shook the community in and around Llanberis, who feared that it might do untold harm to their newly established prosperity. By then the whole of Snowdonia was fast developing into an important tourist area, with hundreds of people coming every year to fill their lungs with clean mountain air. It was thought very health-giving and it became as fashionable to visit the hills of north Wales as to go to one of the spas flourishing at that time in many parts of Britain. It was natural that some of the local people were quick to grasp the opportunities of the boom in tourism and make some money, often at the expense of gullible strangers, most of whom were wealthy beyond the dreams of the local mountain folk. To cater for their tastes, the hotels being built in Snowdonia were the last word in luxury.

It was against this backdrop that in September 1845, a 31-year-old curate from All Saints Church in Northampton, Reverend Henry Wellington Starr, made his first visit to Snowdon. He had been born in Wiltshire, the son of tradespeople in Trowbridge, and had obtained his BA degree at Magdalen College, Oxford in 1842. There is no record of him previously having had any leanings towards mountaineering, but he walked to the summit of Snowdon for his own satisfaction. That is precisely what he achieved, for he was on the summit as dawn broke on 11 September, and he was greatly affected by the sight of the blood-red sun creeping up over the distant skyline. He clearly discerned the hand of his Creator in what he saw, and it was a profound spiritual experience for him. Although he would probably not have achieved fame as a poet, he expressed his feelings in the following short verse:

> When morning broke, and day
> Once more assumed his brilliant sway,
> I saw - but words can never tell —
> That fire-line on the horizon creeping,
> At once upon my knees I fell,
> And from my very joy fell weeping.

After he returned to his parish in Northampton, Henry Starr's health deteriorated, and by mid-summer he had been suffering for several months from a nervous disorder. According to his sister Emily, with whom Henry had a very close relationship, he was persuaded by his doctor to take a holiday where he could relax and get plenty of fresh air into his lungs. At the beginning of September 1846 he returned to Snowdonia and it is perhaps appropriate to mention here the theme of the sermon he preached in Brampton Church, Northampton on Sunday 6 September before he left for his holiday. 'Our bones', said the psalmist, 'are scattered at the grave`s mouth' and, as David said to Jonathan, 'There is but a step between me and death'. Henry Wellington Starr could have had little realisation of how much truth there would prove to be in those words.

On arrival in north Wales he travelled on to Holyhead before returning to Bangor and he wrote to Emily from both places. He spent the night of Monday 14 September in Caernarfon, moving on to Llanberis the next day where he spent the night in the *Dolbadarn Hotel*. On the morning of Wednesday 16 September he walked over from Llanberis to Llyn Cwellyn and was seen by Robert Owen, mountain guide and mine host at the *Snowdon Guide Inn*,[1] situated on the north-eastern side of, and half-way along, Llyn Cwellyn. According to Owen, Henry Starr was sitting with his pipe in his mouth on the wall of the bridge over the stream from the watershed to the east. He asked Robert Owen to show him the way to the summit of Snowdon, but Owen advised him not to attempt to go up as 'the mist was on the mountain'. Henry Starr, however, said that he intended to go and Owen then pointed out the track leading from the *Snowdon Guide Inn* to Bwlch Cwm Brwynog. He was last seen by two farm workers on the flat ground between Llyn Ffynnon-y-gwas, just below the bwlch, and the start of the steep climb up to the mist-covered higher slopes.

Emily Starr did not receive any more letters from her brother, and after two weeks she became convinced that he was ill or that something sinister had happened to him. During this time both Emily and her mother had written several letters to Henry, and having received no reply they decided to journey to North Wales to look for him. They arrived in Caernarfon on the last day of September and immediately set about trying to get information about his movements. Eventually Emily got confirmation that her brother had spent the night of 14 September in Pool Street which he had left early the following morning saying that he was going to Llanberis: he had left a travelling bag and one of his gloves in his room. At the Post Office in Caernarfon, she found the letters she and her mother had written to Henry lying unclaimed in poste

---

1. Now the Snowdon Ranger Youth Hostel.

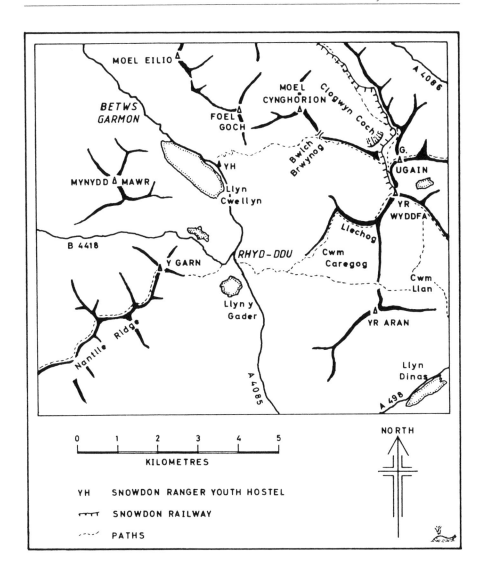

MOEL EILIO

BETWS
GARMON

MOEL
CYNGHORION

Clogwyn Coch

A 4086

FOEL
GOCH

G.

UGAIN

Bwlch
Brwynog

MYNYDD MAWR

YH

Llyn
Cwellyn

YR
WYDDFA

Llechog

B 4418

RHYD-DDU

Cwm
Caregog

Cwm
Llan

Y GARN

Llyn y
Gader

YR ARAN

Nantlle Ridge

Llyn
Dinas

A 4085

A 498

0   1   2   3   4   5

KILOMETRES

NORTH

YH   SNOWDON RANGER YOUTH HOSTEL

SNOWDON RAILWAY

PATHS

Llyn Cwellyn. The Snowdon Ranger is on the extreme right.

restante. Emily's account of what happened during the next two weeks is very interesting, and one can imagine how difficult it must have been for her, unable to speak or understand Welsh. She mentions that she was greatly helped by John William Rowlands of Plastirion, Llanrug, a JP and a much respected figure in the community, and his untiring perseverance in trying to find Henry Starr was given high praise in the reports in the local paper. He acted as interpreter between Emily and the local people, but in spite of his help and the support of one or two others, she was met largely by a wall of silence and mystery. John Rowlands was instrumental in persuading the magistrates to post 'missing person' bills round the area offering a reward of 50 pounds for information leading to the discovery of the Rev Henry Starr. This sum had been put up by *The Caernarvon and Denbigh Herald*, and was a small fortune in those days, but the offer was to no avail. He also organised a massive search by upwards of 900 men, aided by the 'well-trained pack of hounds' belonging to H R Williams Esq of Penrhos. The search continued for several days covering the mountain tops, the slopes and gorges, cliffs and rivers, of the Snowdon massif and the Glyders. Snow came early that year, the mountains were soon covered by a white blanket, and the search was eventually called off. At the time, this must have been the biggest mountain search ever organised, but one must remember that most of the 900 people were not mountaineers and probably went along for the reward rather than from a sense of duty. The use of foxhounds is an interesting point though one wonders how a hound would have indicated its 'find' to the handler as today's search and rescue dogs are trained to do, and whether it would have resisted its natural instinct to eat its quarry. Henry Starr seemed to have disappeared from the surface of the earth, and now suspicions and doubts as to his fate caused a great stir in the area.

When closely questioned about his meeting with Henry Starr and what had subsequently happened, Robert Owen gave two different stories. According to his first account, Starr had set off alone along the track from the inn to the summit and followed it as directed to Bwlch Cwm Brwynog; then, as the path rose steeply, he disappeared into the mist. After a couple of hours he returned to the *Snowdon Guide Inn* and then set off along the road towards Beddgelert. For some reason, after a few days Robert Owen changed his story and in his second account he denied that he had seen Henry Starr returning. He said that the last time he had seen him was when he disappeared into the mist covering the slopes of Snowdon, and he then was carrying a red knapsack on his back.

John Hughes, a quarryman from Llanberis who worked occasionally as a guide, told a different story. He claimed that he had met Henry Starr walking along one of the paths on the Glyders above Cwm Ffynnon late on the evening of 16 September, and had warned him not to go climbing the mountains at night. It was then nearly dark, but Starr ignored his advice and continued on his way. Hughes had noticed that he was wearing only one glove, and that he was wearing a red scarf. On 10 October *The Carnarvon and Denbigh Herald* published an account under the heading 'Llanberis Awful Event', concluding that the young man must have lost his way on the mountain and died. The paper made much of the various theories about Henry Starr's disappearance, including rumours that he had been the victim of foul play, and declared that they suspected very strongly that some of the local people knew more than they were prepared to divulge. Emily Starr had come to the same conclusion.

After six weeks Emily, frustrated and demoralised and no nearer to solving the mystery, gave up her quest and returned to her home in Leamington Spa. The weeks dragged on through the winter of 1846/47 and there was still no sign of Henry Starr's body, or information to explain what had happened to him. The winter was proving to be a very hard one, with the whole area being covered for several months under a deep layer of snow. Nothing more could be done until the snow had thawed, when arrangements could be made to start searching for Henry's body even though there was no evidence to indicate whether it might be on Snowdon, or on the Glyders, or indeed anywhere else.

At the beginning of June 1847 the remains of Henry Wellington Starr were found at the end of Cwm Brwynog at the foot of the precipice of Moel Cynghorion. The snow had then long since melted, and there a smallholder, by name of William Hughes, who was also huntsman to H R Williams of Penrhos, was out with his dog when it found a red scarf and a piece of linen, and scattered around the area some bones and items of personal equipment. Hughes took the scarf and the bit of cloth to the *Dolbadarn Inn*, and Mrs Evans at once identified the scarf as having belonged to Mr Starr. It then came to light that a month earlier John Edwards, a tenant farmer in the valley below where the scarf was found, had discovered Starr's knapsack. The next day everything was collected together under the supervision of John Rowlands, JP, and others, including Mr George, the governor of the county gaol in Caernarfon, and Mr Rees, proprietor and editor of *The Carnarvon and Denbigh Herald*.

On their way to the scene of the discovery, they met Will Boots (William Williams), returning from the mountain, and he showed them pieces of linen he had collected, which were probably the upper part of a shirt. He turned and went back up the mountain with Mr Rowland's party, and they started to search the cliff down which it now seemed certain that Henry Starr had fallen, as they were able to pick up various items of Starr's personal possessions. At the bottom of the first precipice, Mr George and Will Boots left the rest of the party, who had decided to climb round to the top of the cliff, while the two of them descended to the valley below. As they went down, Mr George elicited from Williams that only a short time before he met the party that morning, he had picked up a small silver watch close to the spot where the 'mangled remains' had been found. The glass was broken and the watch had stopped at half-past six — the time at which Robert Owen had last seen Starr before he disappeared into the mist. Mr George apparently thought little of this but put the watch in his pocket to be used as evidence at the inquest. A few days later Williams found Starr's missing pencil case and a pocket handkerchief embroidered with the initials 'HWS'.

It should be noted that Williams, who at the time of Starr's disappearance had a secure job in the quarry, suddenly left Llanberis and went to work in Chester, only returning to Llanberis some nine months later, shortly before the body was found.

A detailed account of the finding of the 'mangled remains of the unfortunate tourist' and his personal possessions appeared in *The Carnarvon and Denbigh Herald* on 5 June 1847 under the heading 'Discovery of the Remains of the Rev H W Starr on Snowdon'. The paper quickly sold out, and the article was reprinted on 12 June 1847.

Emily Starr was informed that her brother's remains had been found, and she returned post-haste to Llanberis. She soon realised that every effort was being

Moel Cynghorion. Bwlch Brwynog is in the foreground.

made to find a simple and plausible explanation for what had happened to Henry, and in the account which she wrote later about the whole affair entitled 'The Remains of Henry Wellington Starr' (a copy of which is held by the National Library of Wales) she emphasises dissatisfaction with the evidence being presented and in particular with the stance taken by *The Carnarvon and Denbigh Herald* in the report of 5 and 12 of June. The newspaper claimed that the guide John Hughes had been lying when he said he had seen Starr on the Glyder mountain, and that the evidence of Robert Owen, who claimed that Starr had been on his way to Bwlch Brwynog near where his remains had been found should be accepted. 'We are fully convinced,' the paper stated, 'that every person who may examine the mountain as we have, will come to the conclusion that Mr Starr's death must have been purely accidental. After he passed the farm servants on the boggy ground before he reached Llyn Ffynnon-y-gwas, he must have turned to the left, to reach the path leading along Bwlch Brwynog to ascend the mountain; but not finding it, owing to the fog which at that time enveloped the whole mountain, he continued his upward course to the left, until he reached the table land of Moel Cynghorion. Here, probably, he became bewildered, and, in the density of the fog, fell over the frightful precipice amidst the rocks, on the side of which he died.' The newspaper deliberately set out to dispel all the rumours which had been circulating ever since Henry Starr disappeared about the possibility that he had been murdered, and the report finished with the statement, 'It is a melancholy satisfaction to know that the suspicion hinted against our mountain peasantry had no foundation.' This before the inquest was opened! There was one particular incident which Emily Starr found very disturbing, and about which there was very little mention either in the newspaper report or at the inquest held a few days later — the arrival of the guide William Williams at the spot where the body was found, and his finding of Henry Starr's watch.

Emily was determined to get to the root of the matter, but the only way of doing this was to prove that the facts being presented were incorrect. According to one expert witness the watch which Williams found was in perfect working condition with no corrosion on it whatsoever; after being wound up it kept accurate time. Emily Starr insisted on having a medical opinion on the `remains' and according to that opinion, all the bones, including the skull, ribs, arms and legs were intact with no fractures. This was extraordinary when we remember that Henry Starr was reported to have fallen at least 60 feet onto sharp rocks down the extremely steep slopes of Moel Cynghorion. A third unexplained fact was that neither Henry Starr's purse nor his money were found although handkerchiefs and other small effects were still in his pockets. At the inquest at Caernarfon Court an attempt was made to raise some of the most obvious questions, but this was ignored as were some of the witnesses themselves. For example neither of the two guides who claimed to have seen Starr during his last hours, Robert Owen and John Hughes, were even called to give evidence.

Emily herself was given no chance to present her evidence about the watch and absence of bone fractures, and in fact the only person to be questioned was William Williams. He was called to account and reprimanded by the coroner for not admitting having found Starr's watch until some hours after he and Mr George had been on the mountain searching together. He failed to explain why he had returned from Chester, nor why he happened to be at the site at the lower end of the valley of Cwm Brwynog when John Rowlands and his party arrived there. Furthermore nobody asked him why he had disappeared to Chester so suddenly nine months earlier, although he had — by coincidence — been asked by a Mr Johnstone of the *Royal Victoria Hotel* to help him to move his goods from Llanberis to Chester.

As far as William Williams' reprimand by the coroner went, he was told that he had conducted himself in a way that would create a suspicion on his integrity and that he would be mistrusted because of his actions. It became clear that because the hotels now being developed were so dependent on the tourist industry, people were determined that nothing should be done to harm that industry by giving the area and community a bad name: the coroner's judgement was final, and in his opinion at some time between 15 and 16 September 1846, Henry Wellington Starr had died as a result of an accident, and he declared that no other person had been involved in his death. Although it was impossible to say exactly what had happened, he thought it very likely that he had fallen off the mountain in the mist and darkness. When Emily expressed her dismay at the coroner's decision, he told her that he congratulated himself, and his country, that the stigma of a tourist meeting his death by foul means had been completely removed. He concluded 'It is my conviction that so foul a deed as deliberate murder has not been committed and the fact is that whatever faults the peasantry of this Principality may be guilty of, they shrink with horror from the shedding of human blood'.

The jury took their cue from the coroner's summing up and after only a few minutes' consultation they returned the verdict that the Rev H W Starr had 'died on the mountain without any hurt or injury having been done to, or committed upon, him by any person or persons whatsoever'. They added that they were unable to say precisely how he had died, but inclined to the view that his death was caused by his accidentally falling over a precipice during the hours of darkness.

Gravestone of William Williams (Will Boots).

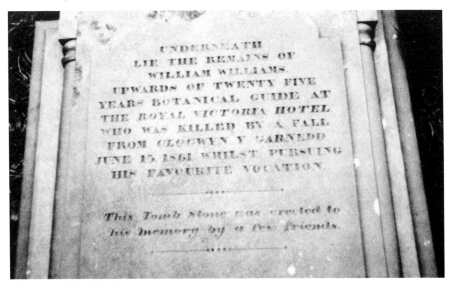

The remains of Henry Wellington Starr were buried by the Rev William Wales from Northampton in the peaceful little graveyard in Nant Peris. A slab of local slate covers the grave which is by the side of the pathway close to the ancient church of St Peris. It is inscribed:

> *Sacred*
> *to the memory*
> *of the*
> *Reverend Henry Wellington Starr B. A.*
> *Curate of All Saints, Northampton*
> *who perished on Snowdon*
> *while on a tour through North Wales*
> *September 15 1846*
> *aged 32 years.*
> *and whose remains, discovered June 1*
> *1847, were interred beneath this stone*
> *June 7 1847*

The final paragraph of *The Carnarvon and Denbigh Herald* report stated that after the inquest the Rev William Wales, accompanied by a Mr Ellis junior, walked up to the spot where Starr's remains had been found. There they had found his purse, containing twenty four shillings in silver and two pence in copper, and, the report stated, if Mr Starr had other money about him the probability is that it still remains among the gravel and earth. The report concluded that 'this was further corroborative evidence of Mr Starr's death having been the effect of pure accident'. It would seem, however, that in their obsessive determination to clear the community, the possibility that someone who realised that his guilt was becoming near to being found out, and had planted the purse and its contents at the place after the area had been systematically and minutely searched by many people over several days, was either overlooked or, like Emily Starr's evidence, not admitted.

That should have been the end of the matter but controversy about it continued for many decades afterwards. There had been great excitement and interest in Northampton, and it is worth mentioning an opinion on the incident by a well-known mountaineer from that town, one J L Cherry, who was only 14 years old at the time of Henry Starr's death. Later on he got to know the Llanberis area and its people well, making his first ascent of Snowdon in 1856, some ten years after the 'Awful Event' which was still a talking point in Llanberis.

In 1909, Cherry wrote a biographical sketch of Henry Starr and was interviewed about it for the local Northampton paper. He was asked if he could say anything about the death of Starr, and replied, 'I can tell you a great deal. The painful sensation caused by the death on Snowdon of the Reverend Henry Wellington Starr in September 1846 is quite fresh in my memory'. And he told the story much as it is set out above. However, he came to a different conclusion about the circumstances of the accident to that set out by Emily Starr. He agreed completely with the finding of the jury and the words of the coroner that, 'the fatality was a mystery and that there could be no reasonable doubt that death was purely the result of an accident'.

As we have seen, Emily Starr was not satisfied on that point and had remarked, 'that the Welsh should be jealous of the honour of their country and greatly attached to their mountainous Principality is both natural and just, and it must be evident to all who read the account of the inquest that the chief endeavour was to do away with any stigma attaching to their character from the mysterious disappearance of a traveller amongst them. If violence or crime has been committed, God will in His own good time and way reveal and avenge it, and in this perfect trust they (his friends) resign the future to His disposal'. Cherry continued, 'Sixty three years have passed since the holding of the inquest, and in that long interval nothing whatever has transpired to justify Miss Starr's rather ungenerous suspicion. The *Caernarvon and Denbigh Herald* reported that on the Sunday following Henry Starr's disappearance, 900 quarrymen and miners had spread themselves over the mountain in search of the missing gentleman.... Nothing could exceed the anxiety which from the first has been shown throughout the neighbourhood in endeavouring to unravel the dreadful mystery, while all, of all classes, whether rich or poor, have shown the deepest and tenderest sympathy in the distress of the bereaved mother and sister of the deceased'. Cherry added that he was at Llanberis in 1874 when a party of these kind-hearted stalwart fellows searched for a Scarborough schoolmaster whose dead body they found eventually on Crib Goch. [1]

1. I am deeply indebted to Ken Jones of Llanberis for his help in researching this story, and his work in translating relevant information from the Welsh. Also to Clive Evan Evans of Rushden, Northamptonshire, for allowing me to include much of his research into the J L Cherry story.

4: The Pattern Develops

The first recorded traverse of the Crib Goch arête, a narrow ridge on the Snowdon Horseshoe route, [1] was safely made in 1847 by C A O Baumgartner, an experienced Alpinist, who came to Britain to seek out and climb the most exposed and difficult crags and ridges. [2]

On 9 July 1853 an incident occurred on Snowdon in which an unidentified man from Birmingham fell and was severely injured. This was the first recorded mountaineering accident in Snowdonia since the demise of the Rev Henry Wellington Starr almost seven years previously. The report stated only the barest facts: 'The said gentleman from Birmingham, while descending Snowdon, missed his footing and fell almost three hundred feet down 'a steep declivity' (sic) on the side of the mountain, thereby sustaining such severe injuries as, we understand, have placed his life in danger. It appears that he, and others who were with him, guided by a boy, had, in order to shorten the distance, incautiously wandered from the beaten path, and were running at the time'. The writer added a rider to the report that, 'The path leading from the *Victoria Hotel* to the highest peak offers a perfectly safe, and the situation considered, even an easy means of ascent'. Further research found no further mention about the ultimate fate of the injured man. It is interesting that the party should have engaged a young boy to guide them when there were so many grown men in the area anxious to make their living as mountain guides.

Throughout the rest of the 19th century, and well into the 20th, recorded incidents in the mountains of Snowdonia are to be found at fairly regular intervals. Most of the reports of fatal accidents appear in either local newspapers or in the Coroner's inquest records. Other incidents of interest to fellow mountaineers were described in various visitors' books such as the 'locked book' at *Pen-y-gwryd Hotel*, usually by members of the party involved. [3]

The next recorded incident happened six years later, on 14 August 1859, when

1. see pages 94-5.

2. C.A.O Baumgartner was born in Geneva in 1825. He died in 1910.

3.This is the original hotel visitors' book. Arthur Lockwood applied the lock to prevent certain individuals tearing out pages containing entries by famous people.

Crib Goch (R–L): Bwlch Moch, Pinnacles, the Ridge.

George Henry Frodsham, a clerk from a merchant's shipping office in Liverpool, said to be 'a young man of very fine physique', slipped and fell to his death. The full story of the accident was told to the coroner by Francis Alfred Nicholson, a member of the ill-fated party:

> I and the deceased, with four others, viz Thomas Clayhill, James Snape, Alfred Gardner and James Goodier, left Chester on Saturday evening with the intention of visiting Llanberis and climbing Snowdon before sunrise on Sunday. We reached Llanberis about midnight and finding the hotel closed, decided to make our ascent at once. We started all together. It came on to rain before we had gone more than 100 yards and we sat down under some trees on the roadside and took our supper of cold meat which we had with us. We gathered a few sticks and ferns and made a fire, and there we remained for about an hour until the rain was over.

As it was getting much brighter, we thought we might safely proceed and we started again. Clayhill, Gardner and Goodier were soon in advance again, Frodsham for a short time going with Snape and myself, but he very soon rejoined the other three. Snape and I … presently came to a part where the road branched off in two directions, one to the left which leads to the top of Snowdon, and one to the right which leads to a copper mine called Clogwyn Coch mine. We passed the junction of the road without observing the other four and proceeded a short distance on the right-hand branch. It struck me that we were on the wrong track for I found it gradually sloping downward. Before we had gone much farther I caught sight of a house and became convinced that we were on the road to the mines. We struck across to the right path saying to each other as we went up that the others would have a good laugh at us for having mistaken the road. The part of the ascent between the two roads was very steep and we stopped for a moment to rest. We shouted to raise an echo from the cliff and to our surprise our shout was answered from below. We shouted again and threw up a light, it being rather dark. We waited for a reply but heard none and a few minutes later three of our companions, Gardner, Clayhill and Goodier, came up the very way we had come, Gardner and Clayhill being two or three hundred yards in advance of Goodier. Goodier shouted for us to wait for him and I did so. When he came up very much winded I asked him where Frodsham was and he said he had gone up the path leading up that part of the mountain which is just behind the mine. Goodier told me he had gone some way towards the path but thought he was going wrong and therefore stopped. He called Frodsham back, but he, Frodsham, answered, 'No, I am on the path', and went up very fast, even though he must have been encumbered by his umbrella and bag. Goodier shouted once more, but the reply came, 'No, I am on top'. We, Snape, Gardner, Clayhill and Goodier, then proceeded to the top of Snowdon expecting to see Frodsham there before us but to our surprise he was not there nor had he been there. We waited about three quarters of an hour and as I felt uneasy, I went down to look for him with a guide from the top. We made a diligent search in the direction he was last seen without finding him. From that time, 4pm on Sunday morning, I never discontinued my search until last night, Monday, about nine o'clock when, having walked about 60 miles in and about Snowdon and travelled to Bangor and Caernarfon to make enquiries, I came back again to this place. On my return yesterday I sought for and obtained the most ready assistance of Mr Ellis, the agent of the quarry, who despatched a number of men to search the neighbourhood and I accompanied them as far as the lake.

One of the quarrymen in the search party was William Owen who stated, 'I was directed to go in search of the deceased. I found him quite dead, lying face downwards at the foot of the precipice at a spot called Clogwyn Coch. He was dressed but his cap was missing and it was found 300 feet higher up, as were his bag and umbrella.'

Frodsham's body, it was stated, had been brought down to Llanberis where Mr W R Williams, surgeon, examined it. At the inquest he stated that he had found two skull fractures which in his opinion would have caused instantaneous death.

The coroner summed up by stating that Frodsham had taken the wrong path and had mistakenly tried to scale the cliffs of Clogwyn Du'r Arddu. Then the jury, all local men, brought in a verdict of accidental death. They added 'a strong recommendation to all tourists not to attempt the ascent of Snowdon without a guide on account of the mists in which they may suddenly become enveloped and the danger of the locality.' Frodsham's body was interred in the old graveyard in Nant Peris where his headstone may still be seen.

Only ten weeks after the death of George Frodsham, an inquest was held in October 1859 into the death of R Rogers Cox from Derbyshire. Cox had walked from Caernarfon to Llanberis on Sunday morning, 23 October, arriving at the *RoyalVictoria Hotel* at 11am. There he rested for half an hour before engaging a guide to take him to the summit of Snowdon, descend to the Capel Curig - Beddgelert road in Nant Gwynant and then walk along this road to Beddgelert. The two men set off for the summit of Snowdon but before they reached the top, Cox complained of severe pain in his back and stopped to rest. The guide urged him to continue in view of the deteriorating weather, which had turned extremely cold, and because he doubted that they would be able to reach the road to Beddgelert before nightfall.

The severe weather presaged the onset of probably the most violent storm then recorded in Britain. Within 48 hours of Cox's collapse, in North Wales the storm had reached its climax and the wind was blowing at full hurricane force 12 with gusts of well over 100 mph, and on Snowdon huge rocks were dislodged and sent hurtling down the mountain sides like pebbles. At sea off Moelfre, Anglesey, the clipper *The Royal Charter* of 2,719 tons, carrying gold bullion from the Australian goldfields and bound for Liverpool, was driven ashore and broken up with the loss of 444 lives, there being only 39 survivors. The storm became known as 'The Royal Charter Gale' and the story of the wreck and what happened to the gold is a fascinating one, and is told in *The Golden Wreck* by Alexander McKee.

Eventually they reached the summit and the guide broke open the door of one of the huts locked up for the winter. Cox was totally exhausted and lay down for a few minutes, and the guide had great difficulty in getting him to begin the descent. When they were within two miles of the road in Nant Gwynant, Cox was unable to go further. The guide placed him in a sitting position with his back resting against a boulder, went down to a farmhouse in the valley and returned with two men to help Cox off the hill. They found Cox lying on his back near the boulder where he had been sitting, apparently dead. They took him to the farmhouse as quickly as they could, where his feet were bathed in warm water, but there was no sign of life. Cox was then taken to Beddgelert where the doctor certified that he had been dead for some time. He could find no obvious cause of death and the inquest jury brought in a vague verdict which merely stated that Cox had died descending Snowdon, apparently from exhaustion. Today that would be called hypothermia, and with present understanding of the condition, no doubt the coroner would have commented that if the guide had allowed him to stay in the hut, and had looked after him there, his untimely death might not have happened. But in those days little if anything was known about hypothermia, and it would be unfair to blame the guide for failing to recognise the seriousness of Cox's condition. One might reasonably say that Rogers Cox was the first victim of the Royal Charter Gale which claimed some 800 lives in the course of its devastating passage up the western seaboard of England and Wales.

5: 'A Gentleman Missing on Snowdon'

The following report appeared in the local Caernarfon newspaper on 22 August 1874:

> On Tuesday 11th inst, at 9.00 o'clock in the morning, Mr F R Wilton of the City of London School, left the *Glyn Peris Hotel* in Llanberis with the intention of ascending to the top of Snowdon and then going down via Capel Curig to Betws-y-coed. He has been traced to the top, but nothing has been heard of him since. There is evidence, however, to show that while on the summit, he fell into conversation with two gentlemen, believed to come from the neighbourhood of Manchester, who were making for Beddgelert and one of whom was taken ill on the mountainside and received attention at Rhyd-ddu from Mrs Fraser.
>
> Mr Wilton is 25 years of age and 5′ 9″ in height. He wore a dark coat and light trousers and had a white straw hat on. He was carrying an umbrella and a guide book. £5 reward has been offered by his friends for his recovery, and this has been

supplemented by the offer of a further £5 by a lady visitor to Llanberis, in case he is found alive. A vigorous search has been made and on Sunday the inhabitants of the village turned out in hundreds and spread themselves over the mountain in every direction.'

The *London Daily News* then picked up the story and on Saturday 29 August the paper carried the following report:

> The Missing Gentleman on Snowdon — Recovery of the Body. The body of F R Wilton who left the *Glyn Peris Hotel*, Llanberis, on Tuesday 11th inst, was found at half past one on Monday afternoon last, by an exploring party at a place known as Cwm Glas, a spot two hundred feet below the top of Crib-y-ddysgl and nearly opposite the stones on the Llanberis Pass known as Cromlech. The deceased gentleman, whose body was greatly decomposed, was lying on his back, with his straw hat shading his eyes. The spot where his body lay was very difficult of access; and it was the opinion of one of the guides that the deceased, on leaving the summit and intending to descend to Capel Curig, must have left the regular path and stumbled down a water rut which had the appearance of a path, and that he must have fallen and slipped down the side of the mountain for a distance of about 50 feet, his head coming into violent contact with the stone on which it was afterwards found to be resting. [1]

After the coroner's summing up, the inquest jury, who were all respectable men and whose foreman was a local quarry agent named Menzies, decided that Wilton had tumbled down the slope, a fact which had been brought out by Surgeon H Rees who had carried out the examination of the body. Rees referred to extensive bruising of the legs and back. There was a great deal of gravel between Wilton's coat and waistcoat, and also between his waistcoat and shirt, from which the surgeon assumed that he must have struggled hard to stop his slide down the mountain. There were no fractures or dislocations, but the bruises were so severe as to prevent Wilton moving. 'I think the deceased died from exposure. I think he could have cried out. He might have suffered internal injuries, or concussion, but there were no outward signs.' The jury brought in a verdict of 'accidental death due to the deceased taking the wrong track'.

In the same edition of the local paper carrying the first report, there appeared a lengthy article which had already been published in *The London Daily News*. It gives an interesting insight into how mountain accidents were viewed towards the end of the last century. If comparisons are to be made, a succinct conclusion would be that very little has changed. Today, 120 years on, mountaineers are still widely held to be irresponsible and somewhat eccentric by the general public.

---

1. The post mortem did not support this conjecture. The surgeon found no outward signs of concussion or other death-causing injuries.

Glaslyn, Clogwyn-y-garnedd and Yr Wyddfa. {SNP}

THE MISADVENTURE ON SNOWDON

There seems at first sight something incongruous as well as shaking in the idea of a traveller being lost in a crevasse on Snowdon. It is natural that the great mountains should claim their victims; at least, we have learned by the records of many years to recognise the fact that season after season they exact their tribute of human sacrifice as sternly as Haslone's sea monster. Victor Hugo, in one of his later poems, describes the Jungfrau as 'spitting an avalanche at the audacious invader of her seclusion'. Even the most frequently trodden of the Alpine ascents seem as if they could not be occupied without some annual tithe of life. But without the least desiring to disparage the properties of Snowdon, we must say that it does not look the sort of mountain on which one might expect to hear of lost explorers. To read of a traveller swallowed up in its gorges is at first a little like being told of a wreck in Virginia Water, or of a belated wayfarer starved to death on Hampstead Heath.... Yet it seems that the utmost alarm is felt with regard to the safety of a gentleman who more than a week ago set out to make the ascent of Snowdon, and has not since been heard of. The day it happened was cloudy and the paths were hard to distinguish although other tourists seem to have accomplished the ascent and descent without danger or, at all events, without harm. We have of late been taught to keep very distinct in our minds the facts of a strange disappearance and the necessity of a tragical explanation. The lost have so often been found in such a case, that the public now are by no means likely to rush to conclusion. Still, of course, it is but natural that relatives and friends of a tourist should feel greatly alarmed and should argue the very worst when they hear that he was seen more than a week before on the side or the summit of a Welsh mountain, and that since then no tidings of him have reached anyone in the neighbourhood where he disappeared. In truth, small mountains are not safe in proportion to their smallness. That must indeed be a poor elevation which does not contain clefts and gorges deep enough to make a corpse of an unwary wanderer.... In one sense the smaller mountains are perhaps even more dangerous than their gigantic brethren. No one, even though he be a member of the Alpine Club, attempts alone the really trying and dangerous steeps of Alpine climbing. But almost anybody feels himself equal to Helvellyn, or Ben Nevis, or Snowdon.... The thing which seems perfectly safe to do is attempted, very naturally, without any precaution; and when an accident takes place we all feel a kind of indignation and can hardly believe that such a thing could have happened.... There really is little to be got by climbing a mountain, at least in nine cases out of ten, for the ordinary tourist. Even from such modest elevations as the summit of Snowdon or Ben Nevis, there is rarely much to be seen but cloud and mist. In fact, few people really ascend a mountain for any other purpose than to say they have ascended it, and it becomes almost a pity, save for the austere interests of truth alone, that they could not follow the suggestion of Sheridan to his son about the descent into a coalmine and say they had done it without running risk or taking trouble.

We know, however, that no advice of this kind will ever be followed while it is the fashion to climb a mountain. Therefore those who are themselves given to mountain ascents, or have relatives or friends thus addicted, must only console themselves by the reflection that there are times when Fleet Street is a more dangerous crevasse than most in the Alps, and that the perils of limb and life are rather greater at given moments, while Parliament is sitting, to a pedestrian venturing from Parliament Street to Westminster Hall than to the same individual later in the year as he proceeds to scale Mont Blanc.... We can only say that most people would do well not to climb mountains, but that they who will climb have at least the consolation of reflecting that accidents also occur on the plains. 'Love' says the poet, 'is of the valleys.' So, sometimes, is Death…'

The concern shown by the Press was shared in high places, for within a few years, following a spate of fatal accidents in the Alps, Queen Victoria expressed her anxiety and commanded her personal secretary, Sir Henry Ponsonby, to write to the Prime Minister, Mr Gladstone, to ask whether he felt that she could say anything to mark her disapproval of the dangerous Alpine excursions which had resulted in so many deaths. The year was 1882, and between 19 July and 12 August, three eminent British mountaineers and their guides had been killed in the Alps. Mr Gladstone replied that 'whilst he shared the Queen's sympathetic feelings, he doubted the possibility of any interference, even by Her Majesty, with a prospect of advantage. It may be questionable whether, upon the whole, mountain climbing (and be it remembered that Snowdon has its victims as well as the Matterhorn), is more destructive than various other pursuits in the way of recreation…' The mountaineering fraternity only narrowly escaped a Royal censure!

Five years after Mr Wilton's death another fatality thought to be due to failure to find the correct path occurred on Snowdon. On 26 January 1879, 23-year-old Maxwell Haseler from Birmingham was traversing the Snowdon Horseshoe from Pen-y-pass in a clockwise direction with a party of experienced hillwalkers who were equipped with ropes and ice-axes There is little information available about the weather conditions, but in view of what happened it was probably misty, with a covering of snow on the ground. After safely negotiating Lliwedd the group had descended to Bwlch-y-saethau and Haseler dropped back. He lost touch with the rest of the party on the ridge and must have lost the way in the mist and veered to the right to find himself traversing the steep and slippery slopes of Clogwyn-y-garnedd. On the east face of Snowdon, he slipped on the rocks and fell 600-700 feet to his death by the shore of Llyn Glaslyn where a search party found his body the following morning.

This accident was written up in detail in Chambers's Journal of 1887, and it is worth noting the author's final comment. 'The accident is a terrible warning against dividing a party in a difficult place. The best policy for the leader of a party, when any one separates himself from it in such a position, is to halt, call the straggler back, and if he hesitates, tell him firmly that the party will not proceed till he rejoins it. For a man climbing by himself on a difficult slope, so slight an accident as a sprained ankle may lead to either a subsequent fatal fall, or a night of exposure and suffering. The first rule for mountaineering is, 'Keep together'.

Sunday 23 September 1884 was a warm, sultry day, and a party of tourists from London and Lancashire had successfully reached the summit of Snowdon. They were still on the ridge when a severe thunderstorm moved in on them with frightening speed, and they rushed back to take shelter in one of the huts on the summit. As they entered it, the hut was struck by lightning and Mr Livesey from Ashton in Makerfield in Lancashire was killed. This story was featured in Chamber's Journal of 7 May 1887, with the comment that 'Perils of this kind seem to be very rare on our higher mountains. We do not recollect any other case of a climber being killed by lightning.' But over the decades since that comment was written, there have been a number of fatalities amongst climbers and walkers due to lightning strike. Indeed it must be considered a peril to be expected, and mountaineers should understand that the most dangerous place to be during a thunderstorm is high up on a ridge where the frequency of lightning strikes is at its maximum. Conversely the safest place is at the bottom of a slope in a 'safe zone' which starts three metres from the mountain-side and extends away from it for a distance equal to the height of the cliff.

6: Getting Away from it All?

Suicides are not unknown in Snowdonia, though why someone who has come to the end of his tether should choose to do the final act up in the hills, is a matter for speculation. Is it the final censure on society, knowing that many people would put themselves to a great deal of inconvenience and possible risk to try to find him, or just that, as with a wounded animal, the best place to die is in a quiet and secluded spot? In recent years people have been found with empty tranquillizer pill and/or whisky bottles by their sides, and sometimes with a little note in a pocket 'to whom it may concern'. Probably one of the strangest incidents of this kind happened in 1875, when 32-year-old Edward Grindley Kendall from Liverpool came to a grisly end on Crib-y-ddysgl. Kendall had been a heavy drinker and had been successfully treated for alcoholism, but in spite of the apparent cure of his drink problem he now had periods of depression. He was not married, but he had a close friend, David Warren, with whom he came on holiday to north Wales in June of that year when he suggested that the two of them should 'have a go' at climbing Snowdon. Though Kendall had previously been on the summit, it was to be a new experience for Warren who looked forward to the climb up the highest mountain in Wales.

They arrived at the *Pen-y-gwryd Hotel* on 10 June and planned to make their ascent the next day. Kendall was up very early, and ordered breakfast for the two of them at 7.00am. Then he went outside and for some time walked up and down the road reading a book. The landlord, Henry Owen, watched him through a window until he came back into the hotel when he told Owen that he was going to have a look at the mountains to see if they were clear. Henry Owen then saw him walk down the road towards Nant Gwynant, but did not see him return, and in fact did not see him again. Soon after this, Anne Roberts, daughter of the landlord of the *Gorphwysfa Hotel* a mile up the road at Pen-y-pass, saw Kendall outside their hotel shortly before 8.00am. He came inside and asked for a glass of milk, which he drank before leaving and disappearing down the road towards Llanberis. Meanwhile, at the *Pen-y-gwryd*, David Warren waited for Kendall to turn up and eventually, assuming that Kendall had decided to go up Snowdon on his own, checked out of the hotel expressing his anger in no uncertain terms, and made his way home to Liverpool.

No word was heard from Kendall, and after a few days some of his friends from Liverpool came to look for him at the instigation of a lady friend, as he had not been in touch with her nor had he returned to his home. Since leaving the *Gorphwysfa Hotel*, Kendall seemed to have completely disappeared.

The first clue to his whereabouts was at the end of the month when Mr and Mrs David Moseley and their guide, who were descending from the summit of Snowdon, discovered a pair of wet and mouldy-looking boots on the shore of Llyn Llydaw. Inside each boot was a garter and a stocking with Kendall's name on a label. A number of suggestions were put forward as to how Kendall's boots came to be by the lakeside, such as the possibility that he had been wading and had become stuck in mud, or that he might have slipped into deeper water and drowned. The latter was the favoured theory and as, even in June, the water would have been extremely cold, he would not have survived long in it. If that had been the case, there was no purpose in looking for Kendall anywhere else but the Llyn, and a wider search for him was called off. Ten days later, on 14 July, his body was found uninjured a considerable distance from the Llyn, and the story can best be told by quoting the newspaper report of 17 July,

> Missing Tourist on Snowdon. Recovery of Body
>   The body of Edward Kendall was found on Tuesday last in a naked condition on Crib-y-ddysgl. The body was found in a steep and dangerous place well above the path and it is believed that the deceased had removed his shoes and stockings to enable him to climb certain steep ledges near Llydaw; the clothes were found about 250 feet above the shore-line, and his body was another 750 feet above them.

It was a short and rather sketchy report, but the evidence at the inquest added more detail. A shepherd had found him sitting propped up against a rock about 400 feet above the Pyg track. He was absolutely naked. The Pyg track is 600 feet above the edge of Llyn Llydaw, so that he had climbed about 750 feet without his boots and stockings, which seems very strange. This, together with the evidence of his curious behaviour on the morning he disappeared, convinced the court that he undressed himself whilst of unsound mind and died from

Gravestone of Edward Kendall.

exposure. Although the newspaper report suggested that Kendall had removed his boots and stockings to climb some steep edges, the general feeling was that Kendall had purposely discarded all his clothing in order to die of exposure. But in his case he did not take any pills or spirits to ease the pain and discomfort of his going. The death of Edward Grindley Kendall will remain one of the unsolved mysteries of Snowdonia.

7: The Conquest of Lliwedd

During the second half of the 19th century it was common practice for alpinists to 'keep their hand in' during the winter months either in the Lake District or in Snowdonia, and it is interesting to note that in *Mountaineering* published in 1893, the author, Claude Wilson, states (page 19) that 'The Snowdon District may be reached from Port Madoc, from Llanberis, from Bangor, or from Betws y Coed. It is so near to London, that it has been found possible to dine in town on Saturday evening, lunch on the top of Snowdon on Sunday, and be back at work in London by ten o'clock on Monday morning'. The four places mentioned were reached by rail, but one could hardly do the journey more quickly today in an average car. This easy and quick access was probably one reason why Snowdonia had become popular by the 1880s, especially with the two hotels, the *Pen-y-gwryd* and the *Gorphwysfa*, so close to the start of the Miners' path leading to Llyn Llydaw and the daunting cliffs of Lliwedd. Lliwedd, one of the 'nails' in the Snowdon Horseshoe, lies to the south-east of Snowdon, and its north face viewed from Llyn Llydaw presents a vista of high rambling cliffs and gullies rising to 1,000 feet above the lake, and nearly 3,000 feet above sea level. It is a huge crag and its two dominant features are the East and West Buttresses, separated from each other by the main Central Gully. To the left are East Gully and Far East Buttress, and to the right Slanting Gully and Slanting Buttress (see diagram). Today there are more than 80 different routes or variants on the crag, while the first recorded attempt to climb the north face was made as early as 1872 by T H Murray Browne and W R Browne who wrote the following short account of it in the *Pen-y-gwryd* visitors' book 'Tried to get up Lliwedd direct from Llyn Llydaw up the crags, but failed completely. Mounted eventually to the col on the left. The direct ascent may be practicable, but I shall be glad to hear from anyone who achieves it. It has not, so far as I am aware, been done, and is certainly difficult'. There are no further reports of attempts to

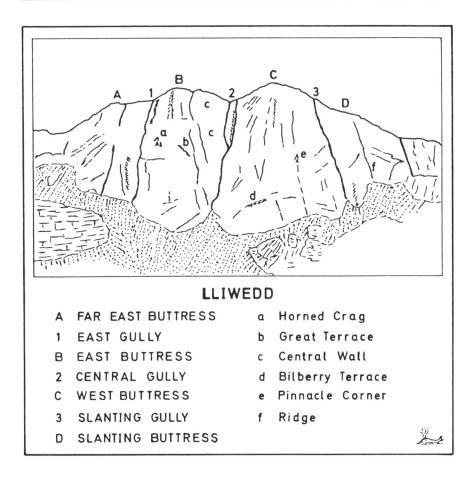

LLIWEDD

A	FAR EAST BUTTRESS	a	Horned Crag
1	EAST GULLY	b	Great Terrace
B	EAST BUTTRESS	c	Central Wall
2	CENTRAL GULLY	d	Bilberry Terrace
C	WEST BUTTRESS	e	Pinnacle Corner
3	SLANTING GULLY	f	Ridge
D	SLANTING BUTTRESS		

make an ascent until 1882 when two experienced climbers, T W Wall, a member of the Alpine Club, and A H Stocker, were 'driven back by rain and the exposed seriousness of the route.' The following year, on 4 January 1883, the same men made another attempt, and there is a brief note in the visitors' book that — 'after two attempts on Lliwedd by Central Gully, ascended north face by buttress west of Central Gully, reaching the arête 13 yards from the summit. No one is recommended to attempt the ascent without at least 60 feet of rope. Height of rocks — about 850 feet; time taken — four hours and a half. Jan 4, 1883'.

East face of Lliwedd.

From then until the outbreak of the Great War, Lliwedd was a magnet to rock climbers and, as the following stories show, several were to have accidents, sometimes serious, on the north face of the mountain.

*

Alfred Evans, a 24-year-old solicitor from Newton Heath, Manchester, was a keen and competent climber who spent a great deal of time in Snowdonia during the late 1880s. On 20 May 1888 he and two friends, W E Corlett from Liverpool and E Kidson from Birmingham who had climbed together many times, planned to climb Central Gully on Lliwedd, descend the Cribin ridge to Glaslyn, ascend a gully on Clogwyn-y-garnedd leading almost to the summit of Snowdon, descend into Cwm Glas, scale Clogwyn-y-Person, and return to the *Pen-y-gwryd Hotel*, where they were staying, by the eastern ridge of Crib Goch. By any yardstick this was a most ambitious expedition and the horizontal distance of ten miles included 4, 666 feet of ascent and 4,933 feet of descent! They proposed to take with them a 100 foot rope, but for some reason the rope they took was only 60 feet long.

The day had a wet start, and before they set out it was suggested that the order of the day`s climbing should be reversed to allow time for the rocks at the bottom of the north-facing Central Gully of Lliwedd to dry. Only one disagreed, suggesting that the route proposed would be too difficult at the end of a hard day`s walking and climbing, especially as none of the party was properly mountain-fit, and all were out of practice. The change of plan accepted, they were then joined by a climber named Bedford, and the four set out at 10am. This route reversal would save the party 284 feet of ascent and 122 feet of descent but it was still an ambitious expedition and, as the one dissident feared, the most difficult and exacting climb was left until the end when they would all be tired. From Pen-y-pass they took the high route traversing the north ridge of Crib Goch into Cwm Glas, but when they reached the foot of Clogwyn-y-Person they were well behind schedule, and agreed that the ascent of Clogwyn-y-garnedd would be left out. After climbing to the top of Clogwyn y Person they followed the ridge over Crib-y-ddysgl, down to Bwlch Glas and then up the ridge to the summit of Snowdon, following the path to the left of what is now the railway track. On the summit they met another friend from Nottingham who joined the party and whilst three of them descended the zigzags to Glaslyn, Evans and Kidson chose to go down the third gully south of Bwlch Glas on Clogwyn-y-garnedd, which is now called Ladies Gully. At the foot they all crossed the stream by the copper works at the outflow of Llyn Glas, and went on down to the upper end of Llyn Llydaw. Corlett, Evans and Kidson then traversed to the bottom of Central Gully of Lliwedd, while the other two watched from near the shore of the lake.

A great deal of energy had been expended in climbing Clogwyn-y-Person, and by this time the forebodings of the member of the party who had opposed the reversal of the original route seemed to have been justified as they all appeared to be tired and perhaps not in a fit condition to tackle a route such as Central Gully. It was decided that because they had brought only a short length of rope, they would not rope-up straightaway, and Corlett, who was in front, carried the coiled rope as they started climbing Central Gully at about 5.15pm. For some distance up the cliff the rocks were water-worn, and water was flowing down the face which made it difficult to climb. Corlett negotiated the lower part and after a considerable struggle reached a ledge about 300 feet above the scree. Evans went next, but stuck when at a point about 80 feet below Corlett's ledge. Corlett climbed down some distance to give assistance with the rope, but it was not long enough to tie round Evans's waist. Not wanting to climb and hold on to the rope at the same time, Evans refused to take it. He remained stuck in the gully for some time, unable to go up or down, even with help from Kidson, who was following. After a great struggle he managed to get down three or four feet, and was then helped by Kidson to a fairly secure and comfortable position where he was able to sit down and rest. This was just out of the gully, and Corlett swung out to the right towards the west buttress and threw the rope down the difficult pitch in the gully where his two companions might be able to use it. Evans eventually moved over to the right and was immediately followed by Kidson. Evans attempted to get over the ledge and climb the gully to join Corlett who was some distance directly above him. He failed to manage this and was helped by Kidson to regain his position. After a brief discussion Evans shouted to Corlett, 'We're going down. I'm clean fagged out'. The latter continued the climb but before reaching the top he noticed that Evans and Kidson had climbed up and traversed a short way, and were near the difficult pitch mentioned above. The ledge had now been successfully passed, and Kidson was sitting on a small, sloping patch of grass on the far side of it. Evans seized Kidson's ankle, lowered himself down, and found a small ledge from where he was able to grasp an excellent handhold on the ledge above. He then worked his way to his right and when he had gone about five or six feet, half the distance of the traverse, his feet slipped. His arms gradually came to their full stretch and with one quickly uttered, 'Oh', he fell. Kidson sprang to his feet expecting to see Evans land on the ledge he had just quitted, but he slid over it, and was deflected outwards from the cliff, landing on his feet almost at the edge of a steep grass slope running up to this part of the cliff. It was about 15 feet long, and from the point where he landed he somersaulted in four or five 'terrible leaps', over and over, some 200 feet to the screes below. After losing his hold, he did not appear to make any effort and beyond the one cry, he fell without uttering another sound. The nature of the spot from which he fell made it impossible for Kidson to give him any help at all, and once he had lost his handhold, even the most determined efforts by Evans to save himself would have been of no avail. The accident happened at 6.55pm, by which time the party had been in the mountains for over nine hours. Kidson very quickly climbed down to reach his friend, but life was already extinct.

In the meantime, Corlett had continued to climb and reached the ridge at exactly 7pm. Feeling rather concerned about his companions he crossed over the top of East Buttress and down the gully to the far side of it. Kidson, who was running down towards Pen-y-pass to summon assistance, shouted up to him that there had been an accident, and Corlett made his way down to where Evans lay. The latter was beyond help, but Corlett waited with him for some three hours until a party of rescuers arrived from the hotel.

An inquest was held on the following Tuesday at the *Pen-y-gwryd Hotel* and Corlett was the principal witness. He told the court that he and Kidson had arrived at Bethesda by train at 4.50pm on the Saturday afternoon and had walked to Ogwen Cottage where they met two friends. All four then walked over the Glyders to the *Pen-y-gwryd Hotel* where they arrived at 9.20 pm. On the following morning, Sunday, they set out at 10am, eventually arriving on the summit of Snowdon, 'but not using the regular paths'. They met another acquaintance there, and at 3.30pm they started their descent to Glaslyn and Llyn Llydaw. The coroner returned a verdict of 'Accidental death whilst climbing' but unusually he made no comment about the rights and wrongs of mountaineering.[1]

During the previous year two successful ascents of the Lliwedd precipice had been recorded, one of them by Corlett and Evans who, in spite of their experience, had become involved in this tragic mishap. It is ironic that at the inquest the coroner remarked, 'it is much to be regretted that a rope is not invariably used in expeditions of this character. Had a rope been used properly on this particular occasion, in all human probability this terrible accident would not have happened and a now sorrowing family would not be mourning the loss of one of its loved members'. The survivors of the party who wrote this account in the *Pen-y-gwryd* visitors' book 'trust that this dreadful accident will be a

---

1. The direct route up Central Gully was finally conquered fifty years later, in 1938, by F J R Dodd and J Menlove Edwards. The route is classified Very Severe(VS).

warning to young and ardent mountaineers, and will induce them to take proper precautions in their climbing expeditions.' They concluded their account by quoting Edward Whymper, author of Scrambles amongst the Alps: 'Climb if you will, but remember that courage and strength are nought without prudence, and that a momentary negligence may destroy the happiness of a lifetime. Do nothing in haste; look well to each step; and from the beginning think what may be the end.'[1]

A cross was erected on a large rock at the foot of Central Gully marking the spot where Alfred Evans lay. It was described in *The Carnarvon and Denbigh Herald* as 'a beautiful, massive stone cross in memory of the late Alfred Evans who died whilst attempting to climb the cliff after a long and arduous day's mountaineering on Snowdon. It stands five feet, eight and a half inches in height, and is of the best Sicilian marble and of a pure white colour. It can be seen from all prominent spots on the Capel Curig ascent to Snowdon and is located at an altitude of 2,100 feet above sea level, about five hundred feet above the lake. It is thought to be the highest monument of its kind in the Kingdom.' It was erected by Evans' two climbing companions, Corlett and Kidson. The stone weighed over 16 hundredweights, and to get it across the slopes to the rock on which it was erected was no easy task. Sadly the cross was soon swept down by a rock avalanche, and it was re-erected on a rocky knoll some distance from the foot of Lliwedd. Unfortunately the cross was again destroyed soon afterwards, this time by vandals, and lies in pieces by the rock on which it had been re-erected.

*

During 1894 three further attempts to climb a new route on the north face of Lliwedd were made and the accounts of each were recorded in the *Pen-y-gwryd* visitors' book. Each narrative is a detailed account written by a first-hand witness, which makes fascinating reading. It is clear that during the latter half of the 19th century the most popular rock-climbing routes were those on Lliwedd, partly because of its easy accessibility and possibly because the accounts written in the various hotel visitors' books presented a challenge to other guests.

Rather less than six years after the death in 1888 of Alfred Evans whilst attempting to climb Central Gully, four climbers — F Wethered, C W Newton, and E H and H Kempson, set out from the *Pen- y-Gwryd* to attempt Slanting Gully on 9 January 1894. This appears to be the first recorded attempt to climb the gully, which is easily identified as the diagonal fault separating West Buttress

---

1. Edward Whymper, *Scrambles amongst the Alps in years 1860-69*. Murray 1871. Still in print after over a century, with nearly 30 different editions in English and many more in other languages, this book remains a classic of mountaineering literature.

and Slanting Buttress. It is most easily approached by crossing diagonally up the scree below Central Gully, and then keeping along the base of the rocks of the West Buttress. At that time the gully was completely frozen up and under snow varying in depth from a few inches to three feet. Progress was very slow, and during the first four hours the party managed to climb only 375 feet. The party kept in the gully the whole time, usually close against the rocks to the west side. Their slow rate of progress was due chiefly to the large number of steps which they had to cut in hard snow, and to the fact that nearly every handhold had to be cleared of snow. Progress was finally stopped at a point where for some distance onwards the gully becomes a mere crack, formed by the western rocks overhanging an almost smooth slab. As it was already 4pm with very little daylight left for them to descend safely, they turned back and reached their starting point as it became dark at 6.30pm.

Details of the climb, and some words of advice to other climbers, were duly entered in the visitors' book:

> Wethered led the way up, and H Kempson was last man on the way down, these two finding that crampons gave considerable additional safety where the footholds were at all precarious. I take this opportunity of strongly recommending these instruments to anyone winter climbing in this or similar districts, especially when there is so much ice or frozen and snowy grass on the hill-sides. The uniformly steep angle at which Slanting Gully lies may be gathered from the fact that a rucksack dropped from the highest point was picked up at the starting point on the return. In the opinion of most of the party the snow and ice in the gully made it easier to climb the more difficult parts, although if cleared of snow and ice the holds for feet and hands would be more obvious. A fairly strong party with the usual amount of rope would find it a most interesting climb and if an examination of the upper part from the top shows a reasonable chance of success, I believe that before long the gully will be climbed throughout.

> The reference to the use of crampons is an important one, as they were certainly not in general use then, although Oscar Eckenstein — one of the leading alpinists of the time had also extolled the virtues of crampons.

*

> The second attempt to climb Slanting Gully was made by John C Morland, Oliver Morland and Wentworth Price on 26 March 1894. The party started up the scree at 1.55pm and arrived at the 'cave', some 390 feet higher, at 5pm. There was not as much snow as there had been in January and they found the conditions reasonably good with the exception of the gully itself which was very wet from melting snow. Their account reads: 'This gully was difficult the whole way up

and at 2,500 feet a chimney 70 feet long must be squirmed up. We believe it cannot be climbed to the ridge, neither is it possible to leave it when one is in. We tried as far as time would permit to get out of the gully both to the right and to the left in several places. To the right a few steps brought us out on to the face of the precipitous buttress, whilst to the left we were immediately stopped where smooth slabs of rock offered us no handholds or footholds. We anticipated that as in Central Gully, the climbing would have become easier as progress was made. But on the contrary the difficulties increased. We should be pleased to learn whether this gully has been ascended throughout, and if so, how the difficulty at 2,690 feet, which is unmistakeable, was surmounted. We carried two ropes with us, 80 feet and 50 feet, and in one place the whole length of both ropes — 130 feet — had to be utilised before the leader could find a place of safety'.

*

A third attempt in 1894 was made by John Mitchell from Oxford on 30 August. He was the assistant editor of *Dr Murray's New Historical Dictionary*, and had been staying at the *Pen-y-gwryd* for a fortnight during which time he had done several solo climbs including three of the Clogwyn y Garnedd gullies. He had little previous experience but possessed natural aptitude, and during the preceding week on consecutive days he had climbed routes on Clogwyn y Person, leading a party of five, Central Gully of Lliwedd accompanied by H J Russel, and on the third day North Gully on Tryfan, again with H J Russel. He had made it known that he intended to attempt Slanting Gully alone on Thursday 30th, and a party of twelve who were all staying at the *Pen-y-gwryd*, went out with him to witness his attempt. The foot of Lliwedd was reached at about 2pm, and whilst the majority of the party remained on the grass about 300 feet above Llyn Llydaw, three of them ascended with Mitchell 300 feet up the scree to the foot of the gully. From then, Mitchell proceeded alone.

The first pitch was quickly ascended, although Mitchell found it fairly difficult owing to the rocks being wet. He then proceeded apparently without difficulty to the foot of the next pitch which is a chimney. He carefully examined it and the face of the rock on either side, and finally ascended the slabs at the right side. On reaching a ledge 25 feet from the top of the chimney he turned and waved his handkerchief to those watching him down below. On being asked what the climb was like, he replied 'It's very stiff.' At this point he was out of sight of the people at the foot of the gully, though still in view of those on the grass farther down. The next part of the ascent seemed fairly easy, and when next seen by the higher party, he was in the crack, probably at the highest point reached in previous climbs. He started to ascend the face at this point, but after a few steps he came back and rested for some time whilst examining the rocks above. At last he climbed up out of the crack following the line of the chasm as it appears from below. This part of the climb was accomplished slowly and evidently with great difficulty, but he finally reached what appears to be the top of the crack, which is just below an overhang. With his feet on a narrow ledge, Mitchell now seemed to be unable to make further progress and was seen to move his hands in all directions over the face of the rock in search of holds. He then cleared moss and stones out of the top of the crack, apparently trying to get a hold round the corner of the face on which he was standing, but still under the overhang. Whilst doing this he tried several times with his hand and foot in the crack to the right, but had to return to his former position. During this time he was asked how he was and he answered, 'All right'.

Mitchell remained in this position for over 30 minutes and then, as he was putting his right foot into the chasm, having apparently found a satisfactory handhold in it with his right hand, his left foot slipped. His hold in the crack either broke away or was insufficient, and he was unable to save himself. From below, his left hand appeared not to have a good hold, but to be spread out on the sloping face of rock above. It was exactly 4.30pm when Mitchell fell, and he came to rest at least 150 feet below. As soon as he landed at the bottom of the chasm, and loose stones had stopped falling, the three men at the foot of the gully consulted as to what they should do. It was evident that they could not reach the spot where he lay as none of them was capable of climbing the chimney. They descended to the party on the grass and, judging from the nature of the fall that there was no chance of Mitchell being alive, then decided to return to the *Pen-y-gwryd* to raise the alarm and inform his friends staying in Llanberis.

It was too late in the day to make any attempt to recover the body, especially as it was getting dark with the mist enshrouding the mountain, but the next morning, some of the party staying at the *Pen-y-gwryd* went to the foot of Lliwedd where they were joined by the foreman of the copper mine across the valley, who had brought some of his miners to help: they set about attempting to reach the position where Mitchell still lay. One of the miners climbed straight up the gully and shouted that he had found the body. Three others then went up to join him, taking some rope by means of which they lowered the body to the foot of the gully where others were waiting to help.

The narrator of this story was clearly moved by the whole event, and put it on record that, 'the way in which these men accomplished their task is worthy of the highest praise, one of them descending the whole way alongside the body and preventing any further injury, whilst the last man had to come down without any aid whatsoever. The names of these four miners are:– Richard Williams, William Owen, Griffith Williams and Evan Evans'.

Mitchell's body was taken down to Llanberis where an inquest was held the next day, Saturday, and a verdict of accidental death was returned. [1]

8: The Mountain Railway

The prospect of a railway to the summit of Snowdon can be traced back to 1865, but it was not until 1894 that firm plans were prepared and negotiations took place with the Vaynol Estate, over whose land the line would run. Prior to this, in November 1871, a Bill had been presented in the House of Commons to build a railway from Llanberis to the summit of Snowdon, and it was discussed in the House of Lords in February 1872. However, George William Duff Assheton Smith, who owned the Vaynol Estate, was obdurate in his opposition to the idea of a railway being constructed on Snowdon. He refused to sell the land to the proposed railway company, and the Bill was withdrawn.

During the early years of the 1890s, some prominent local figures in Llanberis, spurred on by the fact that a line was being planned to link the North Wales Narrow Gauge Railway at Rhyd-ddu to the summit of Snowdon, renewed their efforts to persuade Assheton Smith to change his mind. At that time the Llanberis tourist industry was somewhat in the doldrums, and this was one of the most telling arguments in favour of the railway — it would attract large numbers of visitors to the village. After a meeting between the protagonists of the railway scheme and Duff Assheton Smith in 1893, he agreed to sell the land to the proposed railway operating company. Plans were drawn up and on 16 November 1894 The Snowdon Mountain Tramroad and Hotels Company Limited was formed under the Companies Act and the first meeting of the Board of Directors was held in Chester. One of the primary considerations was to make the railway as safe as possible, and a number of systems were looked at before the decision was made to adopt a 'rack and pinion' system developed by a Swiss engineer named Dr R S Abt, and referred to as 'the Abt system'. The carriages are not coupled to the engine, and the principle on which the train works is that the engine pushes the carriage up the mountain, with the law of gravity relied

1. Slanting Gully remained undefeated until the first recorded ascent by G P and A P Abraham in 1897.

on for descent. The carriages, descending under their own weight, are restrained by the engine which acts as a brake to stop them going too fast. If for any reason the engine itself has a mechanical fault and starts running away, *ie* over 5 mph, the automatic braking system on the carriage immediately comes into play and the carriage, since it is not coupled to the run-away engine, comes to a halt. [1]

Work began on 15 December 1894 when Enid, Duff Assheton Smith's six-year-old daughter, cut the first turf, but there were many delays due to severe weather. The first steam engine arrived from the Swiss manufacturer seven months later, on 28 June 1895, but it was not until 9 January 1896 that the first train reached the summit. It conveyed a number of officials and workmen on what was a test run and was a complete success in spite of the fact that it was in the middle of a winter so severe that the lake at Llanberis, Llyn Padarn, was frozen over. It came to be known as 'the great frost', and high up on Snowdon the temperature was much lower than in Llanberis as, with every 100 metres of height above sea level, the temperature drops by approximately one degree C. [2]

Initially the Snowdon Mountain Tramroad and Hotels Company purchased four steam engines and in 1922/23 they bought another three. Eventually a number of diesel locomotives were purchased, but most of the original steam engines are still in use today, which is indicative of the high standard of workmanship in repair and maintenance carried out every year in the Llanberis workshop. [3]

As soon as the line was clear of snow more trial journeys were safely completed and the new service started on Easter Monday 1896. It was a fine day, and the first train, with two carriages carrying eighty passengers, left the base station in Llanberis at 10. 50am. A second train followed immediately, and they both reached the summit station an hour later. Cloud had descended over the summit, and the second train to arrive, drawn by the engine named *LADAS*. [4] and driven by William Pickles, set off on the return journey to Llanberis at 12.30pm. As it was descending towards Clogwyn station, on the bend before the start of the embankment, the engine's pinion wheel jumped out of the rack, the engine was derailed and careered down the slope into the bottom of Cwm Glas

---

1. Details of the Abt system and the history of the Snowdon Mountain Railway are given in Three Stops to the Summit by Rol Williams.

2. For example, a temperature of nought degrees C at sea level would be about minus 11 degrees C on the summit of Snowdon.

3. The title of the Company was changed in April 1928 to The Snowdon Mountain Railway Company.

4. The engine was so named to honour Laura Alice Duff Assheton Smith (LADAS), the wife of the landowner.

Summit of Snowdon c1900.

Bach. As the engine left the track the driver and firemen both jumped clear, and the guard in the rear coach immediately applied the safety brake and shouted to the passengers to stay in their seats. Two of them, one a visitor from Shropshire, and the other a hotelier from Llanberis, must have panicked, for they ignored the guard and jumped out of the carriage. The Shropshire man escaped injury, but the local man, Ellis Roberts, hit a rock on the side of the track, rolled back on to the line, and his leg was crushed between the footboard of the train and the rail. He was given immediate first aid, but it was some hours before a doctor arrived at the accident. He declared that Roberts 'had no blood in him' — he had been bleeding profusely from his crushed leg — but the doctor did what he could and injected two quarts of warm saline into him. By this time the relief engine had taken about two hours to get up steam and arrive at Clogwyn station. Roberts was put on to a make-shift stretcher and taken down to Llanberis in the relief train. It was about 3pm when the doctor arrived at the scene, and 6.30pm when Roberts finally reached the Quarry hospital — six hours or more after the accident had occurred. Some time on the way down he died from loss of blood and was declared dead on arrival in the hospital. He was buried in Nant Peris cemetery where his gravestone may still be seen.

The railway was closed down whilst a formal enquiry was carried out and as a result of this a number of technical improvements were made to the railway track. The accident had been a very severe setback to the Tramroad Company, and work began immediately to fit safety guard rails along the whole length of the line.

In spite of another hard winter which delayed the work of fitting the safety rails, the railway was re-opened on 22 June 1897. To the present day, that was the only fatal accident on the mountain railway, and although there have been some minor derailments from time to time there have been no serious accidents — a quite remarkable safety record.

For several years after the railway was re-opened, it was run with an engine and two carriages, the engine pushing the closed carriage up the mountain with an open observation carriage in front of it. The open carriages were very popular in fine weather, but there was a risk of passengers in them being hit by burning cinders from the engine's funnel, and in 1912 a claim was made against the Company for damage thus caused to a passenger's clothing. In 1914, the open carriages were withdrawn from service and from then on every train was restricted to the engine and one carriage.

The effect of the opening of the railway was to convert Snowdon during the summer months from a mountaineers' to a tourists' mountain. Purists deplore this and find it disconcerting to reach the tops only to see the summit of Snowdon covered with people who have come up by train. The feelings of walkers were perfectly expressed by a 12-year-old girl who, having scrambled up from Blaen Nant through Cwm Glas and up the steep slope on to Carnedd Ugain, saw Snowdon ahead of her looking like Hampstead Heath on a Bank Holiday. 'It makes me feel sick,' she said, 'and I want to shout at them that I've come up the hard way.' But does it behove those who enjoy the ascent of Snowdon through their own exertions, to deny the same enjoyment to those who are either too old, disabled, simply do not like walking or who are not fit enough to tackle such a long uphill route?

Early visitors to Llanberis and other centres who wished to walk to the summit would make sure they did so in safety by hiring a guide. The opening of the railway was a cruel blow to the local mountain guides, whose services quickly ceased to be wanted, although a few of them managed to find enough visitors wishing to go off the beaten track, usually by guiding botanists or geologists. There remain many parts of Snowdon where climbers or walkers can enjoy their sport with only the occasional reminder of the railway in the sound of a distant whistle or the puffing of a train steaming up the final steep incline to the summit station. Even this is gradually giving way to the less audible whine of modern diesel engines. In the winter months, walkers not knowing that the railway is closed from November to mid-March, aim for the top expecting to find shelter, food and hot drinks available. But the summit cafe can only function when the trains are running and able to service and supply it.

*

During the summer of 1900, a party of six youths, one of whom was Geoffrey Winthrop Young, who was later to be a legendary character in the mountaineering world, had reason to be thankful for the existence of the railway line. They were friends on holiday together, and leaving two of them in the *Pen-y-gwryd Hotel*, the other four set out for Snowdon via Cwm Glas and the ascent of the Parson's Nose route. They spent a lot of time wandering through the mist in the cwm, vainly trying to find the Nose, and it was 3pm before they found the right spot to start their climb. Before they roped up, however, three of them performed their usual rite of bathing in one of the two small mountain pools which lie one on each side of the Nose, whilst the fourth member decided to keep his clothes on and retain his body warmth. It was almost dark when they emerged on Crib-y-ddysgl, and the thought of tea in the summit hotel being irresistible, they raced down from the ridge and jeered at the railway signal which stood between the top of the zigzags and the start of the Snowdon Ranger path as they followed the railway line to the summit of Snowdon. After a leisurely supper, the party prepared to walk down the zigzags to Pen-y-pass. The host's repeated plea 'You can't get down, you must sleep here' only resulted in a request for a lamp. No lamp was forthcoming, and the party, 'scientifically' roped together, issued forth into the inky blackness. So thick was the mist that the man three feet in front could not be seen. They spent more than an hour trying to find the start of the zigzag path, but eventually they agreed that there was no clearly defined path and being fearful of the open mines below, close to their intended route, they decided that their only sensible course was to make an ignominious retreat to the hotel. But one of the party whispered the word 'railway', although afterwards each one denied strenuously that it was he who had made the suggestion! The ropes were adjusted, and after trying various ways of keeping to the line, they decided that the only feasible method was to keep the central cogs between the feet, and brush them with the ankles each time they took a step — which proved to be a painful procedure. In spite of wind and sleet, the boys kept themselves cheerful by singing and telling stories. At last they reached the station in Llanberis, unroped themselves and arm-in-arm for mutual support they set off over the Pass for *Pen-y-gwryd* where they arrived at 3am. The landlady, Mrs Owen, gave them a warm welcome and they went to bed, to be wakened next morning by the sound of other guests getting ready to go out to search for them. The only redeeming thought the four youths had was that they had completed certainly the first, and very possibly the last, roped descent of the Snowdon Mountain Railway.

*

How did the coming of the railway affect mountain rescue? During the winter months, when it is shut down, it plays little or no part and Snowdon reverts to its true role as a mountaineers' mountain. It is in the summer that on a number of occasions the ready availability of the trains, which on a busy day follow each other only a few minutes apart, has been instrumental in saving someone's life. It takes little over an hour from the station in Llanberis to the summit and the same time for the return journey, whereas a stretcher party could take three hours to reach the valley depending on the weather and ground conditions, and the weight of the casualty! In an emergency the train crews will make room for a casualty to be taken down to a waiting ambulance. In this event, if the train is full to capacity, someone will have to make way for the injured person, otherwise one passenger over the limit will invalidate the railway company's insurance policy, a fact which, in these days of huge compensation claims, must be borne in mind. At times mountain rescue teams are taken up the mountain by train to a rescue, and today the introduction of diesel-powered engines means that if an engine should be needed urgently to bring someone down, no time would be wasted getting up steam. The availability of helicopters from RAF Valley has reduced the use of trains to evacuate casualties from Snowdon, but if the weather or other tasks prevent the use of a helicopter, it is possible that a train could be used instead.

During the early 1960s, Has Oldham, a young member of a Royal Air Force Mountain Rescue Team (MRT), was assisting with an evacuation from the summit of Snowdon in which a Thomas mountain rescue stretcher with a patient was being pushed sideways down the railway line rather unsuccessfully. It occurred to Has, who later became well-known as a team leader of the RAF Valley MRT, that there must be a better way of utilising the railway line. Working on the principle that downward motion depends on gravity, he designed a trolley specifically for the evacuation of casualties by the railway line. As a means of evacuation it would be used during winter, and in summer after the trains had stopped running for the night. The problem of getting the trolley up the mountain was solved by using a frame of alloy tubing and four old aircraft wheels with the tyres removed. The whole trolley weighed only 42 lbs and was made to split into four sections, each of which would be carried by a team member. It was then re-assembled and the stretcher, with its casualty, tied on to prevent them slipping off. Two back ropes were attached to the trolley and the speed of descent was controlled by man power.

The Valley MRT used the trolley on several training exercises, and for a few rescues in the winter months in the mid-1970s: it was never actually used during the summer. During winter-time the trolley had to be carried round the snow drifts especially across the lower slopes of Carnedd Ugain and on Clogwyn Coch. It proved to be a good method for evacuating casualties and on one occasion it was used with two stretchers and casualties on board! Although the trolley was easy-running, there are places on the line where the gradient is less steep, and here a rope was used in front to be pulled to maintain momentum. The whole operation was kept completely 'hush hush' from the Snowdon Mountain Railway Company's owners in case they raised objections, but it was a good piece of engineering by Has Oldham and his RAF colleagues. After Has retired from the RAF and handed over leadership of the MRT to Flight-Sergeant Jack Baines, no rescues were carried out when the trolley might have been used, but it was always there in case of emergency. Flight-Sergeant (now Warrant Officer) Alastair Haveron remembers the trolley being used for training exercises when he was the team leader in the early 1980s, but he has no recollection of it being used operationally. The increased use and skills of the helicopter crews probably sealed its fate, and sadly it has now disappeared altogether and no drawings or photographs of it have survived.

9: Into the Twentieth Century

Following the deaths of Evans and Mitchell, things were comparatively quiet in Snowdonia, but the popularity of the Lake District as a mountaineering venue was growing: then, in 1903, the worst accident in the history of British climbing to date happened on a difficult climb called Herford's Slab, high up on Scafell Pinnacle, resulting in the deaths of four young climbers. It was justly described in *The Climbers' Club Journal* as 'The Scafell Disaster' and it so shook the climbing fraternity that the Club decided that it was time to take a serious look at the whole issue of mountain accidents and the rescue of casualties. As a result, later that year, a supply of first-aid and mountain rescue equipment with full instructions on how to use it, was located at the *Gorphwysfa Hotel* at Pen-y-pass, and two years later this was augmented by a rescue stretcher. Those climbers who preferred the Ogwen Valley, however, were not satisfied with this arrangement. It was at least nine miles from Pen-y-pass to Ogwen Cottage by road; they made strong representations to the Climbers' Club to have similar equipment located at Ogwen Cottage, and this was agreed.

One has to remember that the number of climbers and walkers on the mountains almost 100 years ago, was very small compared with today and whilst the principle that mountaineers 'should look after their own' was generally accepted, it was usually quite impractical to observe it because of lack of numbers. Search and rescue continued to be very much a random affair and as had happened invariably in the past, local people including shepherds, miners and quarrymen were relied upon to assist the friends of casualties to search for them and, once located, to get them off the mountain.

During the early years of the 20th century the number of incidents on the mountains remained fairly constant. Tryfan and Twll Du (The Devil's Kitchen) in the Ogwen Valley became increasingly popular, and for several years there was at least one serious accident in this area almost every year.

*

On Monday 31 July 1900, Edgar W W Palmer and J Longley, both 28-year-old Londoners, walked from Bethesda to Ogwen in the morning, and after lunch at Ogwen Cottage they set out to continue over the Glyders to *Pen-y-gwryd*. They sought advice about the best route from Mr Jones at the Cottage, who advised them to go via Twll Du and Cwm Patric, but after consulting their guide book they decided to go by an easier looking route following the path over Bwlch Tryfan across the slopes of Glyder Fach and down to *Pen-y-gwryd*. Although the weather was fine and clear, somehow they lost their way and climbed to the summit of Tryfan. Thinking that it was the top of Glyder Fach, they began to scramble down the southern ridge to the bwlch in the direction of *Pen-y-gwryd*. Neither man had been on a mountain before, and the difficulties they encountered were far greater than they had anticipated; they very soon realised that they should never have chosen this route.

As they descended, Longley slipped and slithered down about 60 feet and, although he was not badly hurt, he was shaken and unable to get back to Palmer who was not prepared to attempt to get down to his friend. Palmer appears to have climbed back to the summit, meaning to re-trace his steps to Ogwen to summon assistance. He left Longley at 7.15pm although it was unlikely that he would be able to reach Ogwen, return with a rescue party and evacuate Longley before darkness fell.

Soon after Palmer had set off, Longley, having rested for a quarter of an hour, managed to extricate himself by scrambling down and making for the road, reaching Ogwen Cottage at 9pm. Palmer had not arrived, but thinking that he must have sheltered amongst the rocks for the night, Longley was not unduly

Devil's Kitchen.   [Tony Welch]

worried. But when Palmer did not appear next morning, Longley tried in vain to get a party together to help him look for his companion. After an early lunch he set out alone, but failed to find Palmer, and it was not until Wednesday morning that the police were informed that Palmer was missing. A search party went up Tryfan, accompanied by Longley who pointed out the spot where he had last seen Palmer. No trace of him was found, and on the following day another party, including the local police sergeant, his constable and the licensee of *The Bull Inn* in Bethesda, started out from Ogwen at 11.50am and found Palmer's body lying in a gully on the west side of the mountain. His watch had stopped at 7.45pm, half an hour after he had left his companion. He had suffered fractures to his arm and leg, and a severe injury to his head which was the direct cause of his death.

*

On Sunday 7 April 1901, a party of five climbers, Mr and Mrs J H Chaytor, A Fontannaz, Percy O Weightman and J H Milton, set out at noon from Gwern Gof Uchaf at the foot of Tryfan and headed for North Gully which they reached at about 1.30pm. There had been recent heavy snowfall, and several pitches were completely covered, making progress slow. As they reached the top of the gully, the weather closed in and it began to rain. They had a quick lunch before setting off down the North Ridge in thickening mist. They missed the route and deviated slightly to the right which brought them some 50 or 60 feet down to the buttress running east which skirts North Gully. Seeing a precipitous drop below, they realised their mistake but rather than climb back on to the main ridge Weightman went to look for another way down. He was a strong, active and sure-footed climber, and after descending about 30 feet he disappeared from view to the right. By now it was 3.40pm and after waiting some time his companions shouted to Weightman. Receiving no reply, Milton climbed down in Weightman's footsteps, and saw the mark of a slip made by his boots in the snow which ended abruptly on a protruding rock. It was now clear that Weightman had fallen, and the rest of the party made a roped descent down the gully. Some 600 feet below where they had last seen him, they found the lifeless body of Percy Weightman. He had suffered very severe injuries and death must have been instantaneous. In view of the lateness of the hour, already after 5pm, and the deteriorating weather, his body was left where it lay until the following morning.

J M Archer Thomson, a Welshman, and a teacher in Llandudno, was one of the leading rock climbers in Britain at the turn of the century. He was very much a localized climber and became thoroughly familiar with the crags and cwms of Snowdonia. After Weightman's accident, he climbed up to investigate, and concluded that Weightman had slipped on the easy slope, (where Milton had seen the mark which ended on the protruding rock), and lost his balance when he stepped on snow overlying a tilting slab. Archer Thomson declared that, 'the accident was a pure mischance, not due to any blameworthy carelessness, but that it should serve to remind climbers of the advisability of using an ice-axe as a prop or probe in such situations'.

*

On 20 September 1904, a twenty-eight-year-old lecturer at Liverpool University, named Ronald W H T Hudson, set out with a friend to survey the cleft in Twll Du. He had little experience of rock climbing, and after climbing the first pitch he told his companion that he would return shortly. About 20 minutes later, the friend heard an odd noise and thought he saw something fall. He immediately descended and returned with a rescue party which for some reason went first to the top of the cliff — Archer Thomson commented that if Hudson had been at the top of the cliff, he would not have needed their help, but if he was in the chasm, they would have been unable to reach him from the top. The rescue party then went to the foot and started climbing up. With the help of a ladder they eventually reached the foot of the penultimate pitch, and there found Hudson's body.

*

In 1905, another fatality was reported in Twll Du when Douglas Southgate fell on 17 July. Southgate was not familiar with Welsh crags, but he was attempting to ascend Twll Du with a friend. He had almost reached the traverse on the final pitch when his hand-hold broke away and he fell 50 feet to the floor of the chasm, being killed instantly. *The Climbers' Club Journal* published a short report of the accident, stating that 'it should be most clearly and emphatically pointed out that much of the rock consists of lava only loosely attached to the more solid wall, and consequently climbers may run risks in attempting this ascent, against which no ordinary safeguards can prevail'.

In August 1907, Arthur T Reid, aged 23, of King's College, Cambridge, was climbing the Devil's Staircase with a friend to whom he was roped. The Devil's Staircase is a grassy buttress to the right of Twll Du. Reid was a fairly experienced climber, possessed good judgement, and on the previous day had led a party up Route 2 on the East Peak of Lliwedd. On this day, both he and his companion came off and fell to the bottom of the cleft. Reid was killed outright, but his friend, apart from being rendered unconscious, escaped with bruising only. What caused the fall was not clearly established, but it seems likely that one fell and the other was unable to hold him.

*

In 1907, the September issue of the *Climbers' Club Journal* referred to a successful ascent of Twll Du by a party of three led by L W Collinson of Liverpool, and then repeated the above warning about the state of the rock in Twll Du. The Editor stated that whilst accounts of any climbs of note were welcome, the most emphatic warnings should be given against the attempt, by any party, of such dangerous climbs. 'Rotten rock such as this, which consists of volcanic rock loosely plastered against the wall of the Kitchen, may be ascended a dozen times without accident... but it is impossible to say when some portion of the rock may become loose.' Subsequently, because his remarks had been misunderstood, the Editor wrote an apology stating that he had had no intention of criticising the action of L W Collinson and his two friends, but that he had only sounded a clear warning to others who were not so experienced or hadn't the knowledge to decide whether 'the rock is in the condition of a death trap or whether it may be climbed without accident'.

*

A misadventure which very nearly ended in disaster, happened on 17 May 1908 when a visitor from Germany, Baron Von Hahn, set out from the *Pen-y-gwryd Hotel*, to climb Glyder Fawr. It was misty high up, and the Baron had reached what he thought was his goal, but in reality it seems that he had only got as far as Castell y Gwynt (Castle of the Wind). While he paused there, he accidentally dislodged a large rock which fell on to his leg, fracturing it. He made himself as comfortable as possible, and although he had told them in the hotel where he was going, no rescue party came looking for him. Next morning he decided not to wait any longer, but to attempt to get himself back to the hotel. He made an improvised splint from his walking stick, and spent the whole day dragging himself slowly and painfully down the rough slope, his only food being a small piece of chocolate. A second night was spent out on the mountain without food or water, but on the third day his shouts were answered by the barking of dogs. This alerted the hotel staff, and before long Baron Von Hahn, who had almost completed the descent to the hotel, was found by a rescue party near the mountain wall, about half a mile from the road. It was an amazing example of sheer determination to survive, coupled with great resourcefulness.

*

New fashions were emerging, not only in the type of clothing and equipment favoured by mountaineers, but also in their attitudes. In 1909 Leonard Salt, who was a brewer from Burton on Trent, and a lady companion — Miss Hudson — were the subject of an article in the *Climbers' Club Journal*. Leonard Salt was an experienced climber and a member of the Climbers' Club, and he and Miss Hudson, who was also a competent mountaineer and well-known as one of the foremost lady climbers of the time, frequently climbed together. During this year the two of them had completed many of the most challenging routes in Britain, the majority of them in Snowdonia and some of which had not previously been climbed by a lady. In addition to their growing renown as climbers, they also became well-known for their up-to-date clothing and equipment, and the report in the *Climbers' Club Journal* stated, 'The equipment of the party, (which included Miss Hudson's father), was more than surprising. Switzerland and Italy had been ransacked for the newest and lightest pattern of rope. The leader's boots bristled with a brave ferrage of UHU nails and some were provided with scarpetti, (rope-soled climbing shoes), 'indispensable for difficult ascensions'[1]

1. Recently introduced UHU (Stollen) nails, which were screwed on, were very efficient, but required frequent checking to make sure that they were not working loose.

No self-respecting Geneva paper would have hesitated to describe them as 'Alpinistes enrages'. But clothing and equipment, *per se*, offer no passports to safety in the mountains, for however careful one might be there must always be an element of chance; an unfortunate slip, a turned ankle on a loose stone, a snagged rope, or the failure of an item of equipment can make all the difference between a successful climb and failure.

During the Easter holiday the following year, 1910, Leonard Salt and Miss Hudson, together with her father, set out from the *Pen-y-gwryd Hotel* and headed for Llyn Llydaw with the intention of climbing The Horned Crag route on the East Buttress of Lliwedd. According to an account of their expedition in the visitors' book, at the foot of the climb they met two men called Hurst and Hubbock who intended to do the same route and the two parties decided to join forces and do the climb together. Salt was leading, followed by Miss Hudson and the others, and they were all tied on the same new light-weight rope. When they were about 250 feet up the climb, Salt passed round a small shoulder and disappeared out of sight of the rest of the party. Shortly afterwards, the stillness was suddenly broken by Miss Hudson's agonised shout, 'Look out, Daddy!' She felt a slight tug on the rope as Salt, unseen by any of his own party, fell into the East Gully, trailing the end of the rope which had broken only a few feet from him. It was believed that in the run-out the rope had caught round some projecting rock and there belayed itself, thus taking the sudden strain of Salt's weight which caused it to break. Mr Hudson heard a sickening thud and thought perhaps it was from another party above them. He then saw a man sliding on his back down a snow slope in the East Gully. Hudson and Hubbock saw the man hit several rocks before he came to rest, apparently lifeless, at the bottom of the gully. The realization that this was their leader slowly sank in.

Another group which was half way up the West Buttress on the Bilberry Terrace did, in fact, see Salt come off, and decided that they could reach him more quickly by continuing their climb to the summit and descending to him from the top. The fall had occurred at 2.30pm, but it was not until nearly an hour and a half later that the Bilberry Terrace party reached the top of Lliwedd. It took them another quarter of an hour to reach Salt's body, almost at the same time that his companions reached the spot. From the nature of his injuries, there could be no doubt that Leonard Salt could not have lived for more than a few minutes. The body was brought down to Pen-y-pass and thence taken to Capel Curig by his friends.

*

On Good Friday, three days before Salt's accident, Charles Donald Robertson, one of a party of five staying at the *Gorphwysfa Hotel* at Pen-y-pass, was leading up the first pitch on the left wall of the Eastern Gully of Glyder Fach. It was the first day of his holiday, and he had not given himself time to tone up his muscles. But this pitch was well within his normal capabilities and he felt fit enough to lead the first rope. A report of the incident states, 'He elected to ascend the left-hand side of the precipitous slab ... Some 25 feet up, the climbing grew very severe, and he made some apology for keeping the others waiting, saying that his fingers were out of practice on this, his first day. His efforts seemed to those below to be doomed to failure, and they suggested that he should come down and try another less exacting route. He pressed on and for some ten feet he forced his way up inch by inch in silence, relying principally, it seemed, upon his magnificent strength'.

The others were 30 feet below him and they could see what appeared to be an excellent handhold just out of reach. He was seen to make a supreme effort to get both hands over it, but it was deceptive, — sloping and smooth, and utterly useless. For a moment he hung there, his strength gone, made a futile effort to find a foothold and then, after a second's pause, his hands quietly opened, and he dropped silently. 'It is almost certain that the fall was due to momentary suspension of consciousness, induced by the over-taxing of untrained muscle and nerve.' (Accident report *CCJ*) He fell head first about 30 feet on to the rocky ground below, where the rest of his party were standing. He was unconscious, and two of his companions ran down to the first-aid post at Ogwen Cottage to raise the alarm and fetch the stretcher. They brought it up to the spot, and Robertson's friends, helped by a large number of climbers who had been attracted by the shouting and general activity, carried him down to the road from where he was taken in a motor vehicle to the hospital in Bangor. First aid had been given at the scene of the accident, but, in spite of this, Robertson died early the following morning in the hospital, without recovering consciousness.

An article in *The Carnarvon and Denbigh Herald* the following week made a profound judgement on the deaths of Salt and Robertson, the final three sentences of which could well be repeated today to put the often emotional criticism by the general public into proper perspective. The public often throw up their hands in horror and express righteous indignation that mountaineers should risk their own lives, and then expect others to risk their's in going out to rescue them. The writer of the article stated, 'We have carefully reviewed the circumstances surrounding the death of these two cragsmen and we can find nothing left undone which might have been done, to spare their friends and relatives the intense grief they must now be experiencing. Two lives have been lost in a most untimely manner. Two young men went out on the mountains rejoicing in their strength and were brought back, one a corpse, the other fatally injured. It was the purest of accidents. The cragsmen require no moralising upon the dangers and follies of their pastime. They seek it out of deliberate choice because the pursuit of the pleasure keeps their bodies fit, their minds alert, their nerves wrought to glorious tension. When the race becomes decadent we shall not have these dreadful tragedies, but a vastly greater tragedy will have overtaken the British race'.

*

In mid-October of the same year two parties set out to climb Y Garn at Drws-y-coed, to the west of Rhyd-ddu. There are three main climbs on this mountain — the East, Central and West Ridges, and whilst the East and West Ridges were not considered difficult routes, the Central Ridge had not then been climbed. The two parties climbed on two ropes of three, and each was led by an experienced and competent climber. One party, led by T C Ormiston Chant, reached the summit by the East Ridge route without any difficulty, but the other, led by young Anton Stoop, who was described as one of the finest and most promising climbers of his generation, was finding difficulty in making an ascent of the Central Ridge. The smooth, almost ledgeless upper section was too much for them, as was a steep mossy cleft in front of the buttress. They then tried to traverse towards the large gully which splits the cliff from top to bottom, and there they made another unsuccessful attempt to climb directly upwards. Anton Stoop worked his way still further to the left, entered a chimney and made some slow progress upwards. His two companions were together on a grassy ledge which sloped outwards to a 300 foot drop to the screes below. Stoop's movements were screened from his companions by a rock buttress and they didn't see what actually happened, but suddenly there was a tremendous rumble as an avalanche of rocks, with Stoop in the midst of them, came crashing down. Stoop was falling feet first as though he had tried to jump clear of the huge boulders around him.

As Anton Stoop hit the grassy ledge on which the other two were belaying, the second man instinctively tightened his grip on the rope as the leader rebounded over the side. As the rope slipped through the second's fingers, it seemed certain that all three would be dragged down, but the strain was too great and suddenly the rope broke leaving the two men on the grassy ledge whilst Anton Stoop plunged to his death on the screes 300 feet below. The other party, waiting on the summit of Y Garn, realised that an accident had happened and hastened down to the screes but Stoop was beyond help. A well-known member of the Climbers' Club, George D Abraham, referring to Anton Stoop's death, wrote, 'it was an accident typical of many others for which Snowdonia is becoming only too notorious. Why are these accidents so frequent? How is it

Y Garn and Nantlle Ridge. [SNP]

that of recent years more British climbers have been killed on the Welsh mountains than in the Alps? The answer is undoubtedly that the rock-climbing in North Wales is largely undertaken on unsuitable rock. With one or two exceptions the formation is slaty and most unstable. Moreover, vegetation is too much in evidence on these more southerly mountains. The upper reaches of the crags are nearly always loose, whilst in Scotland and the Lake District mountains the opposite is the case'.

Abraham picked out Lliwedd as being 'the most treacherous mountain in Wales, with its bewildering sequences of loose, firm, friable, and vegetation-masked rocks. Despite its unsuitability, Lliwedd has become covered with numerous complicated and excessively dangerous routes. Like many of the other British rock climbs, these are far more difficult than anything ordinarily attempted in Switzerland. In the Alps it is usually hard enough to find the easiest way up a peak; in Wales, especially, enthusiasts outvie each other in finding the most difficult. In fact some think that this is the most insidious cause of many mountain tragedies. The spirit of rivalry must cease to exist or, with the rapidly increasing popularity of rock climbing, the Welsh mountains will become as ill-famed as the Dolomites which have been named the 'Shambles of the Alps'. In conclusion Abraham wrote that safe rock is to be found on the

Ysgolion Duon (The Black Ladders).   *[Tony Welch]*

peaks of Tryfan, the grand rocks of Craig-yr-ysfa, the Black Ladders (Ysgolion Duon) in the Carneddau, or even the Glyders. But even so he urges climbers, 'ever remember the tragic lesson of the past that even the best Welsh crags err in the looseness of their structures. Welsh climbers should, in the words of the Prophet, 'ponder well the path of their feet'.

*

The *Herald*, dated 24 February 1911, carried a headline 'Blown into a Lake — Naval Pensioner drowned at the foot of Snowdon' followed by a report of the inquest on 49-year-old Charles Birkenhead, employed as postman by the Britannia Copper mine. He 'had occasion to take a telegram to the manager of the mine who lived by Llyn Llydaw', and was last seen by Rawson Owen, landlord of the *Gorphwysfa Hotel* at 7.40pm on the night he disappeared. There was a strong gale blowing, and Owen warned him not to go out as the conditions were too dangerous, but Birkenhead replied that he could not shirk his duty however stormy it was. Rawson Owen gave him the best lamp he had in the hotel, but Birkenhead told him, 'My boy, don't trouble; I shall be all right, and I can swim the lake if necessary'. Later that evening it became known that Birkenhead had not arrived at the manager's house, and a search party of eight men set out to look for him. He was not found that night, and the search was resumed the next day when Birkenhead's body was found floating in the lake. There were no marks on the body and foul play was ruled out. A rational explanation for what happened is that as Birkenhead was crossing the causeway, which is about 100 yards long, by 3 yards wide, and divides the lake, he was hit by a vicious gust of wind which blew him into the water. The verdict was 'Accidentally drowned', the jury adding that the causeway was very dangerous and should be railed on both sides for safety. Their views were conveyed to the Inspector of Mines, but the railings were never erected. This incident is the only recorded accident to have occurred on the causeway, and whilst it was not strictly a mountaineering fatality, it did require a search party which had to go out in extremely bad weather conditions.

*

The Easter period of 1913 brought many people to Snowdonia to enjoy the winter conditions, and it turned out to be an eventful weekend. There had been a heavy snowfall and mindful of the growing popularity of climbing, one newspaper announced that 'Mount Tryfaen (*sic*) and the neighbouring mountains are in delightful order for the mountaineer. All the hard places are easy, and the gullies are so filled with ice and snow that there is no need to use handhold or foothold'. One party which took the article at face value, so misjudged their climb up the North Buttress of Tryfan that by 8pm, when darkness fell, they were still 150 feet below the North Summit with a steep snow-slope ahead of them. At about 10pm, some of the guests in the *Pen-y-gwryd* raised the alarm, and shortly before 11pm a search party, which had come round from *Pen-y-gwryd* to Ogwen, made visual contact with the night-bound party who were striking matches to show where they were! They were helped off the mountain soon after first light, and in spite of the intense cold at almost 3,000 feet above sea level, none suffered any ill effects. It had been a calm and dry night, otherwise it might well have been a very different story.

Over the same weekend, two climbers, one of them a lady, also had cause to disagree with the Press report about there being no need for handhold or foothold. They were ascending Nor'-Nor' Gully, (in normal summer conditions one of the easiest routes on Tryfan), and had reached a point near the curious 'Tombstone' rock when they heard a loud, sharp noise above them. The lady, who was leading, shouted a warning and they both crouched down, plunging their ice-axes deep into the snow. Just to their left a small snow avalanche poured into the gully, gathered momentum, and swept them down at least 100 feet, providentially landing them on a ledge above the next steep cliff below, with neither climber suffering any injury.

Snowdon itself was not without its share of the weekend's events, and two climbers who were on Clogwyn-y-garnedd on the Saturday morning came across two men who had survived after being caught in a storm the previous night. They were crag-fast, and told their rescuers that a third companion had fallen sometime during the night. They agreed that as he would have fallen several hundred feet he almost certainly would be dead by now. Having got the two men to a more secure position, they descended to search for the third man, but without success. Then all four set off for Llanberis where they arrived several hours later. The rescuers took the two survivors to where they were staying only to find the third man fast asleep in bed! They found him just in time to stop the search party which was about to go out to look for them. Miraculously, he had survived his fall, and finding that he had no voice contact with the others had made his way back to their lodgings.

*

The next fatal mountaineering incident to be reported in the Press occurred in 1915, the first full year of the Great War; a brief report was published in the 1920 issue of the Climbers' Club *Bulletin*. It stated that Miss Byford, who was on holiday from Chelmsford in Essex, had fallen from Crib Goch and was killed. She was with a party which had come across Crib-y-ddysgl from Snowdon and was descending the North Ridge of Crib Goch. At about 4.30pm Miss Byford slipped in the 'notch', and fell down a gully for about 250–300 feet. It was almost dark when news of the accident reached Pen-y-pass, and it was reported that the lady had fallen down the west side of the ridge into Cwm Glas. Three men in the party climbed down and examined Miss Byford and as all of them were sure that life was extinct, and in view of the very bad weather, they left the body where it was until daylight. A recovery party from Pen-y-pass and Pen-y-gwryd, supported by a number of soldiers who were guarding the power station in Cwm Dyli, eventually found the body on the east side of the ridge, and not the west side as had been reported the previous evening.

From then on mountaineering, like so many other of the country's leisure activities, was continued at a much reduced level until the end of the war, for almost every man able-bodied enough to climb mountains found himself in uniform in the trenches, or at sea, unless his conscience dictated otherwise. It is interesting to note that Mr Owen, landlord of the *Gorphwysfa Hotel*, in spite of being severely wounded in the Boer War, was a splendid example of one man who in August 1914 immediately volunteered once again to serve his country. He was to serve in Gallipoli, Palestine, Mesopotamia and in France before being demobilised fit and well. Whilst he was away, Mrs Owen and her children strove gallantly to maintain the standards of their hotel throughout the five long years of war. The *Bulletin* of 1920 stated without comment that of the rather more than 50 climbers who had attended the Pen-y-pass meets in past years, 20 had been killed and 16 wounded during the war years.

Towards the end of hostilities in July 1918, a young man called Reginald Bedford, aged 18, was staying at Pen-y-pass. He set off early on 3 July to climb Snowdon, and that was the last time he was seen alive. He failed to return that evening, but as manpower was very scarce only a perfunctory search was carried out, with negative results. A fortnight later a lone shepherd came across Bedford's body on the south side of Glaslyn at the foot of Clogwyn-y-garnedd. It was thought that the most likely cause of his death was that whilst scrambling up the zigzags he veered off to the left before he reached the Bwlch Glas ridge, and that he then pressed on across the ever-steepening slope, finally losing his balance and falling several hundred feet to his death. There was no evidence about the weather conditions, but if the foregoing assumption of the route Bedford had taken is correct, it would seem likely that there would have been considerable cloud cover over the mountains. If visibility had been good, no one would have taken a short cut across the slopes of Clogwyn-y-garnedd when they could clearly see the ridge only a short distance above. There is the possibility that Bedford had deliberately left the Pyg track well before he reached the zigzags, decided to scramble up one of the Trinity gullies, lost his footing and fell to the bottom where his body was eventually found. As there were no witnesses the true cause of the accident will never be known.

10: The Inter-War Years

During the 1920s and 1930s, public interest in Alpine and Himalayan mountaineering increased, largely because of the publicity surrounding successive attempts to climb Mount Everest, and the publication of mountaineering and expedition books by eminent mountaineers such as Geoffrey Winthrop Young, Frank Smythe, George & Ashley Abraham, Arnold Lunn and Dorothy Pilley. The ever-growing popularity of climbing in areas such as Snowdonia went largely unnoticed, though the Climbers Club published three rock-climbing guides to the area. The reporting of accidents by newspapers, notably *The Times* and *The Manchester Guardian*, created some interest in mountaineering in Britain, but their reports were sometimes misleading: it is a problem which persists to this day, and is sometimes due to an over-eager reporter trying to get a good story, but more often because witnesses of the accidents are traumatised. Another source of inaccurate information can be the casualty department of a hospital. A casualty, probably in shock, is asked what happened, but cannot give a true picture of the course of events, and the resulting story may be over-dramatised and far from the truth. In articles published in the *Rucksack Club Journal* in the 1930s, and in *Climbing in Britain* (1949), published by the British Mountaineering Council, it was suggested that it is better for someone involved in the rescue to give reporters an account of what occurred rather than let them piece together bits of information gained from a number of sources, often resulting in an inaccurate story being published. Journalists are often looked upon with suspicion and mistrust, and all too often rescuers refuse to have anything to do with them which only serves to make matters worse and leaves the journalist to make up his own version of the story. Happily, in many mountainous areas, including Snowdonia, there are reporters who always strive to uphold the principles of good reporting and to which their balanced and accurate stories bear testimony. The late Emyr Jones of Bangor was respected and admired for his truthful and balanced reporting over 45 years of mountain rescue incidents, and this tradition has been followed by Gerald Williams of Caernarfon, and others.

*

On Whit Monday, 16 May 1921, a party of four mountaineers, 64-year-old

Reverend W E Durham, rector of Trusham, South Devon, and prebendary of Exeter, and Messrs Bristow of Leicester (engineer), Peacock of Newton Abbott (Durham's friend) and Price, an accountant from Cardiff, were climbing on the Central Buttress on the East Face of Tryfan. This route, 560 feet long, includes two chimneys, the final one of which is distinctly difficult in the middle section where there are only small holds, and it demands strenuous effort. The exit from the chimney comes out very close to the summit of the mountain, and Durham, an experienced climber, who had done this climb several times, was leading up this final chimney, with Bristow, who was only a beginner, roped to him. They were almost at the top of the chimney, past the main difficulties, when Durham appeared to be in trouble, and shouted, 'I cannot get up'. He then asked Peacock to come up and help him, but while Peacock was climbing Durham shouted, 'I can't hold on much longer'. Bristow called to him to hold on, but Durham slipped. Bristow crouched on the slab he was belayed on holding the rope, but Durham fell past him from 20 feet above to about the same distance below him; there was a great tug on the rope, but Durham had landed head-first on a small stone-covered ledge and died at once. Peacock was already very close to Durham when he fell, and had he been able to hold on for another few seconds Peacock might have been in a position to help him. It was stated at the inquest that Durham was a fit and active climber who had done this climb several times previously and that the accident was caused by a technical error. Durham was relying on finding adequate handholds and footholds, rather than wedging himself into the chimney. He could not find the right foothold, and his hands and arms must have got tired as he was placing too much reliance on them alone.

*

When young Dorothy Pilley was being initiated into the sport of mountaineering, a schoolmaster named Herbert Carr, an experienced alpinist, led her up a climb on Lliwedd in perfect weather. After a stop for lunch he continued to climb until eventually he was slightly to her right and about 15 feet above her. While she waited, she recalled a piece of advice read recently in *Climbing in the Ogwen District* , that, in the descriptive phraseology used by the author, Archer Thomson, it was good practice to 'belay the rope around a stook of bollards' (sic) and she proceeded to do just that. It happened to be an ideal belay; not such as was sometimes called a 'coroner's belay', chosen not so much for its reliability as for a survivor to state at an inquest that the party knew what they were doing and did have a belay. Above her, Herbert Carr was cautiously surmounting a steep section, and as he put his arms round the rock in a hugging movement, a block came away and both he and the rock shot outwards from the face. As he and the block swept past her, Dorothy Pilley held on to the rope, and although she managed to hold him, the rope slipped through her palms causing some burning. Herbert Carr hit the ledge on which Dorothy was standing and then fell further down the face until she was able to take the strain. She heard him say in a calm, distant voice, 'I'm all right'. He managed to drag himself back to Dorothy's ledge, suffering from shock, but still showing great calmness and self-possession. It was immediately apparent that he had suffered a broken leg, with the shin bone exposed for five inches. Whilst he rested on the ledge, Dorothy Pilley tore up her blouse and bound up his wounds, but happily there was not a great deal of bleeding. In spite of his injuries, Herbert Carr, believing that Dorothy was not yet sufficiently competent on rock, led up the remaining 400 feet of the climb. After reaching the top, they considered their best course of action and decided to go on to the summit of Snowdon. Carr figured that it would be less painful to drag his broken leg up the slope than to have to put weight on it going down the long descent to Nant Gwynant by the Watkin Path. From the summit they made their way slowly and painfully down to Llanberis, Carr using Dorothy Pilley as a crutch, until eventually they reached a stream where they were able to wash and cool Carr's injured limb. Dorothy then left him by the stream and went down to telephone for help.

After this traumatic experience, Carr spent six weeks in splints. In spite of being forbidden by her family to climb again, Dorothy started climbing with Herbert Carr's father; but as soon as his splints could be discarded, Herbert and Dorothy began climbing together again!

Carr once again figured in a dramatic incident which illustrates the human will to survive in adverse and arduous situations. The event which occurred high up in Cwm Glas on 4 September 1925 must rank as one of the most dramatic.

Herbert R C Carr, MA, a schoolmaster and member of the Alpine and Climbers' Clubs, a Fellow of the Royal Geographical Society and later the author of the *Climbers Guide to Snowdon and the Beddgelert District* and other books such as *The Mountains of Snowdonia*, set out early on that morning to climb in the cwm with a friend named S B Van Noorden, who was President of Cambridge University Mountaineering Club. They had met in Beddgelert and taken the local bus to Snowdon Ranger from where they walked to Clogwyn Du'r Arddu which they reached by 11am. After doing some pitches on the Far West Buttress of Clogwyn Du'r Arddu they completed the East Wall Climb from the Eastern Terrace and reached the top of the cliff soon after 1pm. They walked across the railway line and the Llanberis path, and dropped down the steep slopes into Cwm Glas. What had started as a fine day had by now deteriorated and thick cold mist enshrouded them. They had intended to climb on Clogwyn-y-ddysgl but in view of the weather decided that it would be too risky and they descended towards the road where they correctly assumed that conditions would be more favourable. They headed for Bryn Goleu farm which they reached at 3pm, and then walked up to the rocks at the bottom of Gyrn Las ridge on the western side of the cwm. These rocks are about 400 feet above the farm, and 500 yards to the west, and are within easy walking distance of the road. But they are off the beaten track and not much used by climbers, a fact which has considerable bearing on what then occurred. Conditions had become dry and fair, and after completing four pitches of a much higher standard than anticipated, they arrived at a ledge covered with heather and sporting a holly bush. Van Noorden led from here up a 20 foot chimney, but Carr decided to try a corner to his right. As he made his way towards it, he stepped on some heather which gave way and his weight came on to the rope, but he continued to fall and lost consciousness. When he came to he was lying among some boulders about 40 feet from the foot of the crag, and saw Van Noorden some feet away from him. As he gathered his wits he realised that he had dragged Van Noorden down with him when he fell. They had fallen violently down the rock face, striking it several times before falling amongst boulders on a grassy slope. When Herbert Carr eventually came round properly and his senses returned, his limbs were painfully stiff — he thought with bruises and cold - and he was unable to move. The reality of it was that he was suffering from a broken jaw, wrist and pelvis, and he also had spinal compression. Van Noorden, still roped to him, was lying several feet away and it was clear from his injuries that he had been killed outright. During the next two days and nights misty rain fell almost continuously. Any food that they had brought with them had been lost in the fall, and the nights were bitterly cold. Down below the alarm had been raised, and a number of fellow climbers spent much time looking for the two missing men. Since it was known that they had started their expedition from Snowdon Ranger, the search was concentrated to the west of Carnedd Ugain and Cwm Glas, taking in the summit of Snowdon and the mountain railway line. Some parties did descend into Cwm Glas but although they passed within earshot several times, they were searching a good deal higher up on the more popular climbing routes. Carr heard the voices of the searchers, and tried to attract their attention, but his voice was too weak, and a little rock-wall under which the two men lay is not visible to anyone approaching from the road, and it also effectively screened his plaintive cries for help. Herbert Carr became progressively weaker from the effects of the wet and cold, and of hunger, but after dark at the start of his third night out, although still hardly able to move, he was found by sheer chance. A farmer and his wife, Mr and Mrs Ellis from Blaen y Nant Farm below, were looking for some of their cattle which had strayed towards the top of Cwm Glas, when she said to her husband that she thought she had heard someone calling for help. He told her she was imagining it. Both listened carefully for a short while, then they both heard Carr's feeble cries. Mrs Ellis called to him, 'Where are you?' and he replied, 'I am here. I think my leg is broken. One of us is dead.' Mrs Ellis then shouted, 'We are coming.' and Carr cried, 'God bless you.'

Carr, by this time suffering from exposure, was later stretchered off the hill to the Quarry Hospital in Llanberis and Van Noorden's body was removed to the mortuary there. The inquest was held at the hospital on Saturday 7 September and a verdict of accidental death was returned. A friend of Van Noorden told the Coroner that he (Van Noorden) was an intrepid mountaineer who used to say that 'to follow the beaten track is like waltzing upstairs to one's bedroom. It might take longer, but the best way is to storm up the front of the house.'

Carr admitted that the initial error — 'an unguarded move on precarious holds' — was his. He was not belayed nor was he belaying Van Noorden; he was moving at the same time as the leader. Once again it behoves everyone to remember that 'a momentary negligence may destroy the happiness of a lifetime'.

In addition to the report of the accident and the inquest proceedings, the local paper considered the event worthy of an editorial which stated, 'It is an astonishing thing that Mr Carr should have lain on the mountainside roped to a dead man for two nights in stormy weather, wedged between two rocks and trussed up in his own rope. Searchers had passed above him and failed to hear his feeble calls and it was only Mrs Ellis, the farmer's wife, calling the cattle home from the scene of the tragedy, who providentially heard Mr Carr.

By the way, no climber or walker on Snowdon should be without an alarm whistle'.

There was no evidence that Carr was 'wedged between two rocks' or that he was trussed up in his own rope. His injuries were so severe that they alone were enough to prevent him moving from the spot where he came to rest. In December of that year (1925), in spite of the injuries he had sustained in this tragic accident, Herbert Carr was present at the opening of Helyg, the Climbers' Club hut in the Ogwen Valley, which he had worked so hard to get established.

It is interesting to note that some of the men searching for Carr and Van Noorden came across a memorial stone to the north and just below the summit of Crib-y-ddysgl, which refers to a fatal accident which had occurred 66 years previously, (see chapter 4). The inscription reads:

Sacred to the Memory
of my old friend, C H Frodsham,
who died here, 14 Aug 1859.

But in fact Frodsham was killed on the rocks below Clogwyn Coch, much further down the mountain.

In the 1920s and 1930s, walking and scrambling became increasingly popular pastimes, resulting in more incidents involving twisted ankles and sudden sickness such as heart attacks, asthma or exposure. Fatal accidents became more common amongst walkers who slipped and sometimes slid hundreds of feet, hitting rocks as they careered down the mountain-side. In many of the less serious incidents, the casualties were rescued by their colleagues, aided if necessary by other walkers in the vicinity. Only those accidents serious enough to need a stretcher and extra man-power found their way into the records. Many years later when the mountain rescue service was properly organised, the regular recording and analysis of all mountain incidents became an essential part of the rescue work.

11: The Giveen Affair

On a typically raw November day, in 1927, an event took place in the Ogwen Valley which shocked mountaineers and others throughout Britain. A party of four young men, F W Giveen, Norman Stott, Arthur Taylor and W H T Cayleur, who were staying together in the Climbers' Club hut at Helyg, mid-way between Capel Curig and Ogwen Cottage, set out on Sunday morning, 20 November, to climb Great Gully on Craig-yr-Ysfa. Giveen had recently been proposed for membership of the Climbers' Club and although he was said to be an excellent and experienced mountaineer and completely without physical fear, he had been blackballed by a member of the Committee named Raymond Greene, who happened to be staying at Helyg when Giveen arrived with his three friends on the Saturday. Raymond Greene, the brother of the writer Graham Greene, was a doctor at St Bartholomew's Hospital and was subsequently the medical officer on two major Himalayan expeditions, Kamet in 1931 and Everest in 1933. In spite of having been refused membership because of Greene, Giveen greeted him warmly as an old friend, and they seem to have spent a pleasant evening together.

Of the three others, only Stott had done any rock-climbing and Taylor and Cayleur lacked even experience of hill-walking. In spite of this, Giveen was not to be deterred from leading them up Great Gully, which was then one of the

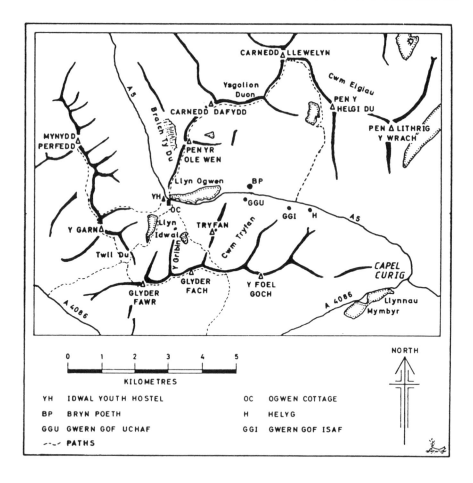

longest and stiffest climbs in North Wales. Even on a dry, warm day it can tax the ability of inexperienced climbers: in winter, snow or wet conditions can make the route extremely arduous. North and west of Helyg a long straight track (now a tarmac private road as far as Llyn Ffynnon Llugwy), leads steadily uphill in a NNE direction for one and a half miles before turning due north, skirting Llyn Ffynnon Llugwy at 1,800 feet above sea level, and finally zigzagging steeply up on to the Pen-yr-Helgi Ddu ridge at a point just SE of the top of Craig-yr-Ysfa. The distance from Helyg to the top of the ridge is 2 miles with an ascent of c. 1500 feet: there is then a steep descent of 750 feet into Cwm Eigiau to the bottom of Craig-yr-ysfa. The long trudge through bitterly cold wind and driving rain must have been dispiriting for them all, but especially for the two inexperienced men. All four would have been wet through before they even started the climb.

In the prevailing conditions Great Gully would have been a series of cascading waterfalls, and these, together with rain and wind, wet clothes and chilled bodies, so slowed their progress that it was after 6pm, and dark, when Giveen finally reached the top by the light of a candle-lantern. He was well used to such conditions, and being mountain-fit seems to have taken it all in his stride. Whatever one might think about the decision to press on with such an arduous climb, Giveen's leadership must have been of a high order for the party to complete the climb. Once on the ridge, there would have been some satisfaction at having done so, but their only aim then was to scramble down and find the track which would lead them to Helyg and food, warmth, and shelter. The going was rough and they stumbled down the rock-strewn slopes in a southerly direction towards Llyn Ffynnon Llugwy, making slow progress even downhill.

Of the novices, it seemed that Cayleur was the most seriously affected and it was he who accidentally dropped their only compass. Aided by the failing light from the lantern, they searched for it amongst rocks, heather and bilberry bushes, but to no avail, and when the candle finally went out altogether, they stumbled on in complete darkness. Walking blindly on, Stott and Taylor fell into the unseen lake, but Stott managed to scramble out on to the bank: then, hearing Taylor, whom he knew could not swim, floundering in the icy water, he dived back in and after an immense struggle managed to get him to the shore. Utterly exhausted, they both collapsed face downwards on the boggy shore of the lake where they lay too tired to move. In any context, Stott's reaction to this dreadful situation can only be described as heroic.

Giveen and Cayleur, who had been falling behind Stott and Taylor due to Cayleur's distress, now caught up with them and Giveen should have realised at once that what had been an unpleasant predicament, was now fraught with danger. According to his own account, he appreciated that as leader it was his duty to save his companions, and he declared that he believed that Cayleur would certainly collapse unless he soon reached proper shelter. He therefore dragged Stott and Taylor behind a rock, as far as possible out of the wind and driving rain, and then, leaving them on their own, he assisted Cayleur, now in a very parlous state, down to Helyg. Because of Cayleur's weakness, they took four hours to cover the one and a half miles to the hut, which they reached at

2.15am. Giveen's account went on to say that they were in Helyg only long enough to eat some food, after which they drove the 6 miles to the *Pen-y-gwryd Hotel*, raising the alarm in Capel Curig on the way. Giveen stated that they arrived at *Pen-y-gwryd* at 6.25am. The hotel owner, Arthur Lockwood, was a mountaineer himself and had been involved in a number of rescues during the many years he had been running the hotel: he set about organising a search party to go out at first light. They knew exactly where to start looking and, as they approached the Llyn, they were attracted by the croaking of a number of ravens slowly wheeling above the far shore where they quickly found the bodies of Stott and Taylor.

Subsequent evidence revealed, however, that Giveen's account was not true and what in fact had happened came out only after the inquest. Giveen had stated that on finding Stott and Taylor lying exhausted on the boggy ground, he realised that he must get the two men into shelter from the wind and rain, try to restore their circulation, and give them any clothing he didn't immediately need himself. The later evidence revealed that what actually happened was that the urge for self-preservation took over, and Giveen and Cayleur left their two companions lying where they were, still face down in the bog, without making the slightest effort to help them. When they reached Helyg, probably two hours later and not the four hours which Giveen said it took them, they ate a good meal and went to bed. It was nearly 6am when they awoke and, finding that Stott and Taylor had not returned, they decided that something should be done. Instead of seeking help from the nearest farm which was only ten minutes' walking time away - and there were other farms nearby within almost the same radius - they drove to the *Pen-y-gwryd Hotel*, passing through Capel Curig on the way but without making any effort to raise the alarm there. On arrival at the *Pen-y-gwryd* at 6.25am, the first thing they did was to have a good breakfast; and this before they told Arthur Lockwood, the hotelier, that two of their companions were missing near Llyn Ffynnon Llugwy, and even then they conveyed no sense of urgency to him.

At the inquest, held in the Helyg hut on the evening following the disaster, Monday 21 November, Giveen's was the only evidence produced. The coroner commented about the wisdom of proceeding with the expedition itself, saying that it was 'an unusual decision to set out on such a morning as Sunday, as the weather was unreliable, and the day short.' A verdict of 'death by exposure' was brought in, and a certain amount of sympathy was expressed for Giveen. That seemed to be the end of the matter, but there was disquiet in some quarters as to why the discrepancy between Giveen's story and the evidence of the rescue party was not questioned at the inquest, and why Giveen was not challenged by the leader of that party. It must have been crystal clear that one of the versions of the events that night on the shore of Llyn Ffynnon Llugwy was not true. Not only were the two deceased men lying face down where they had collapsed, but their rucksacks were still on their backs and Taylor's face was actually in a pool of water: he had drowned in it though he would surely have died of exposure anyway.

Stott's father was profoundly dissatisfied with the inquest verdict. He expressed his views most forcefully, accusing Giveen of gross irresponsibility in attempting such a severe climb with three inexperienced climbers and insisting that Giveen should have aborted the expedition in view of the atrocious weather conditions. At first little notice was taken of his complaints, which many people thought were the outpourings of a grieving father, but the more Stott's father thought about it the more certain he became that something was seriously amiss. He discussed his misgivings with friends, and persuaded a group of them to go with him to Llyn Ffynnon Llugwy to examine the place where the tragedy had happened, which must have been a very emotional undertaking for him. Whilst the group of men were standing on the spot where the two men had been found, one of them picked up a pocket watch. It was identified as having belonged to Taylor, and had clearly lain there in the bog since the fateful moment when Stott and Taylor had collapsed after struggling out of the freezing water. The watch had stopped at 6.40, the approximate time the tragedy happened.

If there were any doubts remaining in Stott's father's mind, they were now completely dispelled and he and his friends challenged Giveen and Cayleur to explain precisely what they had done during the twelve hours between the event occurring and when they arrived at the hotel, sat down to breakfast, and then almost as an afterthought asked the hotelier to send out a party to look for their companions. As often happens in incidents of this nature, the news spread like wildfire and was very quickly embellished with sinister rumours. The pressure on Giveen and Cayleur became intense and it was the younger man who cracked first. He had been completely overawed and dominated by Giveen, but under questioning on his own he denied that he had been in the distressed and exhausted state his leader had consistently alleged and he finally refuted the whole of Giveen's story as 'a damned lie.' It was only at this stage that the discrepancy between Giveen's story of how he had left the two men behind a boulder and how the rescue party had found them became public knowledge and the truth began to dawn. It seemed likely that Giveen had panicked and, putting his own safety first, set off down the hill, ordering Cayleur to follow him. Subsequently Stott's father proved beyond doubt, by means of measuring distances and timings, that the story now admitted by Cayleur was true.

There was a great depth of feeling against Giveen in mountaineering circles, and for his part it seems that he nurtured an obsessive hatred against Raymond Greene for blocking his entry into the Climbers' Club. He collapsed under the weight of loathing against him, and shortly afterwards was declared insane and admitted to a mental hospital. He was eventually discharged, but he still could not face his peers who continued to cold-shoulder him. Various accounts of the incident were written within a few years of the event, and all suggested that at that time Giveen was already verging on the insane. His decision to take three inexperienced climbers on such an exacting expedition in bad weather was an error of judgement, but that on its own does not indicate insanity. No doubt, in the bars and common rooms people would have said it was 'a mad thing to do', but only as a figure of speech. However, at the time of the actual incident, when he showed such callous indifference for the lives of two men who were clearly in great danger, he, like them, had endured the battering of wind and rain for a whole day. Perhaps Giveen himself was suffering from hypothermia and his judgement was thereby seriously impaired. It would be magnanimous to think that.

There was a dramatic sequel to the story. Some time after Giveen had been discharged from hospital, Raymond Greene, who was then living in Holywell in Oxford, received a telephone call from the Warden of Giveen's old college telling him that Giveen was in Oxford, and that he had been overheard saying that he was in Oxford to 'get' Raymond Greene. Greene (a tall man), apparently did not take this seriously, but a few nights later Giveen followed a tall man down Holywell and out of the city to Port Meadow, where he shot the man, who turned out to be a complete stranger, in the back. He then committed suicide by turning the gun on himself. The stranger, thankfully, was not badly injured and survived. Clearly Giveen's obsessive hatred of Raymond Greene had finally turned his mind , but he had mistaken the stranger for Greene, who lived to tell the tale in his book *Moments of Being*.

*

During the 21 years between the two World Wars, the steady increase in the number of mountain accidents continued and in 1932 the Rucksack Club set up a 'Stretcher Sub-Committee' consisting of A S Pigott and B S Harlow to consider how best to carry an injured person down a mountainside. The Fell and Rock Climbing Club of the English Lake District also set up a committee consisting of Dr C Paget Lapage and L H Pollitt with similar terms of reference; shortly afterwards the two committees came together under the title of the 'Joint Stretcher Committee' and were joined by the Manchester surgeon, Wilson H Hey, FRCS (Fell & Rock Climbing Club and Rucksack Club), and Eustace

Thomas, (Fell & Rock Climbing Club); he had an engineering company in Manchester and played a major part in the design of the 'Thomas Mountain Rescue Stretcher' which soon became standard equipment in Rescue Posts. The main features of this stretcher are:-

1. It has telescopic carrying handles which are normally pushed back inside the frame when they are not needed. They are retained there by a catch, which also prevents the handles slipping back inside the frame when in use. Their primary advantage is that when extended the rescuer at either end can see where he is putting his feet.

2. There is a yoke harness at each end through which the rescuer puts his head, thus distributing the weight more evenly.

3. The lightweight frame is made of aluminium, and stretched across it is either a canvas bed or, more commonly nowadays, a plastic covered steel net.

4. The stretcher is fitted with wooden runners which are designed to allow sufficient ground clearance for it to be lowered down rock, scree, grass or snow. It is not strong enough to be dragged over very rough ground.

5. The stretcher can be adapted so that it is divided across the centre into two halves each of which is fitted with carrying straps and becomes a one-man load. The two parts of the stretcher are locked together by wing nuts. This adaptation is called the Split Thomas stretcher.

6. A Thomas splint can be fitted to the frame as can a wire mesh head guard.[1]

Both Wilson Hey and Eustace Thomas were keen and experienced climbers, and Wilson Hey was subsequently elected chairman of the First-Aid Committee. Soon afterwards he was involved in a mountain rescue when he and two of his medical friends were climbing on the Glyders. Near the summit of Glyder Fach they came across a man who had broken his leg and needed urgent attention. Leaving one of their number with him the other two went down to get help and a stretcher from the rescue post at *Pen-y-gwryd*. On the way down they came across a gate which they 'borrowed'; mindful of the fact that saving time was all-important, they took the gate up to the ridge and after making the injured man as comfortable as they could, they put him on it and set off down the mountain. The journey was traumatic for the casualty: the gate was most uncomfortable, they had been able to apply only a makeshift splint to the broken leg which caused him intense pain, and there were no pain-killing drugs available. When they reached the road there was a long delay until an ambulance arrived, and

---

1. Even today the original design of the Thomas stretcher is still in use though some modifications have been incorporated. Major ones have been head guards, patient restraining nets, and foot plates.

while he waited Wilson Hey made up his mind that his committee would ensure that the equipment held in posts must be improved. He was convinced that morphia must be held in every post, though he realised that because of the strict drug controls it was going to be very difficult to get his proposal approved. He fought a long campaign to get official authorisation for morphia to be carried in rescue first-aid kits and for it to be used by rescue teams: it was to take fifteen years before he achieved his goal. Although in 1934 the Home Office had refused permission for morphia to be supplied to mountain rescue posts, Wilson Hey continued to supply it, keeping very careful and complete records, from 1935 until his campaign culminated on 14 August 1949, in a lost court case. Wilson Hey was found guilty of supplying morphia without prescription and was fined £10. His daughter Dorothy, now Mrs Lewtes, was working for him at the time and had first-hand knowledge of his discomfiture at the result. He was furious that his sentence was so light as he had been determined to make the outcome very dramatic and thereby add strength to his campaign. Thwarted by such a small fine, he refused to pay and was determined to go to prison to draw more attention to his cause. When the Rucksack Club paid his fine for him, his fury knew no bounds!

The case did, however, have a positive side; it had done a great deal to create a more understanding relationship between mountain rescue and the authorities as, before the end of the year, on 14 December 1949, the Home Office reversed their decision and permission was granted for morphia to be held in mountain rescue posts. Ogwen and Glencoe in Scotland were to be allowed a larger supply than other posts due to the greater frequency of accidents in those areas. Since 1949 the Mountain Rescue Committee has appointed a medical officer to be directly responsible for the supply of morphia to posts, the first being Wilson Hey himself. This arrangement continued until the early 1990s when the responsibility for the issue of morphia to MRTs was transferred to local general medical practitioners who keep detailed records, which is a legal requirement.

*

The pattern of mountain accidents which would evolve after the end of the Second World War began to take shape during the 1930s. On 22 February 1931, Colin Kirkus, one of the leading British pre-war climbers, had completed a climb up the 'long gully' on Clogwyn-y-garnedd on Snowdon with his friend Graham G MacPhee. They were on their way down the zigzags above Glaslyn when they came across a party of three walkers, Mr and Mrs Wright and their friend Dick Irwin, who had fallen on the frozen snow and suffered injuries. In his book *Let's Go Climbing*, Colin Kirkus refers to this incident in which he and Graham

MacPhee had to cut steps all the way down for the injured party. It was a typical self-rescue of the era, but does not appear to have been officially recorded or reported in the local newspapers.

Another typical accident happened in 1933, when a lady named Mrs E Watson was walking up the Pyg track when she slipped on the path and broke her leg. She was carried down to Pen-y-pass by other walkers but, unlike the previous incident, this was reported in the local paper as a serious accident.

In May 1933 a walker named Wood, who lived in Rhyl, was a member of a party of 14 which set out to climb Snowdon. Not one of them was wearing adequate footwear and, finding it very difficult to walk up the rough and steep path from Glaslyn, they all gave up at some stage and turned back; all, that is, except Mr Wood, who was the only one to reach the ridge at Bwlch Glas. The party saw Wood wave to them from a point about 300 yards from the summit, probably at the top of one of the gullies. Exactly what happened is not known, and whether he lost his balance, or walked on towards the summit and went too near the edge, is a matter of conjecture, but he was seen by other climbers to fall over the edge within a couple of minutes of waving to his friends below. He fell down a sheer drop of some 400 feet and was killed.

*

The scene now shifts once again to the Ogwen Valley, when Tryfan was the scene of a fatal accident in March 1935. A party of four, two members of the Oxford University Mountaineering Club and two girls, had completed their ascent together and decided to come down by different routes. Mr J N Mills and Miss Pritchard, who was a novice, climbed down the North Buttress, whilst the other two descended by the North Ridge. After completing their climb down the buttress, Mr Mills and Miss Pritchard unroped and proceeded to scramble down to the Heather Terrace. Mills was using his shoulder as a foothold for Miss Pritchard at an awkward step, when for no explicable reason she suddenly slipped off his shoulder and fell ten feet on to her head and was rendered unconscious. Mills was a medical student, and after giving his companion first aid he put her in as comfortable and secure a position as he could and went for help. When he returned with a rescue party, Miss Pritchard was no longer where he had left her. It was dark by this time, and getting no response to their shouts and finding no sign of her, they decided to return early the following morning to search for her. Her body was found a considerable distance below the point where she had been left, and it was thought that she must have recovered consciousness and wandered about perhaps in the dark, until she had a fatal fall. At the inquest a verdict of 'accidental death' was brought in.

*

The following year, 1936, an extensive search took place on the Carneddau for Doctor Gwendoline Limmex, aged 33. She had recently had an operation to remove her tonsils, and had come to Snowdonia with her sister to convalesce. They arrived at Ogwen Cottage on Wednesday 1 July, and set out the next morning to climb Carnedd Llewelyn, but after going only a short distance, Dr Limmex's sister decided she was not up to the ascent and turned back, leaving Dr Limmex to go on alone. According to Miss M E Limmex, her sister had 'a good mountain sense and had done some climbing abroad and in other parts of Wales, but not in this district before'.

When Dr Limmex did not return to Ogwen Cottage that afternoon, the alarm was raised and throughout Friday and Saturday a large number of people searched over a wide area of the Carneddau, but without success. On Sunday more searchers were recruited from the local villages and it was estimated that upwards of 250 people took part. It was an organised search on a sector basis, and the plan was for all the searchers to meet later in the day and make their reports. Dr Limmex's father hired an aeroplane to fly over the Carneddau to search for his daughter, but the aeroplane was grounded by low cloud and unable to take off. This was probably the first instance of the idea of air support being used in a mountain search and rescue. The sector search had not been successful, but late on Sunday afternoon Dr Limmex's body was found by a local farmer, Griffith Roberts of Braich Ddu Farm, who was searching along the Braich Ddu ridge above the Nant Ffrancon Pass. The body was lying by the side of a stream about 200 feet below the ridge, barely half a mile from Ogwen Cottage, and it seemed probable that on her way back towards the valley Dr Limmex had lost her way in mist, tried to follow the stream down, and had fallen down the precipitous water course to the spot where she was found.

*

On 8 December of the same year, a Cambridge undergraduate called N Beaumont-Thomas was leading a rope of four on Bochlwyd Buttress when he slipped and fell forty feet, landing on rocks just below the stance on which the last two men on the rope were belayed. Although there was no warning, the second man on the rope reacted instinctively, and attempted to arrest the leader's fall. In the process he suffered head and hand injuries himself but he managed to retain his position on the belay until he was able to get down safely. Beaumont-Thomas suffered a fractured femur and extensive bruising, but happily he recovered.

*

In February 1937, two young doctors, A S J Bradford (26) and E G L Latham (24), were killed when attempting to climb Javelin Gully above Idwal Slabs.

Their bodies were found roped together at the foot of the slabs, and it was assumed that one of them had come off and dragged the other with him. Both men worked at St Thomas's Hospital in London, and Bradford had just qualified as a Member of the Royal College of Surgeons.

Since 1903, the number of Rescue Posts had been increased and the amount and type of equipment held in them had been updated. In the *Mountaineering Journal*, Summer 1936, page 142, there is an article entitled 'New Equipment'. It is interesting to note that 'the new mountain stretcher evolved by members of the Rucksack Club during the last few years', (with a diagram and specifications), was listed for the first time in the 1936 catalogue of R Burns, of Manchester. The cost — a mere £15! A new Yak tent 'which was purchased by the Everest Expedition this year for use at the highest camps' is also mentioned. The price — £12!

Although the *Gorphwysfa* and *Pen-y-gwryd Hotels* had, since 1903/5, been unofficially regarded and used as the fore-runners of mountain rescue posts because of their geographical locations, it was not until 1933 that a number of mountaineering clubs and organisations, including the Climbers' Club, the Rucksack Club and the Fell & Rock Climbing Club, formed a committee which came to an agreement with Arthur Lockwood, landlord of the *Pen-y-gwryd Hotel*, that he should be co-ordinator of search and rescue operations in and around the northern part of Snowdonia. In 1935, the Joint Stretcher Committee was re-formed by a number of clubs as the 'First Aid Committee of Mountaineering Clubs'. The aim of the new Committee was to promote co-ordination between member clubs so that all important points in climbing areas would be supplied with first-aid equipment and that regular care and inspection, necessary repair, and replacement of equipment would be carried out. C P Lapage was elected the first chairman, and A S Pigott was the first secretary of the Committee, serving in that capacity for many years. By 1936 there were nine clubs represented on the committee throughout Britain. In North Wales three clubs were involved — The Climbers' Club at Helyg, the Rucksack Club at the Ogwen Youth Hostel, and the Midland Association of Mountaineers at *Pen-y-gwryd Hotel*.

The leading clubs in Britain continued to set the pace in the field of MR, and in 1938 the Climbers' Club set out in the Club *Journal* what had been achieved thus far. It was a very detailed list of all the mountain rescue posts and items of equipment held in each one, and of all essential information which could be needed quickly in emergency. But these posts alone could not possibly be the whole answer. In the event of an alarm being raised, climbers and walkers in the area at the time would be recruited, but there was no guarantee that enough of them would know how to use the equipment or be sufficiently experienced for the work. Out of season the situation was even more difficult, with miners, quarrymen, local farmers and shepherds being called on to make up the numbers. It was becoming obvious that with an increasing number of people taking to the hills, a much more sophisticated search and rescue organisation needed to be developed. However, before the end of the decade the country was at war, and as had happened between 1914 and 1918, the level of mountaineering activity in Snowdonia was reduced significantly. This was due to petrol rationing, to large tracts of mountainous country being taken over by the War Department to be used as battle training areas, and to many of the country's climbers volunteering for the armed forces. For the next few years, therefore, there was little further development in civilian mountain search and rescue but not far away from Snowdon at a small airfield by Llandwrog, just south of Caernarfon, things were happening which were to have a profound effect on the MR service once the war was over.

12: Royal Air Force, Llandwrog

For the first three years of the war, those Royal Air Force units located in or near mountainous areas, such as Llandwrog in North Wales, had to improvise when the call came to search for missing aircraft; and the calls quickly increased in frequency as the air war over Europe intensified. It was a case of relying on a regular group of volunteer airmen, many of whom had no previous knowledge or experience of mountain rescue, but would go out at any time and often in the most violent weather, to look for crashed aircraft. There was often difficulty in getting enough rescuers together, but those who did come forward soon learnt the basics of going safely in the mountains.

The history of those pioneering years is detailed in Frank Card's book *Whensoever: 50 years of the RAF Mountain Rescue Service 1943-1993* (Ernest Press 1993) and suffice it to say here that it was not until 1943 that what had already developed into a MR Service, albeit completely unofficial and still rather ad hoc, was recognised by the Air Ministry. They found out about it when, after the Harpur Hill team had found and rescued an American pilot in the Peak District, the US Army Air Force wrote to thank the Ministry for the services of the RAF Mountain Rescue. But by the time that the Air Ministry had recognised the importance of what until then had been a purely voluntary service, pioneer RAF MRTs had been involved in a very large number of search and rescue operations all over the country. The Llandwrog team alone had been called out to eleven crashes in Snowdonia, and had rescued no fewer than 12 aircrew and brought down 35 bodies. Improvisation was the name of the game, from clothing, which consisted of ordinary uniform and either marching boots or 'wellies', to vehicles which included an old ambulance.

The majority of the crashes in Wales during the war years were on the Carneddau, or on Snowdon's satellite peaks. The 3,000 foot plateau from Carnedd Dafydd to Drum, having attracted no fewer than seven crashes, became known as Graham's Graveyard, so called after Flight Lieutenant George Graham who, as the young medical officer at Llandwrog, first became involved in MR in 1941. He is remembered by those who knew him as a friendly man whose warmth extended, unusually, to the most junior ranks. George Graham had had some mountaineering experience in the Alps before the outbreak of war, and he was able to adapt this knowledge to mountain rescue. It was due to his ability to improvise, his determination and persistence, and his direct approaches for better equipment to the Air Ministry, that in January 1943 he was awarded the MBE for his rescue work but, more importantly, in July of that year the Air Ministry approved the establishment of a regular, properly equipped and trained MR Service. George Graham moved on from Llandwrog, but his epitaph must be that he was the architect of the RAF MR service on which many of the post-war civilian Mountain Rescue teams were based.

In 1945, air activity began to diminish, but the pioneering work done by the RAF teams in the early years of the war had established a legacy of skill and experience in mountain rescue practices. Over the next few years the number of RAF MRTs in Britain was reduced, but those left operational included that at Llandwrog which was then re-located to RAF Llanbedr near Harlech in the summer of 1945, and then in 1949 to RAF Valley on Anglesey. Valley is not as close to the mountains as are Llandwrog or Llanbedr, but with the increased use of helicopters in MR in the late 1960s, it proved to be a convenient base as the flying time from Valley to Snowdon is only about ten minutes. It must be remembered that the terms of reference for the highly trained and skilled RAF MRTs were to search for crashed aircraft and the rescue of their crews and passengers, but their involvement in the rescue of civilians was considered to be an essential part of their training and over the years, RAF Valley MRT has played an invaluable part in helping to find and rescue many lost or injured climbers, and indeed the crews of crashed aircraft, civilian as well as those of the RAF.

When the war ended, mountaineering in Snowdonia gradually resumed its old pattern; likewise the still inadequate civilian MR service, as is seen in the chapter 'Country Doctor.' But the lessons learned from the RAF MR service during the war years had not gone unheeded, and in 1946 the First-Aid

Committee of Mountaineering Clubs, formed in 1935, altered its name to the Mountain Rescue Committee. Its terms of reference were enlarged to include a wider range of interests, and to the original nine representative members of the First-Aid Committee were added the Youth Hostels Association, the Ramblers' Association, Caving organisations and University clubs.[1] The MRC immediately set about grappling with the organisation of the service, and civilian MR as we know it today had been born; but it had a lot of growing-up to do.[2]

13: Farmers, Shepherds and Quarrymen

By the time the Second World War began, rock-climbing and hill-walking were developing as a popular recreation, and misadventures continued to occur. But searching for missing people or rescuing casualties was still regarded as the responsibility of those taking part; there was still no organised rescue service and it was sometimes beyond the capability of the casualty's companions to get him or her safely off the mountain. Fortunately the tough quarry-men, who were skilled in swinging at the end of a rope across sheer rock faces in the quarries, were always ready to turn out to rescue fallen or crag-fast climbers. In a search for a missing person, the obvious people to lead search-parties were those who knew their way about the mountains — the farmers and shepherds. They could always be relied upon, but the development of organised groups of mountaineers as mountain rescue teams eventually replaced them. Even today farmers and shepherds are ready with advice about the terrain and routes in remote areas with which they are probably a lot more familiar than anyone else, and this is their on-going contribution to the succour of people on the mountains. But when the war began, their replacement by organised civilian rescue teams as the first line of defence was not to come about for many years.

An incident which occurred in mid-August 1938 illustrates the often

1. The original members of the First-Aid Committee were Fell & Rock Climbing Club, Rucksack Club, Alpine Club, Scottish Mountaineering Club, Yorkshire Ramblers, Climbers' Club, Midland Association of Mountaineers, Wayfarers' Club and Gritstone Club.
2. In 1950 the Mountain Rescue Committee was formed into a charitable trust; in May 1993 the name was changed from Mountain Rescue Committee to Mountain Rescue Council.

incredible feats performed by local quarrymen. Glynne Jones was 31 years old and earning 50 shillings a week as a quarryman in the Penrhyn slate quarry, Bethesda. He was on his way home from the quarry when he was told that a climber was lying on a narrow ledge on Ysgolion Duon, the very large cliff below the summit of Carnedd Dafydd. On the way up to the cliff he passed a party of police and climbers from local youth hostels, and from them he got a first-aid kit which he strapped to his waist. In thick mist, without a rope and in his working boots, Jones slowly climbed up the cliff. After two and a half hours climbing he had reached the narrow ledge where he found Robert Leslie Beaumont, a 25-year-old Oxford tutor, who had fallen 50 feet, and had been unconscious for some time. Jones started to give first-aid to the injured man and he was then joined by other rescuers including Dr Pierce Williams and his partner Dr Mostyn Williams, who were in practice together in Bethesda. Dr Pierce Williams attended to the injured climber and then Jones, the two doctors and the other rescuers, one of whom was a brain specialist from Liverpool named Edwards, carefully bound Beaumont to the stretcher which had been brought up from Ogwen Cottage. Jones and Dr Edwards lowered Beaumont down the cliff at the rate of a yard every ten minutes. Then, guided by the light of storm lanterns, Jones helped the other rescuers to carry Beaumont down mountain tracks well known to himself and other quarrymen in the party. Only when the injured man was safely in hospital at Bangor did Glynne Jones think of home and his worried wife. Exhausted, hungry and soaked, he reached his home at 4am. Two hours later he set out again for his work at the quarry, and when asked about the rescue later that morning, Glynne Jones replied, 'It was the worst climb I have ever had. When I reached that ledge I wondered how I'd got there. My only worry now is that my jacket, which I had left at the bottom of the mountain, was gone when I'd got back. It had 8 shillings in it, all the money I had'. Dr Pierce Williams later gave his opinion that, 'if there is any praise for this rescue, it should go to the quarrymen. Without them the rescue would have been impossible'.

14: A Country Doctor

One afternoon in the early 1940s, Dr Rees Pritchard was relaxing after completing his morning rounds in Bethesda, at the foot of the Nant Ffrancon Pass on the A5 road, when two climbers knocked on his door and told him that a teenage boy had slipped somewhere near the summit of Tryfan — that 3,010-foot dramatic rocky peak in the Ogwen Valley — and was unable to move. Medical assistance was needed and they urged him to go up there with them.

Although the doctor was in practice in a mountainous area, he was not, and had no pretensions to be, a mountaineer. The nearest he ever came to climbing a mountain was in the vast Penrhyn slate quarry just south of Bethesda, where accidents to quarrymen working on rock faces or in deep caverns were not uncommon. But exposure to the elements was not in any way comparable there to what it could be 2,500 feet higher on Tryfan. Doctor Rees Pritchard agreed to go with the two men, saying that he would drive up in his own car and meet them at Ogwen Cottage at the top of the pass. When the doctor arrived, to the surprise of the two climbers he emerged wearing his town overcoat, a Trilby hat, and an ordinary pair of leather shoes with smooth soles. In his hand he carried his badge of office — a little black bag.

As they made their way up the mountain, progress was slow, but they pressed on, the doctor's leather soles providing no grip whatsoever, and causing him to slip with almost every step he took. The two climbers stayed very close to him and gave him every assistance as the three of them made their way, followed by a crowd of other willing rescuers, up towards Llyn Bochlwyd. After a short rest, the party skirted the lake and soon arrived at Bwlch Tryfan. High above them, near the summit, the accident site was clearly visible and once again they set off, scrambling up the steep rocky slope to reach the injured boy. For those who do not know this mountain, it is said to be one of the few peaks in Britain which cannot be scaled without using the hands at some stage, and for a non-mountaineer carrying a bag in one hand and wearing smooth leather footwear, it was a great achievement to get to the top.

In the doctor's own words, 'the boy had been secured by other climbers who had chanced upon the scene, and he was roped to a large rock on the actual summit of the mountain and his knee was firmly wedged in a cleft in the boulders. I had never been up Tryfan before, and ... I was wearing anything but

Whirlwind helicopter winching stretchered casualty   [SNP]

proper climbing gear. In spite of this I thought I was doing pretty well, but when we were about a hundred yards from the top, I think I must have had an attack of vertigo and I said to my guides, 'Look, I can't come any further'. So they tied a rope round my middle and more or less pulled me up with them, and I felt a lot safer. The higher I was going, the better views I got, and I was able to look down and see the Nant Ffrancon Pass far below on one side, and over the mountain peaks towards Llanberis on the other. It was all very strange and I realised that I have got a phobia of heights, to my cost, so it was really quite an experience for me.'

Notwithstanding, Dr Rees Pritchard was not found wanting, and when he reached the boy he assessed the situation and managed to manipulate his leg out of the cleft and set him free. Happily there was no serious injury but there was some fairly bad bruising round the knee. The boy tried flexing the joint, found it was sound, and without even a 'Thank you' he walked away down the mountain.

Idwal Slabs.   [Tony Welch]

There was a curious sequel to this incident. About six months later, Dr Pritchard was called to an accident at Half Way Bridge on the A5 road, one and a half miles north-west of Bethesda, where he was told that a cyclist had collided with a bus. There was a body entangled with a badly bent bicycle under the bus and one of the ambulance men told the doctor that the lifeless body he was looking at was the same boy he had rescued on the summit of Tryfan.

Some four years later, shortly after the end of the war, Doctor Rees Pritchard was called out one afternoon to take part in the rescue of a fallen climber on the Idwal Slabs. Once again he put the welfare of the casualty before his own comfort and safety. He put on his overcoat and Trilby hat, picked up his little black bag, and followed the climbers to Ogwen Cottage. They walked up the path to the east of Llyn Idwal until eventually they saw a group of people at the base of the crag. On arrival he examined the casualty, who turned out to be a man in his early thirties, and diagnosed a broken femur with '...the leg lying in the typical twisted position'. The man was clearly in shock and great pain, but one of the quarrymen who had turned out to help in the rescue operation, had had the foresight to bring with him a metal leg iron called the 'Thomas Splint', so-called after Hugh Owen Thomas who was a pioneer in orthopaedic surgery in Liverpool. This splint is very suitable for fractured femurs, and I applied the splint to the casualty's leg so that he could be carried down on a stretcher to a waiting ambulance with as little pain and discomfort as possible'.[1]

The doctor finished his story, 'I well remember asking the injured man what his name was so that I could complete my paper work, to which he replied, 'Major John Hunt, Sir'. But of course in those days the name meant nothing to me at all; it was only about five years later when the same man, as Lieutenant-Colonel John Hunt, had led the first successful ascent of Mount Everest that I realised who I had treated high up the mountain on Idwal Slabs. In his foreword to *Countdown to Rescue*, John Hunt, now Lord Hunt of Llanfair Waterdine, wrote that 'accidents also happen to those of us who have enjoyed a life-time of experience as mountaineers. I have been the victim of two serious accidents, and two very near escapes, in North Wales'— but that is another story.

---

1. The Thomas splint is not to be confused with the Thomas stretcher, though a version of the splint was made to fit a Thomas stretcher.

15: The Calm and the Storm

In 1946, Penguin Books published *Climbing in Britain*, edited by John Barford.[1] It was an instructional book prepared for the newly formed British Mountaineering Council and included a chapter on 'Mountain Rescue and First Aid' produced by the First-Aid Committee of Mountaineering Clubs. In the opening paragraphs it states: 'Unfortunately, everyone is capable of making mistakes, not only the beginner but the expert as well, and this book will have served a useful purpose if it helps in reducing the number of accidents due to ignorance. Sooner or later nearly everyone who walks or climbs in British hills will be confronted with an accident with which he or she will have to deal ...but in the mountains the difficulties of movement may cause a delay of many hours between the time of the accident and the arrival of the victim in hospital.' The chapter also deals with first-aid posts, essential first-aid, equipment, stretchers (including the Pigott rope-stretcher), general information about mountain accidents, search parties, and distress signals. Under the heading 'Assistance and Evacuation' the section on first aid posts includes details of the whole of Britain. Scotland had twelve Posts, the Lake District seven, Derbyshire three (two of which were 'to be installed'), and Wales had five posts:

Youth Hostel, Idwal Cottage.	Supervisor: Mr R S Duncombe.
Climbers' Club Hut, Helyg.	No supervisor, but key available at Gwern-y-gof Isaf Farm.
Pen-y-gwryd Hotel.	Supervisor: Mr O E Ridett.
Glasfryn, Rhyd-ddu.	Supervisor: Mr F H Thompson.
The Outward Bound Sea School, Brynmeddyg, Aberdyfi.	Supervisor: Mr F J Fuller.

The details given for each post included the type of equipment held, name(s) of doctors and hospitals, ambulances and police, and other relevant information about the best evacuation routes from each main climbing area. It was a most helpful little book with a wealth of valuable information packed into very few pages. It was an excellent start, for from 'tiny acorns do mighty oak trees grow'.

---

1. John Edward Quintus Barford, born 1914, was killed in a climbing accident in the Alps in 1947. He was the first secretary of The British Mountaineering Council.

When war broke out in 1939, the hotel business died away, and in 1940 the *Pen-y-gwryd* was occupied by a small preparatory school for boys from Bexhill-on-Sea. There were only thirty-five boys in the school, but it was all very cramped and not very satisfactory. Within three years the number of pupils had dropped to such a low level that the school was forced to amalgamate with another school in Westmorland, and Arthur Lockwood was able to re-open *Pen-y-gwryd* as a hotel. But he had lost his zest for being a 'mine host' and after only two years, in 1945 he moved to the house next door. The *Pen-y-gwryd* was taken over by Mr and Mrs Owen Ridett and as soon as necessary repairs had been completed it was re-opened, although to begin with for only a limited number of guests. Owen Ridett had retired from business due to poor health, and was to find his new occupation as landlord of 'the Gwryd' too much; in 1947 he sold the hotel to William Hampson, who installed a manager.

As the MRC busied itself with the post-war problems of morphia, first-aid, equipment, and radio communications, in which the RAF at Valley were extremely helpful, Wilson Hey foresaw that sooner or later a rescuer would be killed or badly injured, as a result of which he or his relatives might suffer hardship. He approached a number of insurance companies, but they asked such large premiums that it would have been beyond the means of individual rescuers, or the MRC itself, to pay them. The Committee therefore accumulated a reserve Emergency Fund from which *ex-gratia* payments could be made to exceptional cases, but they would be small and probably totally inadequate. This continued for a time, but following an accident in the Lake District when a rescuer was killed and several of his colleagues injured, the Committee had to re-assess the insurance problem. It was not until 1951, however, that any progress was made in this direction.

During the extremely hard winter of 1946/47, there do not appear to have been any deaths on the mountains of Snowdonia, but later in 1947 there was a resurgence of mountain accidents which coincided with the arrival at the *Pen-y-gwryd Hotel* of a 34-year-old Yorkshireman, Chris Briggs, as the new manager. After two years, he had grown so fond of the hotel and the Welsh mountains that he decided that this was where he would like to spend the rest of his life and he bought the *Pen-y-gwryd*.[1]

Chris and his wife, Jo, endeared themselves to generations of climbers and walkers who enjoyed the friendly hospitality of the hotel where Chris lived and worked until his death forty-four years later. The Briggs tradition has been continued to this day by their daughter, Jane Pullee.

---

1. Christopher Bastin Briggs, BEM, 1913–92.

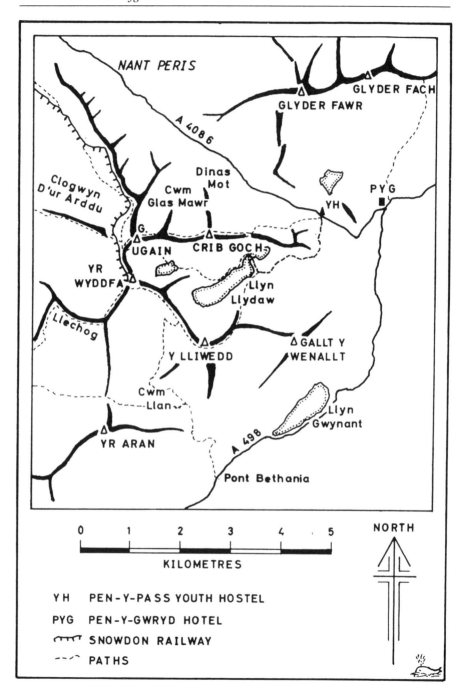

NANT PERIS

GLYDER FACH

GLYDER FAWR

A 4086

Clogwyn D'ur Arddu

Dinas Mot

Cwm Glas Mawr

PYG

YH

G. UGAIN

CRIB GOCH

YR WYDDFA

Llyn Llydaw

Llechog

Y LLIWEDD

△ GALLT Y WENALLT

Cwm Llan

Llyn Gwynant

YR ARAN

A 498

Pont Bethania

| 0 | 1 | 2 | 3 | 4 | 5 |

KILOMETRES

NORTH

YH   PEN-Y-PASS YOUTH HOSTEL

PYG   PEN-Y-GWRYD HOTEL

〜〜〜   SNOWDON RAILWAY

---   PATHS

Chris Briggs assumed some responsibility for MR on Snowdon from the previous owner, Owen Ridett, and the hotel became the focal point of MR activity for the whole of Snowdonia. It was not long before he was involved in organising his first rescue operation as the new landlord of the *Pen-y-gwryd*. A frequent guest at the hotel for many years, Paul R Hermanson, an experienced climber, and a regular visitor to Snowdonia, arrived in the middle of the month to spend a climbing and walking holiday there. On his first morning, after taking an early morning swim in the lake opposite the hotel, he set out to walk the Snowdon Horseshoe. This is a classic ridge walk, starting and finishing at Pen-y-pass at an altitude of 1,096 feet asl. The route follows the Pyg track as far as Bwlch y Moch, turns right and ascends the rocky east ridge to the summit of Crib Goch, crosses the narrow exposed Crib Goch ridge, then goes down to Bwlch Goch, up the Crib-y-ddysgl ridge, then down to Bwlch Glas and on to Snowdon. Thence it drops down the Watkin path to Bwlch-y-saethau before the ascent of Lliwedd and descent to join the Miners' track at the eastern end of Llyn Llydaw. The route is horseshoe-shaped, and the summits of Crib Goch, Crib-y-ddysgl (Carnedd Ugain), Snowdon and the West Peak of Lliwedd are the 'nails' in the Horseshoe. The average time taken by a reasonably fit walker is about 6 hours, covering a horizontal distance of seven miles with 3,390 feet of ascent and approximately 3,240 feet of descent.

On Monday 22 May 1948 the weather was fine and mild, but at about 11.30am a sudden snowstorm developed and covered the peaks with a white blanket. This quickly melted and had completely disappeared by 2.30pm. When Paul Hermanson had not returned in time for dinner at 7.30pm, there was considerable concern for his safety. At 8.30pm Chris Briggs went up to the *Gorphwysfa Hotel* to enquire whether anyone there had seen him, but there was no news. Without any specific clue as to where to start looking, Chris Briggs organised a search party from the guests in both the hotels, and the decision was made to start early the next morning. At first light the party set off and spent all day scouring Crib Goch, Crib-y-ddysgl, Snowdon and Cwm Glas, but by nightfall they had not found any trace of him. They set out again early on Wednesday 24 May to search the lower slopes of the north-east face of Lliwedd, and at about midday his body was found lying at the foot of East Gully. He had apparently fallen from a great height and the nature of his injuries suggested that he must have died instantly. What happened to him was never established, for there were no witnesses.

In October of the same year, there were portents of an early and hard winter when an unusually heavy fall of snow blocked the mountain railway for a week, trapping a party of railway staff in the summit building. An appeal to Chris

Chris Briggs, rescue completed.   [Jane Pullee]

Briggs from the Mountain Railway Company brought a swift response, and a party of volunteer climbers acted as 'sherpas' carrying food supplies daily to the five men on the summit until the snow disappeared and they were able to escape down to Llanberis. The expected hard winter did not materialise, and the comparative lull continued for the next three years, until a 'storm' broke which was to make up for the years of relative quiet.

From the autumn of 1950, there was deep snow covering the mountains of Snowdonia, and as the winter progressed, with extreme cold, snow and strong winds becoming a permanent feature of the weather, the snow got deeper and deeper. By the turn of the year, the snow lay so thick on the summit of Snowdon that it was possible to walk from the end of the station platform on to the roof of the building, a condition not to be seen again until the harsh winter of 1979. The snow which fell on the mountain tops was blown over the ridge between Carnedd Ugain and Snowdon to form gigantic cornices estimated to be about 15 feet thick. To add to this unusual ground condition, the windward slopes where the snow had been blown off were fully exposed to the freezing winds, and from early in the winter any slope above 2,500 feet became a virtual ice-cap. Alternate days of freeze and thaw, then more snow, followed by freezing winds made the conditions truly Alpine, if not Arctic. The tracks from Glaslyn to the ridge were covered with ice, and the safest way up the mountain was the knife-edge ridge of Crib Goch from which all the snow had been blown, leaving bare rock with little ice or frozen snow. With snow completely filling the railway cuttings, and the slopes above Clogwyn Du'r Arddu covered in ice, the railway track became the most hazardous route on Snowdon, and in Chris Briggs's words, 'impossible to negotiate without an ice-axe'. But walkers, then and since, have made the simple and often fatal mistake of thinking the opposite because in normal conditions that route is the easiest and safest way to the summit. The fact is that the path from Llanberis runs directly across the northern slopes of Carnedd Ugain, and with ground conditions as described, it is like walking over a glacier. The line of the railway track is the more dangerous of the two routes, being a narrow cutting packed with frozen snow with a drop of 750 feet immediately below. But occasionally an unsuspecting walker has slipped on the icy Llanberis path above the railway cutting, been unable to arrest his slide and accelerated down the slope, finally shooting clean over the railway track to suffer serious injury or death down in Cwm Du'r Arddu.

As 1951 began, the harshest winter probably ever recorded in Snowdonia showed no sign of easing. On New Year's Day, after further heavy snowfall, one climber was killed and four others injured in an avalanche on Y Garn (Ogwen Valley). This was triggered by two parties, one of two climbers who were roped, and one of three unroped. Both were trying to tunnel through a huge cornice said to be as big as those on Snowdon. The party of two had succeeded in completing their tunnel, but the other party, rather than following them through it, decided to dig another tunnel about 30 yards away 'just for practice'. They had penetrated to a depth of 6 feet when the party of two started to dig a third tunnel in between: almost immediately the whole length of cornice between the two outside tunnels collapsed and all five climbers were swept by the avalanche down the gully through a mass of protruding rocks. One of the party of two smashed his head on rock and was found buried under five feet of avalanche debris. He had suffered fatal head injuries, but the other four escaped with nothing more serious than minor cuts and abrasions.[1]

The party of three admitted that none of them had any experience of tunnelling through a cornice, but it is not clear which party had actually triggered the collapse. Chris Briggs stated that, 'the sun had melted the snow where the cornice joined the main mass on the ridge, and this was evident by a

---

1. No helmets were worn in those days.

four or five inch difference in the level which was quite distinct from the top side, but not evident from below'. He also said that the roped pair, perhaps because of the rope, did not appear to ride the avalanche as well as the others. The RAF Valley MRT assisted Chris Briggs and his team in this rescue operation.

*

Less than three weeks later, on 19 January, a party of thirty-seven walkers from Derby set off to walk to the summit of Snowdon via Crib Goch, although the weather forecast should have warned them that conditions would make even that route hazardous. Their decision to attempt the climb on that day was even more ill-advised in view of their total inexperience of winter conditions and of their lack of ice-axes or ropes. Six of the group reached Snowdon in spite of gale force winds which whipped the lying snow into blown spindrift and caused virtual blizzard conditions. The other thirty-one were a long way behind, but they eventually reached the summit where they sheltered in the summit building, at that time left open all year round as a mountain refuge.[1]

Meantime the six had wisely decided not to descend the zigzags, and had set out along the railway track to Bwlch Glas. From here they tried to walk down the route of the Llanberis path above the railway track, but almost immediately one of the walkers, Donald Pounder, slipped and slid 450 feet down the icy slope before he managed to stop himself. One of his colleagues, Alan Corden, tried to get down to him, but he also slipped and just managed to arrest his slide before he would have plunged over the edge into Cwm Glas Bach. He tried to get back to the path, but slipped again and decided to give up and make his way down to Nant Peris in the valley below. Cwm Glas Bach was filled with deep snow, and Corden floundered his way down to the road at the lower end of the Llanberis Pass. In the meantime the other four members continued to walk down to Llanberis, and it was not long before they found Pounder who had climbed back up to the railway track. The five of them eventually reached Llanberis from where Pounder was driven to hospital. Once down in the valley, they raised the alarm for their thirty-one colleagues still, as far as they knew, on the summit of Snowdon. The RAF Valley MRT, led by Pilot Officer Mason, together with a party of students from University College, Bangor, started out from Llanberis for the summit, but the weather conditions were so bad that the attempt was abandoned. The weather relented in the evening, and the rescue operation was planned to re-start the following morning. The original party, consisting of the RAF MRT and the students, had been considerably reinforced by civilian climbers and when it set out again carrying food and drink it

---

1. The summit building is now kept locked during the winter because of vandalism.

numbered around sixty people. The thirty-one were found safe and reasonably well in the circumstances, and they were brought down to Llanberis. The leader of the RAF team, Pilot Officer Mason, commented that 'To go climbing on Snowdon in this weather without an ice-axe is sheer suicide'.

*

On 10 February Chris Briggs and his team were once again in action, this time to rescue four experienced climbers two of whom were known to Chris. All four were properly equipped with ice-axes and ropes, but there was no mention in the reports about crampons. At that time crampons were not yet in general use in Britain and very few people possessed a pair. This is not really surprising since at the time the majority wore nailed boots, and were accustomed to step-cutting; crampons were not readily available, even to those who could afford them. Right up to the 1960s they were actually regarded as an unnecessary luxury.

The first two climbers involved in this incident were Doreen Harrison, a 22-year-old laboratory assistant from Wallasey in Cheshire, and her boyfriend, Anthony Bolger. They were roped together, and had just started to descend from Bwlch Glas down the zigzags using their ice-axes, when Doreen slipped and shot away down the steep slope. It happened so quickly that the slack in the rope was taken up almost immediately, and Anthony Bolger was dragged down with her. The two of them fell about 500 feet before coming to a stop. Doreen Harrison lay unconscious and bleeding, and all that Bolger could do was to secure her by scraping a level area in the snow and to make her as warm and comfortable as possible.

High above the two young climbers were the two older men, Doctor Anthony James Warren Woodroffe, MB, MRCS from Chester, and A S Turner. Dr Woodroffe was a member of the Climbers' Club and he and Turner were staying at the Climbers' Club hut — Ynys Etws — near Pont y Gromlech in the Llanberis Pass. They had been to the summit of Snowdon and were returning to Pen-y-pass over the ridges of Crib-y-ddysgl and Crib Goch. They happened to be looking back towards the zigzags when they saw the two young people fall. Seeing that the girl did not move, Dr Woodroffe realised that she must have been seriously injured, and he and Turner started down towards them, cutting steps in the frozen snow slope. In the meantime, one of a party of three which was also on the ridge set off for *Pen-y-gwryd* to alert the rescue service and his two companions followed Woodroffe and Turner down. After some time Woodroffe and Turner realised that as cutting steps was so slow, there would be no chance of them reaching the accident site before dark. They were still 300 feet above the casualties, and decided to do a roped-glissade (a controlled slide down a snow slope using an ice-axe as a brake). They were roped together and each in turn used his ice-axe to belay the other doing the actual glissade. After one or two successful glissades, Woodroffe realised he was going much too fast. As he drew level with Turner, he shouted to him, but it was too late for Turner to take any effective action. The rope ran out, Woodroffe's full weight was transferred on to the belaying ice-axe which was jerked out of the snow, and both men careered down the slope, eventually stopping near the platform Bolger had scraped out of the snow. Bolger had been unaware that the two men were making their way down until he noticed bits of ice falling around him and almost at the same time heard Woodroffe's shout. The situation was disastrous — Dr Woodroffe was killed in the fall, and Turner was seriously injured. Bolger could only wait with the two injured people and hope that a rescue party would reach them soon, but his hopes were dashed as it grew dark, it began to snow, and the cloud base lowered. The man who had gone down for help had made very good time, but it also takes time for a rescue team to be assembled. It was going to be a difficult and risky operation, and there could be no question of including anyone in the team who was not capable of dealing with the appalling conditions they were bound to meet. As soon as the team had been briefed by Chris Briggs, they set out, but because of the bad visibility the only way they could locate the exact position of the accident site was to home in on Bolger's whistle blasts. It was after 11pm when the first stretcher party reached the scene. Doreen Harrison was still alive, and as she was clearly the more seriously injured of the live casualties, she was made the priority stretcher case. The rescue party lowered her on a stretcher down the icy slopes, and carried it along the track to Pen-y-pass where they arrived at about 3am, but unfortunately by this time the girl had died. Following them down was the second stretcher party with Turner, who had head and facial injuries in addition to a broken pelvis, and the unfortunate Anthony Bolger who was now suffering from severe shock and hypothermia.

Following the incident, Chris Briggs, writing in the *Climbers' Club Journal*, drew the conclusion that 'an ice-axe belay, even though it is well in, will only stop a man sliding down a steep snow slope if the weight comes slowly to bear on it'.

At the inquest the Coroner expressed his admiration for Dr Woodroffe's selflessness in immediately going to the assistance of the girl and her boyfriend, and he said, 'His children, as they grow up, will be consoled, at least, by a sense of pride in the memory of their father, and if this tragedy results in less risks being taken and more lives saved, then it may have served a purpose'.

The Mountain Rescue Committee handbook includes a page headed 'Distinguished Service' which records with gratitude the names of some thirty people to whom the Committee has awarded Certificates in acknowledgement of the debt owed by all mountain lovers, mountaineers and hill-walkers for outstanding service in the rescue of the injured in the mountain country of Britain. Anthony Woodroffe heads the list: 'he lost his life going to the aid of someone injured on Snowdon' and there are others whose work was specific to Wales, such as Johnnie Lees and Chris Briggs.

Dr Anthony Woodroffe was the first rescuer to be killed or injured since the end of the war, and his family was given some compensation from the MRC's Emergency Fund, but it was very little and no more than a gesture. As a result of Dr Woodroffe's death, an approach was made to the Home Secretary, James Callaghan, and through his great efforts a scheme was established whereby rescuers would be insured through the police service.[1] It had at last been accepted that mountain rescuers were temporarily doing police work and should have the same insurance cover as the police themselves. Hill-walkers tend to regard Easter as the start of their season but when winter is prolonged, they face the choice of forfeiting a long weekend in the hills or of taking a chance with the conditions. In 1951 Easter came early and there was never much doubt what conditions would prevail. The situation had not even begun to improve. Good Friday was on 23 March, and in spite of the Alpine conditions, or perhaps because of them, great numbers of walkers and climbers converged on Snowdonia for the weekend. The post-war boom in mountaineering being well under way, it was not surprising that so many should seize the opportunity to get in some real Alpine climbing without the expense of travelling to the Alps. The climbers were for the most part well equipped and experienced; it was the walkers who were to cause problems, for they took risks with little idea of the consequences.

*

What was to become known as Black Easter began on Maundy Thursday, 22 March, when a party of seven experienced climbers were descending South Gully on Tryfan. They carried ropes, but were coming down unroped even though the going was difficult. The gully floor was covered with hard-packed frozen snow and ice, and most of the group were using the edges of the gully where there were adequate rock handholds. One of the party, Miss Norah Batty, chose to descend the ice-chute in the middle of the gully, and not surprisingly slipped and slid 500 feet to the bottom of the gully where her companions found her body. Good Friday passed without incident, but at 1pm on Saturday, 24

---

1. James Callaghan, who was later Prime Minister and now sits in the House of Lords, was a close friend of Chris and Jo Briggs, and occasionally stayed at the *Pen-y-gwryd*. As Home Secretary he was also responsible for making radio sets available to MRTs.

March, Chris Briggs received information that two people had slipped on the icy slopes of Carnedd Ugain, and fallen several hundred feet into Cwm Du'r Arddu. A rescue team was quickly assembled and, carrying first-aid equipment and a stretcher, the party set off for the accident site where they found a man and a young woman who had fallen from the railway track above. They had been attempting to walk down the Llanberis path, in winter conditions one of the most dangerous routes on Snowdon. The man, T J Orrell, had severe head injuries and was already dead, and the girl, named Harrison, who also had head injuries, was in a serious condition. She was carried down to Llanberis and rushed to hospital; happily she eventually recovered. Both these walkers were wearing proper boots, but in spite of all the warnings, neither had an ice-axe.

Having delivered the two casualties to a waiting ambulance in Llanberis, Chris Briggs and his party were making their way back up the Llanberis Pass towards the *Pen-y-gwryd*, when they were intercepted at Pen-y-pass and told of an accident, this time on Clogwyn-y-garnedd. Three well-known and experienced climbers — Gilbert Peaker, Peter Koch and R Clegg — had been ascending Trinity Gully, and had made good progress without undue difficulty, cutting steps in the hard snow. After climbing about 600 feet, the snow turned into very hard ice, and at the same time the wind began to gust strongly, making the going precarious and exhausting. They decided to retreat and started to retrace their steps, but found that the steps they had cut on the way up, whilst being suitable for ascending, were too far apart for them to use safely going down. They had to cut more steps in between those they had already made and it was no easy task swinging an ice-axe from above to strike the hard snow below their feet in what was by then a gale-force wind. Eventually Peaker, who was leading, was caught by a gust of wind in the middle of a stroke and was blown off, dragging his two companions from their stances with him to the bottom of the gully. Peter Koch was killed instantly, but Peaker and Gilbert suffered only minor cuts and bruises and were able to walk off the mountain. Briggs and his team stretchered the dead man back to Pen-y-pass, and then walked down the road to the *Pen-y-gwryd* with the two 'walking wounded'.

The nightmare scenario continued, as on his arrival at the hotel, Chris Briggs was told of yet another accident at the spot where he and his team had already carried out the first rescue of the day. G Hall, walking alone on the same icy stretch which had caused the first accident, and again without an ice-axe, had slipped and fallen to his death.

This was not the end by any means. A short time later another lone walker, named Dale, slipped on ice when ascending the last 800 feet of the Watkin Path and fell about 50 feet. He was found lying some way down the slope by a party of Boy Scouts from Dublin, and as the man had a nasty injury to his leg, these boys set about making a rope stretcher on which they carried him to the summit. They started to walk down the railway track towards Llanberis but, after proceeding as far as Clogwyn Coch, they found the going too hazardous and returned to the summit building. There they were joined by another party including two very experienced mountaineers — Jack Longland and Alan (A B) Hargreaves, who had come up the zigzags from Glaslyn and, after trying to descend by the same route, had thought it wiser to stay in the summit building overnight. By now there were at least twenty-one people seeking shelter inside the building, and Jack Longland took charge of the whole party. Soon after dawn the following morning, they set off down the path towards Llanberis, leaving just four people with the injured Dale in the summit building. They were able to cut good steps right across the difficult stretch, and once they reached Clogwyn station they speeded up and soon reached Llanberis. At the police house they met Chris Briggs and his party, plus the RAF Valley MRT, ready to go up to the summit to bring down the five men still up there. Conditions were still dreadful high up, and on the way down, in order to avoid crossing the icy slope with the stretcher, Chris Briggs led the party down the sky line above Cwm Glas Mawr and Gyrn Las which required very accurate navigation.

On that Easter Saturday there were other accidents, mostly involving walkers who were not carrying ice-axes, but thankfully the injuries sustained were not serious and the casualties were able to get themselves down aided by their companions. The RAF MRT, based near Bethesda for a training weekend, did sterling work both in the Ogwen Valley and on Snowdon throughout the Easter holiday. They recovered at least three bodies and four injured walkers, the result of three incidents, and when not actually involved in rescues they helped parties in difficulty on the icy paths or advised others about the safest and easiest routes to follow. Chris Briggs was generous in his praise of the well-trained volunteers of the RAF MRT over this terrible weekend, and they in turn complimented him for 'turning out at any time and anywhere, not with a 'trained' team of alpinists, but ad hoc volunteers from his hotel and bar!' The part played by the RAF MRT gave a clear indication of the value of having a trained team ready to turn out at a moment's notice, and provided a blueprint of what was to develop in the area within the next two decades.

*

On Sunday, 25 March, the Clogwyn ice claimed yet another victim. A man and his girl companion were trying to cross the slope when they slipped and fell, coming to rest on the railway line. They were seen by a group of Boy Scouts, climbing from Llanberis to the summit of Snowdon, which managed to reach them only to find that the man was already dead and his girlfriend badly injured, but still alive. Rather than waste valuable time trying to get back across the ice and then descend to Llanberis to raise the alarm, the boys started to send semaphore messages requesting immediate help. It was a remote possibility that someone would see and read the messages, but in fact they were lucky and the message was seen and understood by another group of walkers who sped down to Llanberis to raise the alarm. In the meantime, however, the accident had also been seen by other walkers who alerted Chris Briggs and once again he set out with a hastily assembled team. He decided it would be quicker to go up the Miners' track to Clogwyn Coch via Glaslyn, rather than go via Llanberis. At Pen-y-pass a motor cyclist came towards him over the brow of the hill, and Chris Briggs immediately stopped him — a complete stranger — and persuaded him to take him on the pillion up the Miners' track as far as they could go. The man, Peter Hodgkinson from Penrhyn Bay, who happened to be an experienced climber enjoying a quiet ride round the mountains, agreed to do so and also volunteered to help in the rescue. At Glaslyn they were joined by the rest of the rescue team, but as they climbed up towards the Pyg track intersection, they met a stretcher party of other climbers and walkers which had been assembled in Llanberis as a result of the Boy Scouts' semaphore signals and was already coming down from Bwlch Glas with the injured girl. Chris Briggs accompanied the stretcher party down to Pen-y-pass, but three of the team and Peter Hodgkinson carried on up to Bwlch Glas. As they ascended the path towards the ridge, they saw what was unmistakeably the outline of a man's head and shoulders several hundred feet above them. He was motionless, and after watching him for a few minutes they shouted, and in response could just hear a faint voice. Immediately above them there was about 400 feet of very steep snow and ice, beyond which there was 100 feet of bare rock. Three of the men roped up and started to climb, cutting steps into the hard snow, which was tough work and very time consuming, and Peter Hodgkinson followed them up. It took them nearly an hour and a half to reach the man, whom they found lying on a ledge near the top of the rock band with congealed blood on his face. He told the rescuers that his name was George Hall, and complained of severe pain in his back. The rescuers were presented with a problem, for the ledge on to which Hall had fallen was narrow, and he was in an insecure position. Very little could be done for him in that exposed situation, and the choice was whether to lift him to the ridge above, which would have been very difficult especially as there were only four of them, or lower him down the slope. The man was clearly in shock and in spite of the risk involved in trying to get him to a more secure position, the four men were agreed that he could not possibly survive the night in the

Chris Briggs and his daughter Jane.   *[Jane Pullee]*

intense cold, and that fact alone outweighed the risk of moving him. They decided to lower Hall to the snow-field below the rock band, and this was done by one of the rescuers named Thomas climbing down beside and supporting Hall whilst the other three paid out the rope. Once in a secure place, Hall was made as comfortable as possible, covered with spare clothing and given hot coffee to try to warm him up, but he did not respond and eventually he lost consciousness and quietly died.

All these tragic accidents were fully reported in the local paper, *The Carnarvon and Denbigh Herald*, with particular reference to the part played in them by Chris Briggs. One of the reports read: 'Mr Briggs, who had been in three rescues in twenty-three hours, with hardly any sleep, was drenched to the skin. It had rained incessantly... and ice had formed on the stretcher'. In addition to the actual rescue operations in which he was personally involved, Chris Briggs hardly slept at all during Easter Saturday night because, in his own words, 'All through the night the telephone at *Pen-y-gwryd* rang continuously informing us of people missing from hostels, and inquiries poured in from Manchester, Liverpool and London as to the whereabouts of 'our Willie' '.

*

The severe conditions had not improved by the next weekend, and on Monday 9 April, a lone walker from London, 44-year-old Joseph Berry, went missing on a walk on Snowdon. The following day two climbers, ascending the steep snow slope to the ridge at the east end of Bwlch Glas, noticed a large hole in the cornice about 400 feet above and slightly to one side of them. It looked far too big to be a man-made tunnel and, wisely deciding it made the cornice unsafe, they traversed to enable them to reach the ridge where the cornice was undisturbed. As they passed underneath the hole, they discovered a man's body lying partially covered by avalanche debris: that of Joseph Berry. It seemed that he must have wandered on to the cornice which collapsed precipitating him 400 feet down the snow slope. He had suffered quite severe injuries, but the inquest verdict was that he had died of exposure.

There had never been so many accidents on the mountains of Snowdonia in such a short space of time, and much the same picture emerged from other mountain regions in Britain. The total of fatalities on Snowdon over the Easter weekend was nine; by the end of the year the number killed had risen to 14. The Press had a field day, and it was not surprising therefore that there was a public outcry, echoing the remarks of the coroner after completing the last of the Easter inquests. He summed up in a few very critical comments what he thought about the weekend's events. 'These mountains,' he said, 'were invaded during the Easter weekend by an army of what I call novices, who were more equipped for a day on Hampstead Heath than the rigours of these mountains.' His remarks were given great coverage in the national press and inevitably letters to the Editor flooded in, adding criticisms to those made by the coroner, and embellished by many of the reporters. Nothing really changes, and one of the main points of condemnation then, as today, was that climbers from 'over the border' were putting at risk the lives of 'locals' who had to go out to rescue them although, as Chris Briggs pointed out, only one local man had in fact volunteered and taken part in the rescue operations over the Easter weekend. An outraged correspondent, with remarkable foresight perhaps, suggested in the strongest possible terms that climbers and walkers should be responsible for carrying out their own rescues, and that there should be a 'party of twelve or so members of the Climbers' Association standing by to do it'.[1]

Chris Briggs, recognised by the MRC as the organiser for search and rescue in Snowdonia, sprang to the defence of the climbers and walkers, pointing out that the majority of the accidents involved what he called 'ordinary tourists', or casual walkers, who were not members of climbing or rambling clubs. Perhaps

---

1. No such Association has ever existed.

echoing the remark made in the local newspaper following the deaths of Salt and Robertson in 1910, that 'When the race becomes decadent we shall not have these dreadful tragedies, but a vastly greater tragedy will have overtaken the British race', Chris Briggs quoted Blake 'Great things are done when men and mountains meet, that is not done by jostling in the street', adding that when young people no longer seek for adventure, such as climbing mountains, that previously mentioned tragedy will indeed have overtaken our race. In a final summing up of his experience during the tempestuous period during the first few months of 1951, Briggs wrote that, 'A rescue party, in my opinion, should consist of eight or ten experienced climbers and for preference should include some or all of the following:- Bill Osborne, Roy Beard, John Disley, Tony Moulam, Peter Harding, Dave Thomas, Ralph Jones, Alan Manger, Ian Macdonald, Peter Hodgkinson, S Fry, and J Neill, all of whom have done a splendid job of work on recent rescue parties'.[1]

Following the Easter weekend, there was concern that some sort of restriction might be imposed on access to Snowdon, especially during severe weather and difficult ground conditions, but those who put forward the suggestion had no idea how such an imposition could possibly be enforced. Climbing and walking clubs were urged to do everything possible to ensure that members were properly equipped and did not exceed their individual capabilities, especially in winter conditions. One suggestion which came out of discussions that took place during the summer was that there should be a system of 'scouts' whose job would be to report on conditions in the mountains, and when necessary to issue warnings to the public through the BBC and the Press. Within a year there were to be National Park wardens throughout the mountains of Snowdonia who did just that.

*

It was about this time that organisations such as schools and youth clubs started to go to the mountains in large numbers. The 'explosion' which was to continue over the next two decades had begun, and the pattern of mountain incidents gradually changed. During the summer of 1951, there was a fatal accident on 21 July when a group of Boy Scouts from Middlesex started to climb the cliffs on Clogwyn Du'r Arddu and one of them, 15-year-old Geoffrey Spencer, fell. The group was in camp at Llangollen, and five of the boys had

---

1. Chris Briggs's assessment clearly refers only to those actually involved in the technical part of a rescue and not in a long stretcher carry. On anything other than a short stretcher carry, at least two relief carrying parties will be needed, numbering at least eighteen people in all.

come over to Llanberis with their Scoutmaster to walk to the summit of Snowdon. Soon after passing the 'Halfway' brew-shack, the boys requested that they should do a bit of rock climbing. The Scoutmaster told the Coroner that he had done some climbing in Austria, and he had chosen a place where, in his opinion, there was no apparent danger. From the description of the accident site given to the Coroner by the police who attended the incident, the boys were little more than 200 yards from the ascending Snowdon path; the route was not very steep and was one up which they could either scramble or walk. It was 'the least severe part of Clogwyn Du'r Arddu' and the cliff was grassy with protruding rocks and boulders. According to the inquest report, the Scoutmaster was leading but none of the party were roped; all were well-shod, however, with studded boots which at that time was quite the norm. He had given instructions to the boys to keep to the left and follow him, avoiding any grass. They were scrambling on firm rock, when the Scoutmaster heard a shout and saw Spencer falling. He hit a series of boulders, eventually coming to rest at the foot of the grassy cliff, having fallen about 200 feet. He was already dead when his companions reached him. The coroner decided that it was an unavoidable accident due to Spencer's foot slipping and that no blame could be placed on the Scoutmaster. He therefore brought in a verdict of accidental death.

*

Only three weeks later another fatality occurred when a party of three were rock-climbing on Clogwyn y Grochan in the Llanberis Pass. 21-year-old Patrick Montague Brown, who was leading, was said to be a very keen and experienced rock-climber, and he had done the particular route twice before. The other two were belayed and as Brown attempted to climb a small overhang, his companions heard him say 'I can't make it... I'm coming off.' His second took in the slack but almost at once found himself holding the end of a loose rope. Brown had first crashed into the rock, then the rope had broken at a running belay; he hurtled headlong past his companions to the bottom of the crag. He suffered a fractured skull and died immediately. At the inquest, experts called by the coroner gave their opinion that the hemp rope used was past its best, and although it seemed reliable, it was not good enough for a severe climb of this sort. The coroner referred to the growing list of fatalities on the mountains, declaring that it had thus far been a phenomenal year, and there was very real cause for concern.

Soon after this accident there was another incident on Snowdon, this time on the Watkin Path when a 52-year-old man slipped and slid just a few feet down the slope. This, however, was not a climbing accident, but was a fall due to natural causes. The man had had a heart attack and was probably dead before he hit the ground, but as far as the MR service was concerned, it was another operation which involved getting a team together and carrying the victim off the hill.

*

A major incident occurred on 10 January 1952 when a Dakota aircraft belonging to Aer Lingus crashed on the western slopes of Moel Siabod whilst en route to Dublin. The alarm was raised shortly after 7pm when a farmer from Nant Gwynant heard a crash and, looking towards the direction of the noise, saw a red glow. He climbed up the slope to Bwlch y Rhediad and about half a mile from the road came across the remains of the aircraft which was still burning. It had made a large crater in the boggy ground and there were bodies scattered round the area. The farmer, William Williams, hastened off the hill to raise the alarm, and by 8.45pm the RAF Valley MRT was on its way to the *Pen-y-gwryd* where they met the farmer, police and fire brigade. Chris Briggs was not directly involved in this operation except in the very early stages, offering what help he could: it was an RAF responsibility, and he had to stand aside, although the crash was literally on his own doorstep. The sight which met the rescue services was a grisly one, with personal possessions and a number of badly broken bodies littering the surrounding slopes. It took three days to complete the clearing-up operation, but of the twenty-three people on board, only 12 bodies were recovered as the remainder had to be left inside as the aircraft was slowly sucked down deeper into the bog. The area was at first guarded by the RAF until a fence was erected to keep sightseers away, but such is the morbid interest in disasters of any kind that a plaque erected in memory of the three crew members and twenty passengers was stolen soon afterwards, presumably as a souvenir. The ground was consecrated by two priests from Ireland, and it is now given a wide berth, being a place of sad memories. RAF Valley MRT was presented with a Thomas stretcher by Aer Lingus for their part in the rescue operation. The 12 bodies which were recovered lie together in a mass grave in the Llanbeblig Cemetery in Caernarfon; the headstone gives their names and the date of the crash, but no other details of what happened.

*

On 1 February 1952, 31-year-old George Quiggley from Liverpool was walking with his friend George Oliver on the Pyg track somewhere near Bwlch Glas when they were caught in a severe snowstorm. The weather was racing in over the ridge and, unable to make any progress upwards, they turned back. There was already a lot of snow on the ground, and the heavy fall now taking place added to their difficulties. Visibility was virtually nil, and the two men, having struggled through deep snow drifts for a number of hours, eventually found their way down to Llyn Llydaw. Quiggley had been nearing the end of his physical reserves and just as they reached the lake, he collapsed. George Oliver dug a snow hole, and having managed to get him inside it and out of the blizzard, he did everything he could to get some warmth back into him. Darkness fell, and the temperature dropped still further, with the storm showing no sign of abating. It was too much for George Quiggley; at about 3am, Oliver, who was hugging him to keep him warm, suddenly felt him go limp.

In the meantime, it was not until late in the evening that it was noticed that the two men had not returned from their day on the mountain. In view of the appalling conditions, it was decided that nothing could be done until first light. The storm had died down when the party set off, and the searchers soon found George Oliver and his dead companion by the shore of Llyn Llydaw, no more than an hour's walk from Pen-y-pass. Information about George Quiggley revealed that perhaps he was not completely fit, as he suffered from a war wound to his leg. Evidence was also given that his wife was expecting their second child the same week. It was a most distressing incident, and the circumstances of it bear some resemblance to another death from hypothermia on Snowdon some twenty-seven years later. [1]

*

On 14 July 1952 the RAF Valley MRT was on a training exercise on Cader Idris and a team member, David Gwyndaf Thomas, who was only 19 years old, was leading on One Pitch Gully. He appeared to be getting into some difficulty and said to his second, Johnny Barratt, the team driver, that he thought he was going to fall; shortly afterwards he lost his grip and came off, and although perhaps 99% of times the rope would have held him, this time it was cut by a sharp rock as it ran out, and Thomas fell 250 feet to the bottom of the crag. He was killed instantly, and his untimely death, the first fatal accident to happen to an RAF MRT member actually on team duties, was mourned deeply.

Only a few weeks after this sad event on Cader Idris, the RAF MRT was in action on Snowdon. It was a horrendous day, that 11 August; the whole of the mountain was enveloped in heavy driving rain with visibility down to a few yards at best. The trains stopped running from Llanberis station, but there were still two at the summit, one of which, driven by a local driver, George Sellars, set off to return to the village soon after midday with about 60 passengers on board.

---

1. The particular death from hypothermia is fully described in *Countdown to Rescue* — Chapter 12 — 'Point of No Return'.

Aer Lingus mass grave in Caernarfon.

Sellars found it very difficult to see the track ahead of him but as the train was approaching the sweeping left-hand bend below Clogwyn Coch which leads on to the embankment before Clogwyn Station, he detected a red glow. He could feel his train being battered by the gale, and was happy that he had a good load on board, the combined weight of which was acting as ballast to keep the carriage on the rails. Within yards, the glow became identifiable as an aircraft which had crashed on to the track and which was still burning. Sellars jammed on the brakes bringing the train to an abrupt stop. He and his fireman, Robert Owen, got down from their cab and walked carefully towards the burning wreckage, where they saw a body close to the fuselage. Regardless of their own safety, they moved the body away from the fire, and almost at once the plane blew up, covering the area with burning fuel. The train guard, meanwhile, had made best speed down to Clogwyn Station, and telephoned the news down to Llanberis. When the RAF MRT arrived from Valley, other rescuers were already on their way to Clogwyn Station, including Chris Briggs and his team, a local doctor from Llanberis, firemen from Caernarfon, ambulance personnel, and other volunteers.

The crashed aircraft was identified as an RAF Anson which had been flying from its base at RAF Aldergrove in Ulster to South Wales. It had hit the mountain at almost 90 degrees to the slope, and the three crew had been killed outright. The train driven by Sellars had to return to the summit where the passengers joined those of the other train which was still up there, and 120 people had to spend the night in the summit building. The trains were stranded at the summit for several days as the track had to be re-laid; meantime the passengers had to walk down to Clogwyn Station, from where they were conveyed by train to Llanberis.[1]

Chris Briggs's outstanding work in the field of Mountain Rescue was one of the contributions he made to the mountaineering scene in Snowdonia. Another was the part he played in the preparations for the first successful ascent of Everest in 1953, when the hotel was used as a base for training, trying out new equipment, and planning for the attempt to climb the highest mountain in the world.

By the end of 1952, Chris Briggs was respected by many mountaineers for his mountain rescue work. A year or two later, he introduced a special incentive scheme to encourage children under the age of eight, who stayed with their parents in his hotel, to climb to the summit of Snowdon and return to Pen-y-pass 'under their own steam'. There could be no question of 'thumbing a lift' on Dad's shoulders: the climb had to be the youngster's unaided effort. Chris gave each successful child a silver ice-axe brooch, and they were invited to have a drink, (strictly non-alcoholic, of course), from one of the Everest climbers' mugs which still hang behind the bar. This was always done in the evening to the applause of whoever might be staying in the hotel at the time - very often well-known mountaineers. It was typical of Chris Briggs to encourage the young in this way, and many parents were grateful for the 'push' the incentive scheme gave their sometimes diffident children.

For more than two decades Chris Briggs continued to lead *ad hoc* teams stiffened by a few local friends on whom he could rely to turn out at a moment's notice, and in 1956 his exploits, particularly over the 'Black Easter' period of 1951, were officially recognised when he was awarded the British Empire Medal for his work in mountain rescue. Chris Briggs served his adopted country and community in other ways; he was High Sheriff of Caernarfonshire in 1963 and was a Deputy Lieutenant of Gwynedd.

---

1. The bend where the plane crashed is still known to railway staff as *Tro'r 'Aeroplane'* (Aeroplane Bend).

16: The Snowdonia National Park

The National Parks and Access to the Countryside Act was passed by Parliament in 1949 and The Snowdonia National Park came into being in 1951. It was a milestone in the development of Snowdonia from every point of view, but its effect on climbers and hill-walkers was not to be felt for at least the next decade. The terms of reference given to the National Park Authority[1] defined their duties as:

1. to preserve and enhance the natural beauty of the areas, and
2. to promote their enjoyment by the public.

The Park knew that the primary task was the creation of a balanced attitude between those who use the mountains for leisure, and farmers and others who obtain their livelihood from them. They set up an information service for tourists, climbers and walkers, which would give advice to those not familiar with a particular area so that they could get the maximum enjoyment from the mountain without causing damage to the flora and fauna, or to the mountain itself. One of the considerations was the thorny question of waymarking routes. In the Alps and other areas where mountaineering is a major tourist industry, routes are waymarked, sometimes giving the walking-time to the next place on the route, but it was also appreciated that in Snowdonia any attempt to make it easier for people to invade the mountains was anathema to probably the majority of mountaineers. In the knowledge that waymarking could result in frequent replacement of broken or removed signs, and bearing in mind that a profusion of such signs would do much to deface the mountains, it was decided not to proceed with such a plan. The problem was to some extent solved by utilising the strategically-placed cairns which had been created by many generations of walkers. but of course there was a risk that more cairns would be built. The Park maintained a few 'key' cairns whilst cairns which were not considered to be essential were removed. Many years later standing marker-stones were erected at important intersections, mainly on Snowdon.

The question of guiding walkers to their destination led naturally to argument about what the Park was trying to protect — was it the mountains from people, or people from the mountains? The Park decided that its primary

---

1. Known as the Park.

duty was to protect the mountains from people. This policy was challenged in the 1970s when it was suggested that a rather narrow rock step, on the last pitch of the refurbished zigzag footpath just below Bwlch Glas, could be made easier and safer by attaching some form of handrail to the rock. The pro-rail argument was that some casual walkers made the effort to get to the summit of Snowdon along well-maintained footpaths only to be thwarted by the short but narrow rock step which they found too daunting. Others could not face the step on the descent, and walked down to Llanberis instead. A handrail would have made it easier for those walkers to complete their ascent and return safely. In this way, the Park would have been ensuring their enjoyment, without in any way harming the mountain. One anti-rail argument was that a handrail could be damaged or even removed altogether. It would be the responsibility of the Park to maintain a handrail in a safe condition, and to insure themselves against Third Party claims in the event of the handrail failing in any way. After careful consideration the suggestion was turned down.[1]

A similar idea was put forward after a number of walkers had slipped off the railway line at Clogwyn Coch in severe winter conditions, and had fallen into Cwm Du'r Arddu. It was proposed that a safety net should be fixed just below the railway track 'to catch anyone who slipped on the ice or snow'.[2]

The initial cost of erecting such a net, which would have to withstand the harshest weather year after year, and the problems of maintenance and insurance, made it impractical. Signs have now been erected by the Warden Service requesting the public not to follow the railway track in winter conditions, and directing them to the Llanberis path a short distance up the slope.

*

In 1964, Warren Martin who was Head Warden of the Caernarfonshire part of the Park from 1963 to 1966,[3] planned and built a mountain refuge hut just below the summit of Foel Grach on the Carneddau. He received much assistance in the venture from the North Wales Mountaineering Club and from the RAF Valley MRT and its Team Leader, Flight-Sergeant Tony Bennett. The refuge was intended for emergencies only, but over the years it became subject to a great deal of misuse and abuse with parties actually planning to spend the night in it.

---

1. The rock step is now safe as it has been made wider by building up the path on the exposed side.
2. In Japan there is such a net to catch climbers who fall down Mount Tanigawa.
3. Warren Martin was warden for the Countryside Commission for Wales from 1966 until he retired in 1995.

A monolith which replaces a large cairn at the top of the zigzags. [SNP]

On one occasion someone walked over the roof wearing crampons and turned it into something resembling a colander; eventually the roof collapsed. The surrounding area, too, was abused and became little better than a public tip. The same sort of thing happened to several bothies in the Scottish Highlands, some of which were removed in the 1980s in the interests of health and safety. After much consideration it was decided to keep the refuge on Foel Grach and it was refurbished by the Wardens during 1989/90. A baffle wall was fitted inside to keep out any drifting snow and make it a more efficient shelter but this slightly reduced the capacity of the refuge. Before it was re-opened, mountaineering clubs, hostels, the military and youth organisations were sent a letter by John Ellis Roberts, Head Warden of Snowdonia National Park, informing them that the refuge had been refurbished for use in an emergency only and not as an overnight stopping place.

One consequence of the outdoor explosion was the erosion of footpaths,

Footpath restoration at Milestone Buttress.   [Neil Adam]

principally on Snowdon but also to a lesser extent on other mountains within the National Park. Not only were footpaths becoming worn away, and in many cases getting wider year upon year but, with so many people choosing to wander at will over the uplands, the often scarce flora and fauna were suffering damage as well. It was clear that without comprehensive management the damage would rapidly become irreparable, so in 1977 the Park, in partnership with the Countryside Commission, agreed to proceed with a five year programme of work on Snowdon which would concentrate on repairing and improving the condition of the footpaths and the summit, including the building, and the provision of visitor facilities on and around the mountain. The scheme started in April 1979, and at the end of the five years results were so promising that it was decided to carry on the work indefinitely and the end is not yet in sight. The improvements have made the mountain a safer place to walk on, but that was not the primary consideration. By improving the footpaths, the effect has been to channel walkers on to them, and the surrounding slopes have been allowed to start their long-term recovery.

Because Snowdon is accessible both on foot and by train, the bulk of the funding available for the restoration and improvement of footpaths has been devoted to the Snowdon massif. It is appreciated that there are many other mountains in Snowdonia suffering stress from increasing visitor numbers, and on some of these such as Cader Idris, the Arans, Rhinogs, lower level uplands south of Nant Gwynant, and parts of the Glyders and the Carneddau, a certain amount of 'first-aid' footpath work has been done. In the Ogwen valley, where The National Trust owns sizeable tracts of mountain, work similar to that done on Snowdon has been carried out by the Trust, and access has been greatly improved.

Returning to the responsibilities of the Wardens, weather forecasts are included in the type of information they provide, and since 1993 an automatic weather station has been operating on the roof of the summit building. Up-to-the-minute information is radioed hourly to the wardens' centre at Pen-y-pass where it is shown on a screen. The information includes wind speed and temperature, and the rainfall during the last hour; the development may extend to screens at other main tourist centres such as Llanberis and Betws-y-coed.

The welfare of the public, including rescue, is the responsibility of the Police, and the policy of the Park regarding MR has always been to give the fullest possible support to the RAF and civilian MRTs which operate throughout Snowdonia. If an accident is reported, the Warden's job is to inform the police and then render assistance either at base or on the hill. The civilian MRTs, which operate on a purely voluntary and charitable basis, provide a splendid and efficient service. Often based on the information available from the informant, the duty Warden will set the rescue procedure in motion and then, as a voluntary member of the local team, set out to locate the casualty and give appropriate first-aid. He will have a radio with him, will be able to report the nature of the injuries and condition of the casualty, and will guide the main body of the rescue team, or the rescue helicopter, to the accident site. This speeds up the whole operation and increases the chances of the casualty's survival.

17: The Rock Climbers

Pioneer climbers naturally formed groups of kindred spirits and, in 1897, the idea of forming a national club for mountaineers was discussed at a dinner party held at the *Café Monaco* in London at which some 40 regular visitors to the *Pen-y-gwryd* were present: soon afterwards the Climbers' Club was established. It was largely 'Wales-oriented', and one of its declared objects was to encourage all forms of mountaineering from hill-walking to rock-climbing. The emphasis soon swung in favour of rock-climbing, and the Climbers' Club became regarded generally as a club for rock-climbers.

The *Pen-y-gwryd Hotel* was closed at the turn of the century when the Owens, who had been landlords for close on half a century, had both died. Henry Owen died in 1891 and a tablet was erected in his memory in the old church in Beddgelert, on which it stated — 'To the Memory of Harry Owen, For 44 years Landlord of the Inn at *Pen-y-gwryd* ...' C E Mathews, writing about these 44 years in *The Climbers' Club Journal* dated December 1901 under the heading 'Reminiscences of Pen-y-gwryd', stated: 'That period witnessed the birth, the development, almost the culmination of mountaineering. Snowdon and Siabod, the Carnedds, and the Glyders, had of course been climbed before Harry Owen became the landlord, but the era of real Welsh climbing was not yet. Within the period covered by his life, the great playground of Europe had been thoroughly explored'. In 1902, the *Pen-y-gwryd* was bought by Mrs Roberts, the owner of *The Royal Hotel* in Capel Curig.

The choice of accommodation for the climbing groups was then between the *Pen-y-gwryd*, *Gorphwysfa*, which had just been enlarged and refurbished, *Ogwen Cottage Guest House*, and the *Royal Hotel* in Capel Curig. Most of the climbers who had favoured the *Pen-y-gwryd* defected to the *Gorphwysfa*, amongst them Geoffrey Winthrop Young, and the introduction of his Easter 'get-togethers' of well-to-do young climbers quickly made the *Gorphwysfa* 'the place to stay'.

Club members inevitably formed groups based on their home locations; great rivalries built up between groups, and these were roundly condemned by George Abraham. He claimed that they led to a number of avoidable accidents in the early 1900s, and also endangered the unity of the Climbers' Club itself.[1]

Within the groups, however, there was great companionship, and as the

---

1. See Chapter 11.

steam was gradually taken out of the rivalries, club activity once again found its proper level.

In 1909, an electrical engineer working on the Cwm Dyli power station named Arthur Lockwood, married the then landlady of the *Pen-y-gwryd*, Miss Pritchard, and in 1921 he became the landlord; he was closely involved in both mountaineering and fishing.[1]

There had been a long gap since the late years of the Owens' reign and it took a number of years before the Easter parties became a feature of the hotel. Arthur Lockwood took great pleasure in seeing skilled young climbers coming back from the hills and relaxing together in his hotel.[2]

From the last two decades of the 19th century, although heavily outnumbered by men, ladies were part of the mountaineering scene, and Haskett Smith frequently mentions them in his *Climbing in the British Isles*. Because men's clubs were closed to women, the Ladies Alpine Club was founded in 1907, and the Ladies Scottish Climbing Club in 1908. After the Great War was over, more women became interested in the sport, ladies' meets were organised, and a climbing club for women based in the north of England became a possibility. Pat Kelly, with her husband's active support, together with her great friend Annie Wells, set up a meeting place in Manchester, and by 1920 plans were being forged to establish the club. The amount of support from the Press, notably *The Manchester Guardian*, and from leading male climbers was encouraging, no less than the response from women themselves. The inaugural meeting was held at the *Pen-y-gwryd Hotel* on 26 March 1921, and the Pinnacle Club was given a great send-off. Many members climbed in Snowdonia and the club soon acquired a hut in Cwm Dyli. Founder members included Dorothy Pilley, Len Winthrop Young (Chairman), Pat Kelly (Honorary Secretary), and others who are recorded in *Pinnacle Club — A History of Women Climbing* which was written in 1989 by Shirley Angell.

On 17 April 1922, the last day of a three-day Welsh meet of the Pinnacle Club, three parties were climbing Wrinkled Slabs on the west face of Tryfan. Pat Kelly had not felt well that day and did not climb with them, but she joined them later at the top of the climb to see how they were getting on. The three parties completed their climbs and made their way down; it seems that Pat Kelly stayed behind, possibly to coil a rope. No one saw what happened, but Pat's body was

1. During his time at *Pen-y-gwryd*, Arthur Lockwood added one first ascent to the growing list, 'Lockwood's Chimney' on Gallt y Wenallt, not far from the hotel, and approached from Nant Gwynant.
2. The *Royal Hotel*, re-named Plas-y-Brenin, is now owned by the Sports Council and is the National Centre for Mountain Activities.

found later stretched out on the ground some way down the mountainside. She had severe head injuries and her face was badly bruised and cut. One of her climbing boots was missing but in spite of a thorough search it was not found. Pat Kelly was taken to hospital in Bangor where she underwent an operation, but her condition suddenly deteriorated and she died a few days later without regaining full consciousness. Pat did not live long enough to enjoy the fruits of her labours and of her great enthusiasm for her club, and her friends in the Pinnacle Club were devastated. Whatever happened to her high up on Tryfan remains a mystery.

*

In the 1920s, a schoolboy called Colin Kirkus, whose family lived in Liverpool, spent most of his holidays from the age of ten in the mountains of Snowdonia. By the time he left school in 1927 he was 'hooked' on mountaineering, and joined the Liverpool-based Wayfarers' Club. Colin's story is told in *Hands of a Climber* by Steve Dean (Ernest Press). Colin's enthusiasm was such that he would cycle from Liverpool and back for a weekend's climbing in North Wales. During the early 1930s, Colin Kirkus was acknowledged to be one of the leading climbers of his generation, pioneering literally dozens of new routes on all the main cliffs. He knew and occasionally climbed with John Menlove Edwards, another outstanding climber who also made many first ascents. Their styles were markedly different, but each played an important part in the development of rock-climbing in Snowdonia. The story of Menlove Edwards is related in *Menlove* by Jim Perrin.

In 1946 Gwen Goddard began climbing in Wales and by 1947 she had become addicted to the sport. In 1949 she married G Moffat, but the marriage was short-lived and the couple divorced. Gwen kept her married name, however, and became well known as a professional mountain guide and writer of mountain thrillers and other books. At Easter 1952 she met Johnnie Lees, the Leader of the RAF Valley MRT, whom she married in 1956. Before that, however, Gwen had become the first woman to qualify as a British mountain guide, and she was one of only three qualified guides in Wales. In 1961 Gwen wrote her autobiography, *Space Below my Feet*, to be followed three years later by *Two Star Red*, a history of RAF MR. By this time she was devoting more of her energy to writing and travelling than to climbing, but she had made a considerable contribution in the history of women climbers.

Brede Arkless, and her husband Geoff, are both qualified British mountain guides, and both were members of the Llanberis MRT. Brede herself has the honour of being the first Briton, man or woman, to have been awarded the 'carnet' of Bergfuhrer by the International Union of Mountain Guides. This organisation was originally only for Alpine guides, and it was mainly due to the efforts of John Brailsford in the early 1970s that British Mountain Guides were accepted.

*

In mid-January 1953 a party of climbers gathered at the Climbers' Club hut at Helyg. This was not just an ordinary climbing club meet, but was held for more serious business. The meet had been convened by Lieutenant-Colonel John Hunt who was now the leader of the forthcoming Everest expedition. Although John Hunt and his team had been training for some time using the *Pen-y-gwryd Hotel* as their base, this last meeting before leaving for the Himalayas was for the specific purpose of testing various types of oxygen-carrying equipment. The next time that they would all meet again in North Wales was to be after the successful first ascent of the highest mountain in the world — Everest, 8848 metres. Then, members including Edmund Hillary and Sherpa Tensing who were the first humans to stand on the roof of the world, gathered at the *Pen-y-gwryd Hotel* and signed their names on the smoke room ceiling. They each gave Chris Briggs an item of clothing or equipment actually used on the expedition, and these are still on display in a cabinet in the Everest bar, along with the pewter beer mugs with the inscribed names of each member of the team. The 1953 Everest expedition did a great deal to create public awareness, and enhance the image of Snowdonia as a region for hill-walkers and rock-climbers.

18: A Tuft of Grass

Peter Llowarch was 23 years-old and had crammed a great deal of climbing experience into his young life, including a spell as a member of the RAF Cyprus MRT during his National Service. Peter was a fit, strong young man in keeping with his job as a forestry worker near St Albans: he was also a member of the North London Climbing Club and the Liverpool-based Annabassas Climbing Club. On the eve of Friday, 24 November 1961, with a 17 year old friend from work — Ian Rennie — Peter set out for a climbing weekend in Snowdonia, and arrived at Capel Curig shortly after midnight. On Saturday Peter took Ian, who had no experience of rock-climbing, round to Tryfan where they did some simple and easy routes to give Ian an introduction to the basics of rock-climbing. On the next day, they were joined by Brian Clarke who, though only 16 years old, had been rock-climbing for more than a year. The party's aim that day was

Main Wall Climb, a 400-foot Hard Severe route on Gyrn Las which is an impressive cliff on the western side at the head of Cwm Glas Mawr. By modern standards it is not a particularly hard route but it is tremendously exposed and fairly serious. In the 1960s, especially in late November, the route would have provided a serious challenge even for an experienced party.[1]

They scrambled 350 feet above the scree and started climbing at 12.30pm with Peter leading, Brian second and the novice Ian as the third man on the rope. The first two 30-foot pitches were climbed without difficulty, and Peter then climbed up the 80-foot third pitch and belayed. Whilst Ian remained belayed at the bottom of the third pitch, Brian started to climb, but at about halfway he shouted that his hands had gone numb and that he was going to fall off. Peter shouted back that if he did fall, he would be able to hold him. A moment after Peter's shout of assurance, Brian fell about 20 feet but Peter was able to arrest his fall. The force of the fall came upon Peter's waist and pulled him from his stance; he was pulled down until the slack was taken up to the belay which took the strain and held him. He was able to get back on to the stance and shouted to the others to ask if they were all right. They replied that Brian had slipped further down, and they had both become entangled in the rope at the bottom of the third pitch and couldn't move. Peter then untied his rope and climbed down to them but, as he was about to secure Brian on to the belay with Ian, a tuft of grass he was standing on gave way under his foot. He lost his balance and fell some 250 feet to the scree below where he lay motionless.

Brian and Ian were now trapped on Main Wall, but their cries for help were miraculously heard by two climbers from the Royal Marines climbing on Carreg Wastad, 3/4 mile away on the other side of the valley. The Marines responded quickly and were soon at the scene of the accident. It was obvious that Peter Llowarch had very severe head injuries and that there was little hope. Whilst one soldier went for help to the Climbers' Club hut at Ynys Ettws, the other climbed up to the stranded party to secure them until the arrival of the rescue party. The body of Peter Llowarch was recovered and the two young climbers were escorted off the climb to safety. Peter was buried in the churchyard at Nant Peris and the funeral was attended by the two Marines who had come to the help of the trapped party. At the inquest, the Coroner 'wished it to be known that Peter had died whilst trying to assist his friends'.

1. Gyrn Las. The local name for this cliff was Diffwys Ddu, (Grey Horn), but the earliest climbers for some unknown reason changed the name to Gyrn Las by which name the cliff is known today. The rock is not always perfect and even on the easier routes a good deal of competence is needed. The major routes are long and exposed, giving fine expeditions for competent climbers.

19: Fatalities in Cwm Ffynnon Llugwy

There was an early cold snap in November 1962 which caught many people by surprise, and over the weekend of 17/18th, the RAF Valley MRT was on exercise in the Ogwen Valley. Late on the Saturday afternoon a detachment of the team was called out to rescue a party of three who were reported cragfast at the top of the Idwal Slabs. By the time the team reached the Slabs it was growing dark, the snow which had been threatening all day was falling heavily. and conditions were very unpleasant. The Team Leader, Corporal John Tunnah, led the team past the left-hand side of the Slabs below Suicide Wall and up until they were eventually able to traverse to the benighted party. Although it was dark there was no great difficulty in getting them down, although the party, two men and a girl, one of whom was wearing ordinary casual clothes and walking shoes, were all suffering from frostbite and exposure. Having taken them to the sanctuary of Ogwen Cottage, the RAF party made their way to their weekend base at Garth Barn, Dyffryn Mymbyr. While they were having their evening meal, a report came through that a party of climbers was missing somewhere on the Carneddau, believed to be in the Craig-yr-ysfa area. The team was asked to prepare for a night search from Helyg where one of the missing party — Squadron Leader Tony Back — had arrived and reported that his two companions were still 'out there somewhere' on the other side of the road a few hundred yards towards Llyn Llugwy, but he didn't know exactly where. The two missing men were Junior Technician Richard Blatch, aged 24, and Corporal-Cook J P McCann, 36, two members of an RAF party led by Tony Back which had arrived at Helyg on Friday 16 November for expedition training in preparation for a trip to Mount Kenya in February 1963. Dick Blatch was fit and young, and had previously been a member of the RAF Kinloss MRT. McCann was a keen athlete, but was in the throes of a head-cold when they arrived at Helyg; nevertheless he had insisted that he was fit enough to climb the next day.

The party had split into two groups, one of which consisted of Tony Back, Blatch and McCann. This group set out at 8.50am on Saturday 17 November to climb Great Gully on Craig-yr-ysfa. There was snow on the ground, and more had been forecast, but the going was not too difficult during the early part of the day. By 3pm the party was having problems climbing the gully, and at 3.15pm, in deteriorating weather, they retreated down the gully and retraced their steps towards Helyg. Heavy snow started to fall, and they had covered about three quarters of the way back to the hut when McCann started to show signs of exhaustion. Supported on either side by Blatch and Back, he managed to keep going for another 45 minutes, but Blatch himself was also exhausted by this time, and they were unable to go any further. Tony Back asked Dick Blatch if he would go ahead to summon assistance, but Blatch replied that he didn't think he would be able to make it.

Setting off for Helyg, which was only about ten minutes away, Tony Back left his rucksack and torch with Dick Blatch, told him that they must try to eat some food and keep awake at all costs, and to flash his torch as soon as they saw the rescue party returning. When he arrived at the hut, Back collected six men and immediately set off to find Blatch and McCann. In the short time since he had left the two men the wind and fresh snow had obliterated his footsteps, and no torch signals were seen: eventually the search party had to admit defeat and they returned to Helyg to alert the rescue service. The weather had become steadily worse, the snow continued to fall heavily, the roads were rapidly becoming blocked, and the RAF Valley MRT at Garth Barn was sent to Helyg. They had to undergo the unpleasant procedure of putting on their cold saturated mountain clothes, and having reached Helyg with some difficulty at about midnight, they started a sweep search from the A5 road astride the rough track leading to Llyn Ffynnon Llugwy.[1]

They reached the top of the track, turned about and repeated the sweep down the slope towards the road but there was no sign of the missing men. John (Taff) Tunnah decided that conditions had become too bad to continue searching and at 3am he withdrew his men to rest. At 10.15 on the following morning the Valley team, assisted by the Police and Tony Back, resumed the search; by 11.20am Dick Blatch's and McCann's bodies were found lying under a covering of snow in a small hollow just short of the final ridge in front of Helyg, between the A5 road and the leat which runs across the slope: they had made a brave effort to reach the shelter of Helyg, but in the end exposure had claimed their lives a bare 500 yards from safety.

*

Yet another incident occurred in Cwm Ffynnon Llugwy during the evening of 28 January 1978 when two climbers, trying to reach the A5 road ahead of deteriorating weather, slipped down snow-covered rocks and plunged into the freezing waters of Llyn Llugwy. As in the 1927 tragedy,[1] one of them, James Farrel, aged 33, couldn't swim, and it seems that he died almost immediately.

---

1. This was before the tarmac road was laid.

The other man, Rolfe Birch, also aged 33, who was a surgeon, swam for the shore and by good fortune he survived. The story began when the two men, who had already done a rock climb on Crib Goch during the morning, decided to drive round to the Ogwen Valley and spend the night on the Carneddau. They parked their car at the start of the track leading from the A5 road up to Llyn Llugwy, just opposite Gwern Gof Isaf, (commonly known as 'Big Willy's Barn'), shortly after 4pm, as it was their intention to walk up to the mountain refuge on Foel Grach and spend the night there. Before they could reach the refuge the weather quickly deteriorated into a heavy blizzard, and the two men decided to stop where they were, a long way short of the refuge, and build a snow -hole. They were well equipped with excellent clothing, survival and sleeping bags, ice-axes and crampons and they had adequate food. Being experienced mountaineers, and having done many expeditions in similar conditions together, they were fully prepared for a rough night. Soon after 8pm the snow-hole was ready, and they were getting out their sleeping bags to put in the shelter when a violent gust of wind blew Farrel's bag away. This was a serious turn of events, and they decided to pack up and return to lower ground and try to find some sort of natural shelter. By now the conditions were extremely bad, and eventually they reached a spot near the shore of Llyn Llugwy where they sheltered for a while under a large rock. After eating some food, they set off again with Birch leading by the light of his head torch. Farrel's battery had run out and he was virtually walking blind about five yards behind Birch. After about two hundred yards, Birch climbed a little way up a slope to avoid a steep slab of snow-covered rock, and as he tried to get round the top of it he slipped and slid ten feet into the lake. With the weight of his equipment dragging him down, he was at once in difficulties and the wind was blowing him away from the shore. He turned in the other direction and, struggling against the wind, he managed to reach firm ground where he supported himself on a rock slab. He shouted to his companion not to come near the water, but there was no reply, and as he turned to look across the lake he saw Farrel's face about five yards away from him. He had no idea whether Farrel had slipped when trying to get near the water's edge to help him, or whether he had deliberately entered the water to assist him.

Birch climbed out of the water, secured his position on the bank, and shouted to Farrel, but once again there was no reply. He scanned the water with his head torch, but Farrel had completely disappeared. Soon afterward he saw Farrel floating face down about thirty yards from the shore, and being blown out across the lake. He realised that he couldn't possibly make a successful rescue

1. *The Giveen Affair* — Chapter 11.

attempt in such appalling weather conditions, and in any case he thought that Farrel was probably already dead. Birch then set out round the lake to find the track which led down to where they had left their car. The snow was still falling heavily and lay thick and soft, making progress slow and difficult. The car was just over a mile from the lake, and by the time he reached it, he was utterly exhausted. He crossed the road and made for Willy's Barn where he gasped to the astonished farmer, 'my friend ...'. But he collapsed and lost consciousness before saying any more. Farmer Williams realised that the man was in a very serious condition, and without delay he put him in his car, turned the heater on at full blast, and set out into the teeth of the blizzard for Bangor hospital. At that time the road was still open, thanks to the snow-plough crews, and he reached his destination soon after midnight. Birch was given emergency re-warming treatment, and before long he was able to say what had happened, and to indicate where he had last seen his companion.

At 1am on 29 January, the Ogwen Valley and RAF Valley MRTs were informed of the incident by North Wales Police, and a search was organised to begin at first light.[1] A total of twenty-eight experienced mountaineers, which included the two MRTs, and two search dog handlers — Phil Williams-Jones and Neil Adam — took part in this operation, the dog teams going out first at 8.15am, and the remainder, including a diver from the University Marine Science Laboratories at Menai Bridge, setting off at 9am. It was still snowing and the ground conditions were getting worse. At the time, as Neil Adam explained, they were able to walk across the tops of the five-barred gates. Down on the main road the snow-ploughs were in danger of losing their battle to keep even one lane open, and the Highways authority warned at mid-morning that the road would very soon be closed altogether and advised that all personnel should be re-called. It was unlikely that Farrel could still be alive, and in the interests of the safety of the rescue teams, a recall was ordered; everyone was safely off the hill by 12.30pm. As they walked down to the road, even the tops of the gates were no longer visible, and snow continued to fall.

It was not until a week later, on 4 February, that the search could be resumed. On that day the search co-ordinator was Tony Jones and the party included fourteen members of the Ogwen Valley MRT, the same two dog handlers, RAF Valley MRT members and the police under-water search unit which had been airlifted to Llyn Llugwy by 'C' Flight. The dog teams were deployed immediately on each side of the lake, and Neil Adam's dog quickly alerted to something under the surface at the spot where the two men had been in the

---

1. The RAF Valley MRT was based in Bethesda at the time, and Dr Tony Jones was staying with them.

water, but it turned out to be Farrel's rucksack, with the two ice-axes nearby. Farrel's body was found by the police divers at 12.36pm, in 30 feet of water, a few yards from the shore of the lake. The finding of the pathologist was that Farrel had drowned, and a verdict of accidental death was returned.

20: The MRS Takes Shape

During the 1950s, the only MR Post in Snowdonia with an accredited organiser for search and rescue was the *Pen-y-gwryd Hotel* (Post 22). No other posts, including those at Idwal Youth Hostel (Post 20) and Ogwen Cottage (Post 21), had such an organiser, their purpose being to hold essential first-aid and rescue equipment. At this time also, RAF Valley maintained a number of sub-units in Snowdonia, which took on responsibility for assisting with rescue work in the areas where they were positioned.

At the top of the Llanberis Pass, the *Gorphwysfa Hotel* still attracted large numbers of climbers, so that between the two hotels — the *Pen-y-gwryd* and *Gorphwysfa* — there was nearly always a supply of competent mountaineers available to carry out rescues, usually under the leadership of Chris Briggs. On the other side of the Glyders in the Ogwen valley, the post at Ogwen Cottage had been there since 1903, and for many years Ogwen Cottage had been a thriving guest house used mainly as a base by climbers. Colin Kirkus and his colleagues used to favour staying there during the 1930s, and just after the war a new generation of climbers made it their base for it was ideally situated between the Glyders and Carneddau. Towards the end of the 1950s, when the popularity of mountain recreation was gathering momentum, education authorities and others wanted to establish their own outdoor activity centres and were on the lookout for suitable buildings to convert.

One evening in 1954, the owner of the *Royal Hotel* in Capel Curig, Eugene Brunning, decided to sell the hotel with the proviso that he must be the last landlord in its 150-year history, and that whoever bought the building must use it for some purpose other than as an inn. For many decades the 'Royal', as it was affectionately called, had been a popular venue for mountaineers and it had also been a ready source of volunteers to take part in searches and rescues.

John Disley, the Olympic steeplechaser, happened to be in the bar when Eugene Brunning confessed that playing the role of an inn-keeper in such difficult times had begun to pall, and he had decided to sell up. Disley immediately contacted Justin Evans, the deputy secretary of the Central Council for Physical Recreation, as he knew that the CCPR was looking for a suitable location for a mountain training centre in North Wales. He also sought Chris Briggs's help in extolling the suitability of the hotel as a centre for outdoor activities. Within two months the sale had been agreed and on 1 April 1955 the *Royal Hotel* passed into the ownership of the CCPR. It was renamed Plas-y-Brenin, (literally King's House), was to be known as the Snowdonia National Recreation Centre, and with accommodation limited to 40 students, the first courses were held during that summer. John Disley was appointed Chief Instructor and Roger Orgill Chief Canoe Instructor, and together they built up a core of permanent-staff instructors with a pool of experienced mountaineers and canoeists as volunteer staff who could be called upon as required to enable the centre to function efficiently.

From the outset Plas-y-Brenin worked very closely with Chris Briggs at *Pen-y-gwryd*. The students were useful for assisting with stretcher carries and searches, and in many instances assistance was readily given by those who came to the centre for recreation and training. Basic mountain rescue courses were included in the programme for the first time in 1960, and in that year Plas-y-Brenin was designated MR Post No 60. MR involvement was voluntary, even for the permanent staff; on many occasions instructors would turn up for work straight from a rescue or turn out on a rescue after a hard day's work on the hill. From 1963 onwards a few instructors became expert in the use of karabiner brakes, rope mechanics, stretcher lowering and self-rescue techniques. Many team members, youth leaders and instructors became interested in learning more, and because self-rescue and MR was a requisite for the Mountain Leadership Certificate and, at a higher level, the Mountain Instructors Certificate, Plas-y-Brenin was encouraged to offer specific courses for mountain rescue. The rescue programmes, 'suitable for MRT personnel,' were offered in the 1964/65 brochures, and had the official backing of the MRC in the form of additional equipment and subsidised places on the courses. The first MLC course was also held in 1964; part of the syllabus was 'improvisation for evacuation of a casualty from steep slopes, but not necessarily rock faces'. Rescue courses are still run twice a year and liaison between the Centre and various rescue organisations remains very close. Since Plas-y-Brenin was established, some of the permanent staff have been involved in the development of MR in North Wales, notably John A Jackson who was the Director of Plas-y-Brenin for 16 years from 1960 to 1975, and Derek Mayes who for many years represented Plas-y-Brenin on the North Wales Mountain Rescue Association and is still actively supportive of the MR service in North Wales. Over the years, the commitment of Plas-y-Brenin to call-outs has greatly diminished, but at the same time its training courses and special assistance from staff have remained important. The training they give in accident prevention and risk management continues to have a significant impact on accident statistics. Plas-y-Brenin justifiably claims to lead in the field of training guides, instructors and leaders.

In the Ogwen Valley, two keen climbers, Ron James and Tony Mason-Hornby, bought Ogwen Cottage in 1959 and soon afterwards it was opened as one of the first permanent private mountaineering schools. Ron and Tony adopted a policy of complete professionalism and to this end they employed as instructors only competent mountaineers. It was soon realised that Ogwen Cottage was not only an outdoor centre but also a very active MR post, and the instructors accepted this role as part of their job and automatically became members of the Ogwen Cottage MRT, and available for call-out at any time. They were given help and advice in setting up the team by Flight-Sergeant Johnnie Lees, the leader of the RAF Valley MRT, and during the next five years, the Ogwen team carried out many rescues in the area and were often asked by Chris Briggs to help with rescues on Snowdon. Since the school was open throughout the year, there were usually at least six competent mountaineers available to form the core of the team. They worked together to develop rescue techniques, and to assist them the names of volunteers were placed on a call-out list.

In 1964 Birmingham Education Authority bought Ogwen Cottage as a going concern, and for the first time instructors were able to enjoy regular school holidays. During that summer, when most of the instructors were away in the Alps, and Valley MRT was training elsewhere, John Glews, one of the staff who had stayed behind, fell and was badly injured whilst attempting a new route on Clogwyn Du, a crag right at the top of Nameless Cwm above the Idwal Slabs. Someone went for help and whilst John lay there waiting, he realised the need for continuous MR cover involving rescuers other than Ogwen Cottage staff and the RAF Valley MRT, either of whom might be away from the area or otherwise engaged. When a hastily assembled rescue party arrived, John Glews was not over-impressed by their untrained skills and tried to tell them what to do as he lay injured on the stretcher. When his colleagues visited John in the orthopaedic hospital at Gobowen in Shropshire where he was still in intensive care, having heard about his rescue by an inexperienced party, they decided that the need for a more permanent rescue team had become a pressing priority.

RAF Valley MRT over the last 20 years had developed a system for immediate response in contacting and assembling a team for a rescue operation. Ron James and Tony Mason-Hornby decided that the new team would consist of a number of team leaders, mainly the instructors at Ogwen Cottage, with a large pool of skilled rescuers who would be on call round the clock. It would be a charitable and entirely voluntary commitment, for then, as now, no public funds were available to cover the running costs of mountain rescue teams. The Ogwen Valley Mountain Rescue Organisation was formed in the autumn of 1964 as an operational team with Tony as Chairman, Ron as Senior Team Leader and Barbara James as the first secretary: they received much valuable help and encouragement from the Mountaineering Club of North Wales and from RAF Valley MRT. In 1966, Tony Mason-Hornby's cousin died and he left North Wales to take over the family estate in Cumbria. Cedric Milner became Chairman, but a year later he departed for Canada and Tony Jones took over as Chairman. In May 1969 Ron James became the Principal Lecturer in Outdoor Education at the I M Marsh College of Physical Education in Liverpool, a position he held for 16 years until he retired and returned to North Wales in 1985.[1]

They left the Ogwen Valley Team in good hands, a fact which has been born out by its excellent record of rescues during the last 33 years.

During the ten years he had been involved in MR work, Ron James had made many improvements in equipment and in rescue techniques. Essentially an innovator he went to Pontresina in Switzerland for one winter to study the techniques used in mountain rescue in the Swiss Alps. There he met Dr Rudolph Campbell, the President of the International Rescue Organisation, who was most helpful though some of what he told Ron was of marginal use in Snowdonia as it dealt with glaciers and rescuing people from crevasses!. Ron also went to Innsbruck in Austria to meet Wastl Mariner, author of *Mountain Rescue Techniques*, and he acquired a film of *Rescue in the Alps* which Mariner and his team had made. On his return to Ogwen Cottage he used the film to instruct team members in some of the techniques which had not hitherto been used in Britain. The team bought a Mariner mountain rescue stretcher and through Ron's efforts also purchased a Tragsitz, a special rescue harness which enables a rescuer to carry a man on his back as he is lowered down a cliff face. The Mariner stretcher was the most widely used stretcher in the Alps. It can be split into two sections for transportation and can also be fitted with a wheel so that it can be manoeuvred over rough ground by rescuers to make it easier to evacuate a casualty. Its other advantages over the stretchers in general use in Britain at that time were first, that the handles can be adjusted to any angle to make carrying

---

1. Ron James had been Chief Instructor at Ogwen Cottage from 1959 to 1964, and Warden from 1964 until he left in 1969.

The Mariner stretcher (above) on skis, with back rope and (below) using the wheel.
[Neil Adam]

easier, and second, that the casualty can be carried in a semi-sitting position. It also has excellent adjustable splinting for fractures.[1]

Ron also went to the French Alps to meet Edouard Frendo, who had a shop in Grenoble and from whom he bought a Perche Barnarde stretcher. This is another piece of specialist mountain rescue equipment designed to be carried or used on an aerial rope way. It has an adjustable knee splint (see photograph).

Ron was the first to receive the 'Advanced First-Aid as applied to Mountain Rescue' certificate from St John's in August 1967, and his wife, Barbara, was awarded the second. In the mountains Ron James was a master of improvisation, particularly in rescue situations. On one occasion he was driving back from Birmingham when, as he approached the Milestone Buttress, he was flagged down by police who had recognised his car. He was wearing a town suit and leather shoes, but fortunately he had a pair of trainers with him. The police explained that there was a climber in difficulty in Ivy Chimney. The man had slipped and his leg had shot into a crack where the knee had become completely jammed. He had been there for at least three hours, and both the police and the RAF Valley MRT had tried everything they knew without success. Dr Ieuan Jones, who was the senior accident officer at the Caernarfon and Anglesey Hospital in Bangor and a member of the OVMRO, had been called to the scene, and even he was beginning to wonder if he would have to amputate the leg to get the man out. Some of the RAF team members came up with a car jack, intending to place it in the crack and use it to try to prise the sides of the chimney apart to free the leg. Ron was not happy with that solution as there was no way of telling what the effect on the rocks forming the chimney might be. Ron climbed up to the casualty in his immaculate suit, and the patient was manoeuvred into a sit-sling to take the weight off his knee, which then enabled Ron to straighten the leg. He then got himself alongside the patient whilst in a sit-sling so that he was free to move about and use his hands. He asked for some scissors and cut away the trousers in front and behind, and then removed the boot from the stuck leg. Having done that he asked if anyone had any sandwiches; thankfully they had, and Ron smeared the butter all over the casualty's knee. Clipping his waist belt tightly to the back of the patient's sit-sling, he then put his feet firmly against the rock and suddenly straightened both his legs, so that the patient popped out of the crack. Subsequently Ron did two more similar rescues, once using engine oil as no one had any sandwiches left! After Ron had left Ogwen Cottage he frequently came back to Snowdonia with his own students from the Polytechnic in Liverpool, and whilst in the area he

---

1. The Mariner is no longer in use and other stretchers, such as the Bell, have superseded it.

Perche Barnarde stretcher on aerial ropeway.   *[Neil Adam]*

was on call to OVMRO. It was on one of these occasions that a second-year girl student was leading up Flake Chimney on Dinas Bach when she slipped and her knee jammed in a crack. Ron arrived at the site and realised that the situation was unlike any he had dealt with, and that none of his usual techniques were going to work. He couldn't get behind the girl to use his legs to push out with, so he fixed a pulley on top of the pinnacle, manoeuvred the girl into a sit-sling, and got her to straighten her leg in the crack. Sandwiches were duly produced and when the knee area had been well buttered, Ron tied the pulley rope and a safety rope to himself and climbed to the top of the pinnacle. Then, when all was ready, he jumped off the pinnacle, the ropes tightened, and the girl popped up out of the crack like the proverbial cork from a bottle. Ron fell 10 feet before stopping, but the job was done and his reputation saved — apart, that is, from the fact that the chimney was almost unclimbable for about six months due to the grease left on the rock.

In the ten years of his involvement in MR, Ron James took part in 360 rescues, and of these the following is certainly worthy of special mention.

In the summer of 1968, there was a serious accident involving three climbers, two men and a girl, on a route called Soap Gut on the Milestone Buttress. Ron James and Neil Adam from the Ogwen Valley Team were the first on the scene, and the Plas-y-Brenin MRT was also called out. The leader had fallen off when the block of rock he was holding came away, almost severing his foot. The block then dropped on to his second, causing him severe shoulder and chest injuries which might well have proved fatal. The third member was a girl who had been pulled off her stance but was still holding her companions on the rope. Ron James and Neil Adam were lowered down the climb with two stretchers and, after making the leader and his second secure, dealt with the girl by lowering her off. A tourniquet, made with a sling and a karabiner, was then applied to the leader's leg and the necessary first-aid was given to the second. With Ray Greenall lighting up the area with a searchlight, a double lower, controlled by radio by Tony Jones in the Landrover, was carried out with Ron and Neil, each with a stretcher and on separate ropes, being lowered side by side for most of the descent. It was a long and difficult operation, successfully performed by good team work, and it was one which had a happy ending. Some months later Ron attended the wedding of the leader and the girl, with his second as the best man!

In the early 1960s, Dr Ieuan Jones embarked on a campaign to ensure that as many members of MRTs as possible should be competent in Mountain First-Aid. Over the years some casualties had died because those at the scene of an accident had no knowledge of the elementary treatments necessary to sustain life until the injured or sick person could be properly treated in hospital. The impact Ieuan has made on the quality of MR care in the United Kingdom justifies taking a closer look at his work.

Although Dr Ieuan Jones has spent nearly all his working life in North Wales, he was born near Llanelli in South Wales, in December 1935. He did his medical training at Guy's Hospital in London, and first came to North Wales at Whitsun 1960 when he joined the staff of the old Caernarfon and Anglesey Hospital in Bangor. Soon after arriving, Ieuan joined the Ogwen Cottage MRT which at that time consisted of eight members. Before he joined the team, Ieuan had been a keen hill-walker, but had never done any rock-climbing. The members of the team set about teaching him and Ieuan soon became a keen and accomplished rock-climber as it was essential for any one doing first-aid in a mountain situation to be able to solo-climb difficult rock, even in the dark.

In 1961, when Flight-Sergeant Tony Bennett was leader of the RAF Valley MRT, Ieuan became involved with the RAF at Valley as there was a little local difficulty about the supply of morphine to the team. RAF MRTs were permitted to carry morphine as part of their first-aid kit, but team members were required to possess a certificate signed by the Station Medical Officer that they were trained and confident in its use. It was agreed that Ieuan would test the team members and provide the Station Medical Officer with a list of all those who passed, and he would then issue the certificates. Ieuan found that the team members had a poor idea about the purpose and application of morphine, and set up a course specifically to train the RAF team members in its use. The RAF men were keen to learn and asked Ieuan to run a course in general first-aid as applied to the mountain environment. Soon afterwards, Ieuan started a course on 'First-Aid in Mountaineering' in the physiotherapy department of the hospital which was open to everyone who wanted to come, with mountaineers, county ambulance men, St John's Ambulance and Red Cross personnel making up the bulk of the students. The course consisted of a series of lectures and practical demonstrations, and standard first-aid certificates were given by the St John's Ambulance Brigade (Wales) to all those who completed the course. It was a successful venture but his career had to take precedence over the voluntary work he was doing, and Ieuan left North Wales in 1964 to take up a position with the Coal Board in the East Midlands. As part of the job, he had joined the St John's Ambulance Brigade, for one of his tasks was to train colliery officials in first-aid.

In June 1966, Ieuan returned to Bangor as Senior Accident Officer at the C & A Hospital and re-joined the OVMRO. He was approached by Roland Edwards, one of the senior instructors at Plas-y-Brenin, who persuaded him to re-start his courses, but at the University of North Wales in Bangor. These new courses became official St John's courses in 'First-Aid in Mountaineering' in the autumn of 1966, and with the support of a senior St John's Officer — Don Williams — Ieuan asked the St John's Ambulance Brigade Headquarters in Wales to issue a special certificate. The courses continued to be well supported and soon Ieuan was asked to introduce an advanced course as well. While the examination at the end of each course was rigorous, Ieuan became concerned that non-mountaineers could pass the exam without ever having been on a mountain. His fear was that a non-mountaineer holder of the certificate might be drawn into a rescue on a crag and then prove to be a danger to himself and others. He therefore introduced an intermediate theory test which included questions on basic mountaineering such as navigation and compass work; this acted as a screen to filter out non-mountaineers.

There was another screening test which Ieuan introduced for all mountaineers who attended the advanced assessment for the Advanced First-Aid in Mountaineering course. They had to attend the casualty department at the hospital and be involved with casualties. This involved coping with the sight and smell of real injuries, mainly to diagnose the injury; learning how casualties respond to pain and treatment, and, under supervision, the art of handling broken limbs and patients. The popularity of the basic courses was overwhelming; as many as 300 people would attend, some travelling from as far away as Birmingham for an evening lecture. With these numbers it was almost impossible to demonstrate procedures and techniques in a way that everyone could see. To reduce the size of classes, there would have to be many more courses, but Ieuan's time was already being stretched to the limit. The answer to the problem came to him by chance when on one occasion he had an extremely bad cold and had virtually lost his voice. It was clear that he could not take the class that night, so he quickly prepared a tape of his lecture, albeit in a very husky voice, and the course went ahead as planned. He developed this idea, preparing a series of slides of real injuries to illustrate the various wounds that mountaineers were likely to come across. To demonstrate how to examine the patient, the photographs were taken from behind Ieuan so that the slide would clearly show the use of the examiner's hands. The slides were a tremendous success. They have been updated and improved, and the most recent set has been expanded to nearly 500 slides, covering all aspects of the subject. With the taped lecture by Ieuan, they are used on courses held throughout the United Kingdom.

All members of MRTs were, and still are, encouraged to hold the Mountain First-Aid certificate, but Ieuan Jones could not instruct every team member. In November 1968 he ran the first Mountaineering First-Aid Instructors Course, based on the use of tape and slides. This so clearly showed the very high standard of first-aid training in Wales that MRTs from other areas requested Ieuan to put on the same instructors' course for them.

Dr Ieuan Jones's legacy to MR is the development of his first-aid courses, but he made other innovative suggestions. He persuaded Dr David Last, a lecturer at the Electronics Department of the University, to co-operate in a venture to add to existing radio communications, which at that time relied mainly on hill sets such as the Pye Bantam. The idea was to develop a coded audio modulator facility to send back data from the rescue site to be interpreted by a doctor at the hospital. Information to be sent back would include pulse rate, blood pressure, respiration rate and depth, and ECG readings. In the trials there was too much interference for a constant clear signal and eventually the idea was shelved and recourse had to be made to the use of radio sets. On occasions, timely advice has been radioed from Ieuan at the hospital to the accident site on the hill; when a walker had suffered a heart attack on the Glyders, Ron James asked for advice and was told to get the man into a tent, keep him warm and quiet, 'and I will get some pills up to you'. The pills arrived by runner, and soon afterwards it was possible to carry the patient gently down to the *Pen-y-gwryd* where he was transferred to a waiting ambulance. He subsequently made a full recovery.

The next anecdote is from a time when the treatment and prevention of hypothermia was exercising minds. Various instructional documents had been issued such as BMC circular No 380 in November 1964, which was published jointly by the BMC and ASCC[1] and headed 'Exposure — Notes on the Recognition and Treatment'. It was based on the report of a working party set up by the Outward Bound Trust under the chairmanship of Jack Longland, and following a symposium on 'Exposure' held in 1967, it was revised in March 1968 by Tom Price of Eskdale Outward Bound school. In 1972 it was again revised by the BMC Safety Sub-Committee under the chairmanship of John Jackson and Ron James and included more recent work done by Ieuan Jones, and Don Robertson of the Institute of Aviation Medicine.

Peter Ellis, a design student from Birmingham Polytechnic, asked Ieuan to give him some ideas about a project he was doing on the design of a new type of MR stretcher. Ieuan suggested a concept to Ellis that would prevent hypothermia during the evacuation of casualties. The requirement was to ensure that the casualty's environment was controlled during the rescue. Ellis designed a fibreglass cocoon in the shape of a human body which was in two parts, the body and lid. A transparent panel was to be fitted in the lid to provide assurance to the casualty. Hot air from a portable heater would be fed through ducts into the cocoon, and the temperature controlled and adjusted as necessary. The design was developed and the prototype was actually built, but it was too heavy and cumbersome. It ended up as a huge yellow sledge which was once seen floating across Llyn Idwal and was later used as a carriage for Santa Claus! What started out with high hopes, ended up with typical MR humour.

Dr Ieuan Jones's outstanding work in North Wales was recognised in 1974 by the award of the Torch Trophy. The Torch Trophy Trust had been established in 1952 to encourage voluntary work for sport at club level, and Ieuan was nominated by the North Wales Area Committee of the BMC. He was presented with his trophy by John Hunt, the leader of the 1953 Everest expedition. Since that time, Ieuan has extended his work in first-aid training to the whole of the United Kingdom, not only in MR but also to other rescue services such as cavers, teachers, youth group leaders, and expedition parties. 25 courses were run in 1982; in 1988 the number of courses had increased to 68, and catered for 1,060 students of whom 69 per cent passed.

---

1. Association of Scottish Climbing Clubs.

In his 'spare time' Ieuan is a Lieutenant-Colonel in the Royal Army Medical Corps, Territorial Army, and was embodied into the Regular Army in 1991 to serve in the Gulf War.

Barbara James, in the Silver Jubilee News Letter of the OVMRO in 1990, wrote, 'Primarily, however, it is those unlucky enough to be injured who owe the biggest debt to the hand which has guided so many — yet whose name the casualties are unlikely to have known — Dr Ieuan Jones.'

*

In the mid-1970s, the OVMRO had to relinquish the facilities at Ogwen Cottage because Birmingham Education Authority needed the space to expand the centre, but they quickly outgrew the alternative facilities offered at Idwal Youth Hostel nearby, and in 1976 they were able to rent from the National Trust part of an old cottage, Bryn Poeth, to the north of the A5 road opposite Gwern Gof Uchaf. It was well away from the road, bore no large flamboyant signs announcing that it was a MR base, and was entirely in keeping with the organisation's policy of 'playing it in a low key'. The lease of Bryn Poeth was eventually extended to include the whole building and in February 1987, after a great deal of hard work by the team members, sufficient funds had been raised to enable work to start on a 'purpose-renovation' programme. In the summer of 1990, Bryn Poeth was opened as a practical operational base with the latest communications equipment, and a helicopter landing pad just behind the building.

During the late 1960s, the number of Outdoor Activity Centres in Snowdonia was increasing, but none had enough manpower to form a team, nor did all instructors want to be involved. Those who were willing soon found themselves being called on more frequently to take part in rescues. The co-ordinator was still Chris Briggs, but he was not keen on doing anything which might further the radical change, looming ever closer, in the existing system. It is sad to reflect that the development of MRTs on more formal lines such as had been developed in the RAF, OVMRO, and further afield, at Kendal and Ambleside in the Lake District, was not universally approved. Chris Briggs, for example, who had done so much for MR on a purely ad hoc basis felt that the present system, which had served the Snowdon area well for 20 years or more, was good enough and he could see no reason for the MR service to be developed any further.

There are two sides to every argument, and some animosity began to build up between the OACs in Snowdonia on the one hand, and Chris Briggs and his long-established group of rescuers on the other, and it was soon apparent that things could not continue as they were.

In November 1972, the MRC held their annual conference at Plas-y-Brenin, and as a result a meeting of all rescue personnel in North Wales was convened at Plas-y-Brenin on 15 March 1973, when the North Wales Mountain Rescue Association was established. The inaugural meeting of the NWMRA was held on 17 May 1973.

Even before the NWMRA was formed, off-the-record approaches had been made to the MRC Sub-Committee for Wales by the leaders of the various OACs in and around Llanberis with a view to setting up a properly organised MRT in that area. Amongst the centres involved were the Loughborough Outdoor Centre at Glyn Padarn in Llanberis (now the Kent Mountain Centre), The Worcestershire OAC in Llanrug, Hafod Meurig OAC in Brynrefail (now closed), and Aberglaslyn Hall Outdoor Pursuits Centre near Beddgelert. A minute of a meeting of the sub-committee in September 1971 stated that 'there appeared to be a Llanberis MRT operating as a separate entity, and most often never available together'. It was 'not certain whether they wished to be recognised as a team and further discussion on the issue was deferred'.

In the meantime an ad hoc committee consisting of interested instructors from the centres concerned called a meeting to discuss the formation of a Llanberis MRT, and everyone who was thought to be even slightly interested in MR was invited to attend. The meeting was held at Glyn Padarn on 23 May 1968 under the chairmanship of Don Roscoe, Principal of the Loughborough centre, and it was well attended. The Llanberis MRT was voted into being, and Don Roscoe was elected to be the first team chairman. Other founder members included Jesse James, Geoff Arkless, John Brailsford, Dr Ieuan Jones, John Ellis Roberts and the Police Sergeant from Llanberis, whose name is not recorded. Of these Jesse James, Dr Ieuan Jones and John Ellis Roberts were all subsequently Team Chairman. There were other founder members, but the records of the meeting are no longer to be found.

A minute of The North Wales sub-committee of the MRC dated 15 March 1973 noted that the Llanberis organisation was now recognised by the Committee as an MRT, and Dr Ieuan Jones was its representative on the Committee. The Park Authorities agreed to allow the team to use the Warden Centre at Nant Peris as their permanent base, with facilities to keep rescue equipment in the workshop/stores area. It was then formally recognised by the MRC as Rescue Post No 77.

In March 1973, the North Wales sub-committee approved a constitution and change of title to the 'North Wales Mountain Rescue Association'. Brian Grey, Principal of Aberglaslyn Hall OPC, was elected Chairman, John Ellis Roberts, who had been on the North Wales sub-committee as the representative for

SARDA, was elected Secretary, and Dr A S G Jones accepted the position of Treasurer. The objects of the NWMRA were:

1. To establish and maintain co-ordinated and efficient voluntary mountain rescue in North Wales.
2. To meet together at least four times annually and discuss the above.
3. Membership of the Association shall consist of all Rescue Post supervisors, one representative from each recognised MR organisation where these are not synonymous with a Rescue Post, a representative from the MRC and a representative from the North Wales Police.

The Association wasted no time in coming to terms with its task, and within the first nine months of its existence, the following sub-committees were set up:

Sub-committee	Date	Responsibility
Extended Searches	17 May 1973	Plas-y-Brenin
Radio Telephone Equipment	5 July 1973	RAF Valley
Search Procedure	5 July 1973	Plas-y-Brenin
Team Structure	6 December 1973	RAF Valley

Later, on 26 September 1974, another sub-committee — Major Disaster (MR) — was set up, RAF Valley being the responsible organisation. Prior to that a discussion on the Search Panel for Snowdonia held in July 1973 had yielded two noteworthy proposals:

1. By Dr Ieuan Jones that, 'a Medical Officer should be present at Search Control as part of the Search Panel to advise rescuers especially with exposure cases'.
2. By John Ellis Roberts that, 'more emphasis should be made on the use of Search Dogs in both token and extended searches'.

In November 1973, the Snowdonia Search Panel was formally set up with 11 members: Dr Ieuan Jones stood down as the representative of the Llanberis MRT and he was replaced by John Mills who had taken over as the Team Chairman. The following month the Moelwyn MRT applied to join the Association and provisional approval was given. In the meantime a sub-committee divided the main mountain areas of Snowdonia into search sectors, with a total of 264 sectors. The division was:

Sector	Area
001–057	Carneddau
058–099	Glyderau and Tryfan
100–133	Snowdon
134–161	Mynydd Mawr, Cwm Silyn & Moel Hebog
162–192	Moel Siabod & Moelwynion

193–227   Rhinog mountains
228–253   Cader Idris
254–264   Aran mountains

A further minute of this meeting laid down standards for MRTs, the agreed requirement being that half the members must be 'competent' mountaineers, and the remainder should be in possession of the MLC or be able to prove that they had achieved that level of experience and competence. The minimum number of members in an MRT should be 25.

Initially the Association consisted of ten Posts, four MRTs and the Search and Rescue Dog Association which were:

POSTS: No 20 Idwal Cottage; No 21 Ogwen Cottage; No 60 Plas-y-Brenin; No 22 Pen-y-gwryd; No 23 Cwellyn Arms, Rhyd-Ddu; No 62 Aberglaslyn Hall; No 43 Blaenau Ffestiniog Police Station; No 58 Llandudno Police Station; No 24 Aberdyfi OB Sea School; No 47 Dolgellau Fire Station.

MRTs: OVMRO; Llandudno and District Rescue Team; North Wales Cave Rescue Organisation; RAF Valley MRT; SARDA.

By February 1976, the number of posts had increased to twelve, the additions being No 77, National Park Warden Centre, Nant Peris and No 83, Mold Police station. In 1977 post No 83 was transferred to HM Coastguard at Holyhead. The number of MRTs had also increased to 8, the new Teams being : Llanberis; Rhinog; Moelwyn; Plas-y-Brenin.

In 1977 John Ellis Roberts stood down as Secretary, and Dr Tony Jones was appointed to succeed him. Phil Williams Jones was appointed Treasurer in succession to Tony Jones. In September 1977 Chris Briggs, who had attended his first meeting of the Association in February 1974, retired from the NWMRA having been actively involved in MR as a team leader and administrator for 30 years.

Over the years there has been a growing body of opinion that MRTs should be made semi-professional and that the service should be paid for its work, and more than one attempt has been made to bring this about. On one occasion, following a request from the Member of Parliament for Caernarfon — Dafydd Wigley — a meeting was held in Caernarfon between him and members of the NWMRA. Mr Wigley was concerned about the number of mountain accidents and alarming press reports at that time and wanted to know what could be done to reduce the number of misadventures in the mountains and to improve the rescue service. Inevitably the question of MRT members being paid for their work on the mountains was discussed, but the weight of opinion in favour of keeping the MR service entirely voluntary was such that so far the status quo has prevailed. The only exceptions to this are firstly that since March 1973, the Police Authority has provided 100% insurance cover for all team members involved in an authorised rescue, and providing forty-eight hours notice is given that cover is extended to team training exercises. Secondly, radios for MRTs are provided by the Police.

It is a police responsibility to search for, find and rescue people in trouble anywhere, including mountain areas. Further south, in the Cader Idris area, this had long been the responsibility of the Fire Service at Dolgellau. Their commitment was not a voluntary one, but was a special service in the course of their employment as firemen. They had no special mountaineering equipment, but frequently carried out rescues on the steep slopes of Cader Idris. It is worth mentioning that a decade earlier Tom Roberts, the deputy Fire Officer at Dolgellau, was awarded the Stanhope Medal for Bravery for his part in a difficult rescue on Cader Idris. Once again, however, as the number of accidents grew, it became obvious that the demands being made on the firemen were becoming unacceptable.

The Outward Bound School at Aberdyfi already provided a rescue service with instructors forming the core, and visiting students making up the balance of the team. As far as the students were concerned, it was entirely voluntary, and although the team was recognised by the Police, it was run independently of any other rescue organisation until it joined the NWMRA in 1973.

The Cambrian Rambling Club, which was based in Barmouth, had formed an MRT in 1970 to cover the Rhinogs and Cader Idris, and one of their members, Hugh Griffith Roberts, who was a voluntary National Park Warden and had already taken part in several rescue incidents in those two mountain areas, was closely involved in getting the team established. Another founder member was Barry Ellis, who is still involved with the team. At that time the team's base was in the basement of the Youth Club in the town, but subsequently the team moved to the Royal Aerospace Establishment at Llanbedr near Harlech. Hugh Roberts wrote to Chris Briggs asking for his help and advice, which was promptly forthcoming. There were already MR posts in the southern part of Snowdonia at the Police Station in Blaenau Ffestiniog, the OB School at Aberdyfi, the Fire Station at Dolgellau, and Aberglaslyn Hall OPC, and the availability, if required, of RAF MRTs from Valley, Stafford and St Athan. The method used to summon searchers when anyone was reported missing on Cader Idris was to toll the church bell in Dolgellau!

In 1972, a local newspaper published a letter which criticised the performance of the Fire Service at Dolgellau as mountain rescuers. The writer described the impracticability of going out on to snow and ice covered slopes wearing Wellington boots, and however right he may have been, his criticism caused some bad feeling. It was felt that it was a criticism which should have been kept within MR circles and not made public, and the Fire Service, not surprisingly, felt that they had been unjustly snubbed.

In July 1972, Hugh Roberts was appointed Head Warden of the southern part of the National Park which actually covered two thirds of the total area of the Park. Once again he sought the advice of Chris Briggs, and it was decided to hold a meeting of everyone involved, in Dolgellau in November 1972. Hugh Roberts was elected chairman of the meeting, and he was given the responsibility of co-ordinating all available resources and of 'zoning' the areas of responsibility for each team. It was decided that the Fire Service would no longer provide a Rescue Team, and as a temporary measure the Shropshire Outdoor Education Centre at Arthog, in conjunction with Plas yr Antur at Fairbourne, took their place. In addition, Search and Rescue Dog cover was to be provided by the Rev Mike Perrin, Warden of the Christian Mountain Centre at Tremadog, a qualified dog handler.

At the MRC annual conference held at Plas-y-Brenin in November 1972, Hugh Roberts and Barry Ellis of the Rhinog team represented the Meirioneth area, and shortly afterwards intensive training sessions were introduced in which the Police and all the teams in the southern part of the Park took part: these included search exercises with an RAF Whirlwind rescue helicopter from C Flight. Radios, supplied by the Home Office through the Police, had gradually been introduced into civilian MRTs, but they were costly and in short supply. Chris Briggs made two Pye Bantam sets available to the Meirioneth area, but this number was insufficient except for initial training purposes. One of the members of the Rhinog team, Maurice Griffin, who was a radio engineer, actually built his own radio set, and Jo Jessup, who was in charge of Home Office radio communications at Caernarfon, gave much valuable advice as more radios became available to the teams. Some team members bought their own radios privately, but as the use of unlicensed sets was illegal, to get over the problem privately owned sets were taken over by the Home Office and 're-issued' to those who had bought them. RAF teams had always had radio sets as part of their authorised MRT equipment.

Hugh Roberts and Has Oldham, (RAF Valley) who was the Equipment Officer of the NWMRA — a post subsequently held by successive leaders of the Valley MRT — were given the responsibility of inspecting all the equipment held in posts in Meirioneth, and it was indicative of the lack of supervision hitherto that, for example, the ropes held at Blaenau Ffestiniog Police Station were found to be grey and rotting and quite useless. It was also reported at a meeting of the NWMRA a little later that the morphia was missing from the post at the Cwellyn Arms Inn at Rhyd-Ddu and half the split-Thomas stretcher and the casualty bag had been found in a ditch nearby. There was clearly a pressing need to ensure that all the equipment in the posts was maintained in a proper and safe condition, and this is what Hugh and Has set out to do. The new organisation in this part of the Park was soon proving itself, and at Easter 1973 all available manpower was asked to join in the search for four missing schoolboys (see Chapter 24). This did much to boost the morale of the southern MRTs

There was still a gap 'in the defences', and a new team, based at Rescue Post No 43 in the police station in Blaenau Ffestiniog, was established to cover the Moelwyn and Aran mountains. This team was co-founded by Major John Nash, commandant of the Army Training Camp near Capel Curig, and Hugh Roberts. Among the 16 team members were police officers Sergeant Mel Williams, acting secretary, and constables Idris Williams and Terry Jackson, plus Joe Rotherham and T I Thomas who was appointed Team Leader.

On 15 April 1974, the Plaid Cymru Member of Parliament for Meirioneth, Dafydd Ellis Thomas, now Lord Ellis-Thomas, in a speech in the House of Commons, praised the working party and the new MR organisation in his constituency. He himself is a keen hill-walker, and he joined in some of the search and rescue practices. His example was such that four farmers from the Trawsfynydd area joined the Rhinog team.

When the NWMRA was established in 1973 its primary object was to establish, maintain and co-ordinate an efficient rescue service in North Wales. Since that time the Association has become accepted as the body responsible for MR in the counties of Gwynedd and Clwyd, thus covering the whole of Snowdonia and more besides. It fosters effective co-operation between the civilian teams, the Police, the Royal Air Force, HM Coastguard, and others such as the North Wales Cave Rescue Organisation.

The OVMRO covers an area of approximately 125 sq miles, from a line extending west to east along the Glyders–Capel Curig–Betws-y-coed in the south and northwards to the coast, and from the Conwy Valley westwards to Bangor and the Menai Strait. The position of the team base at Bryn Poeth is isolated compared to that of the Llanberis team which is in the village of Nant Peris at the foot of the Llanberis Pass. The area of responsibility of the Llanberis Team is more compact than that of the OVMRO, and covers some 90 square miles.

At weekends and on public holidays, the Ogwen Valley Team base is manned by a team member normally between 10am and 5.30pm so that if there is an incident, the call out of team members can be immediate. Having a radio operator on duty has often helped to save lives which might otherwise have been lost.

The Llanberis requirement is somewhat different. Many of the regular team members live within a few minutes drive of Nant Peris, and only three miles away at the top of the Pass are the Park Wardens' Information Centre and Pen-y-pass Youth Hostel — both with radio and telephone communications. The Information Centre is normally manned during working hours every day, and it is there that an informant coming off the mountain can report an accident. There is therefore no necessity for team members to be on hand to deal with a day-time call-out, and they are able to go about their normal business until they are called out. The exception to this routine is at weekends and at holiday times, especially when weather or ground conditions are likely to result in a number of incidents; some team members then usually go on the mountain 'on patrol'.

The Ogwen and Llanberis teams have developed their respective MR procedures and philosophies to suit their respective areas of responsibility. Both are organised in the same way, being sub-divided into a number of smaller teams of about ten members, each with a leader, but the OVMRO has its own purpose-built base which has separate operations, equipment and briefing rooms, whilst the Llanberis MRT shares the Wardens' centre as its base. Both teams have a fine record of search and rescue work, and between them they deal with the bulk of searches and rescues in Snowdonia.

Snowdon is the magnet for hill-walkers, whilst the Glyders, Tryfan and the Carneddau are popular alternatives. Backing up the civilian MRTs is 'C' Flight, SAR helicopters from Valley, and when local teams are too hard-pressed, other available civilian and RAF MRTs are asked to assist.

All MRTs carry out training exercises, which include radio procedure, first-aid, and working with helicopters. Since the 1980s, search management courses have been open to interested parties other than MRTs and this has been a significant development.

It was in 1980 that Dr Tony Jones, chairman of the OVMRO, after visiting rescue organisations in the United States of America, pressed for the introduction of search planning and management, but it was some years before the first search management course took place. It was organised and run by Peter Howells, Leader of the Morlais (now Brecon) MRT and took place at Crickhowell, South Wales, in September 1988. This course was sponsored by the South Wales Conference committee, and 32 people attended. The concept of having a group of members working to a laid-down and practised system and all applying their knowledge of the area being searched and their experience on

Winch-off from accident site.
[John Ellis Roberts]

the mountain, is designed to take much of the strain off the shoulders of a single team leader, particularly when an incident involves organising perhaps hundreds of searchers.

From the mid-1960s two new 'weapons' had been introduced into the North Wales mountain rescue armoury — RAF SAR Helicopters, which had been in existence for a number of years, but were now being used for the first time in support of MRTs, and SARDA, both of which were to be instrumental in speeding up the finding and recovery of people injured on the mountains. In 1963, John Jackson, then Director of Plas-y-Brenin, was driving from Bangor to Capel Curig, when he saw a flight of RAF training helicopters parked by 'Willy's Barn' in the Ogwen Valley. He had two interests, firstly that he had flown as a wireless operator/air gunner as a member of aircrew in the RAF, completing two full operational tours in Burma in support of the Chindits and the Imphal and Kohima 'boxes', and secondly he had been toying with the idea that Plas-y-Brenin could probably use helicopters in mountain search and rescue incidents. He stopped to speak to the Flight Commander, Flight Lieutenant Whiteley, an instructor at the RAF Central Flying School and also a member of the North Wales Mountaineering Club, who was in the Ogwen Valley on an exercise. They discussed the possibility of Plas-y-Brenin organising a search and rescue exercise involving the use of helicopters, and John subsequently contacted RAF Valley and then the Ministry of Defence. The MOD not only agreed to the use of two of Flight-Lieutenant Whiteley's helicopters in the proposed exercise, but also allowed John to fly with Whiteley.

Not long after the exercise 'C' Flight intervened claiming that if helicopters were to be used in support of civilian as well as RAF MRTs, they should be the ones to fly them, not the Central Flying School. Before long the helicopters of 'C' Flight were being used to airlift casualties off the mountains, and also to airlift rescuers and search dogs as high up the mountain as possible when the cloud base, for example, was too low for the helicopter crew to effect the rescue on its own. Many hours of valuable time have been saved by the use of helicopters, and this has greatly increased the chances of the casualty's survival.

SARDA, too, was instrumental in saving hours of searching by large numbers of team members. It is rightly claimed that in normal weather and ground conditions, one trained search dog, searching with its nose, is equal to at least twenty humans searching with their eyes. When visibility is limited due to fog, rain or snow, obviously the noses have the advantage.[1]

From 1965 onwards search dogs were used by RAF Valley and other RAF MRTs, but it took a few years for the dogs to be accepted by the teams in North Wales and other areas. SARDA's credibility was eventually established due to some classic finds, notably that of two small children benighted high above the Llanberis Pass,[2] and there have been many successful searches by SARDA (Wales) during the 25 years the Association has been in existence. There can be no doubt that there are people alive and well today thanks to being found in time by a search dog and its handler.

---

1. A short history of the introduction of search and rescue dogs into the mountain rescue scene, their training and their operational use is told in *Countdown to Rescue*..
2. The story is told in *Countdown to Rescue*, Chapter 6 — 'The Babes on the Mountain'.

21: Snowdon under Threat

Whilst mountaineering continued to flourish in Snowdonia, towards the end of the 19th century and during the first few years of the 20th, the increased use of electricity as the main source of industrial power resulted in a number of hydro-electric schemes being built to supply the many mines and quarries throughout Snowdonia. These had little impact on either climbing or hill-walking, other than their adverse aesthetic effect, such as lines of pipes traversing serene valleys or descending steep slopes, or serried ranks of large poles firmly concreted into the ground supporting electricity cables for mile upon mile to some remote mine or quarry. The most obtrusive of these schemes was the little power station below Cwm Dyli, which was again the subject of conflict in the late 1980s. The pipes from Llyn Llydaw across the cwm and down to the station were an obtrusive excrescence on the landscape, and the line of double poles which ran up to Pen-y-pass and then followed the road down to Llanberis seven miles away, were a perpetual reminder that even in this beautiful and lonely place, the 20th century had arrived. There was a certain amount of protest, which came to nothing, and the scheme soon became part of the landscape.

Locals and visiting mountaineers alike, however, had been warned of an ever-present threat to despoil parts of the mountain scenery, and a wary eye was kept to ward off any attempt to impose other unsightly schemes on Snowdonia. It was not surprising, therefore, that in 1949 an article in the *Climbers' Club Journal*, warned its members that a new and extremely dire threat to the Snowdon massif and Nant Ffrancon valley existed. The notice in the Journal stated quite succinctly, 'A most menacing shadow has been cast this year over the area with which this Club has its strongest association, by the announcement of the North Wales hydro-electric projects. Members are urged to arouse public opinion to the realisation of what this scheme involves. The secretary's circular to the Club in April of this year, a melancholy but valuable document, is worth repeating here. It says:

> The scheme falls into seven parts of which one, for extending the catchment area of the Dolgarrog Power Station, is believed to be in hand but this is of minor importance to mountaineers. Whilst objections may be taken to others, the heart of the matter for us is the Snowdon and Nant Ffrancon schemes. These would involve:

The Miners' Track with the summit of Snowdon on the left and Bwlch Glas in the centre. [SNP]

1. The erection of a power station in Cwm Llan fed through a tunnel under Lliwedd. This would involve raising the level of Llydaw and probably of Glaslyn. [Author's comment: It did not indicate by how many feet the level of Llydaw would have been raised. It seems clear, however, that the Miners' Path would have been submerged, restricting access to and from Snowdon on the eastern side of the mountain to the Pyg track. Vehicles can now be driven up the Miners' Path as far as Glaslyn, but if the proposal to raise the level of the lake had been implemented, rescue operations would have been very much more difficult as all evacuations from the eastern side of the Snowdon massif would have had to be stretcher-carries down the narrow and sometimes rough Pyg track to the road at Pen-y-pass.]

2. A reservoir on the Nant Gwynant slopes of Yr Aran.

3. A leat on the slopes of Snowdon above Rhyd-ddu delivering water through a tunnel to a power station at the head of Llyn Dinas.

4. Llyn Dinas would be dammed and water taken through a tunnel to a power station near Pont Aberglaslyn. [This would reduce the flow of water in the Afon Glaslyn down the Aberglaslyn Pass to a mere trickle].

5. Water from the Southern slopes of Moel Siabod would be caught and led to a

new power station by Llyn Gwynant which would also be fed by a leat on the Glyders from near Dyffryn Mymbyr to Llyn Cwm y Ffynnon.

6. A dam would be thrown across Nant Ffrancon near the Penrhyn Quarry spoil heaps and the whole valley flooded back to the foot of the Ogwen Falls.

7. A power station, to be fed from Llyn Ogwen and Llyn Idwal, would be built at Ogwen Falls. This would mean raising the level of Llyn Ogwen and, probably, Llyn Idwal.

8. Water would be collected from the southern slopes of Elidir, Foel Goch and Y Garn and fed into Idwal by a tunnel under Clogwyn-y-geifr.

9. Apart from the dams, power stations, leats and tunnels, there would be substantial roadways, considerable lengths of surface piping, transmission lines on pylons from Aberglaslyn to Pen-y-gwryd, from Ogwen to Bethesda, from *Pen-y-gwryd* down the Llanberis Pass, and to Capel and along the Ogwen valley.

No information is available as to plans for disposal of the rock spoil from the tunnels etc. The cost of carting away would be prohibitive.'

This list of proposals was frightening enough, but there were other plans afoot in more outlying parts of Snowdonia, such as another power station at Fairy Glen, and the diversion of water from the tourist spectacular at Aber Falls.

The reaction was immediate and furious. A fighting fund was set up, and mass protests were organised, the most effective being a rally on the summit of Snowdon in early May 1950 when Chris Briggs and some of the leading mountaineers of the time addressed several hundred protesters who had made the effort to be there in adverse weather conditions, and condemnation of the proposals was unanimous. The power of mass protest won the day, and the whole idea was scrapped, but threats to Snowdonia, some of perhaps lesser magnitude, continued to be made.

During the mid-1960s the Youth Hostels Association was planning to build a show-piece hostel in central Snowdonia which would include a National Park wardens' information centre. The favoured site was to be somewhere in the Pen-y-gwryd–Pen-y-pass area to complete a ring of six hostels encircling the Snowdon massif. The site eventually chosen was in a shallow hollow on the hillside behind the *Pen-y-gwryd Hotel*, and an outline plan was submitted to the planning department in July 1965. Opposition to what was almost universally considered to be a monstrous proposal was immense.

A local hill-sheep farmer — Esme Kirby — who had lived at Dyffryn Mymbyr, half way along the Snowdon valley, for more than thirty years, worked incessantly with missionary zeal, drumming up all the support she could get to oppose the wanton despoliation of the wild and lonely beauty of her valley. Her emotion-charged appeals for help produced a deluge of letters to the county council and Welsh Office, and the weight of public opinion against the scheme was so overwhelming that the planning authority refused permission. Esme Kirby, encouraged by her success and supported by many friends, set about forming a society to monitor all future developments within the National Park and adjoining areas, and The Snowdonia National Park Society was established and registered as a Charity in 1967.

Just one mile away from the *Pen-y-gwryd Hotel*, at the top of the Llanberis Pass, was the *Gorphwysfa Hotel*, on the decline but still popular with climbers. It was surrounded by squalid, empty cottages and barns, and was an eye-sore. The YHA, still looking for a site for their show-piece hostel, bought the *Gorphwysfa* and planned to demolish all the dilapidated buildings within the curtilage of the hotel and build an appropriately designed hostel and cafe. The SNPA opposed the plan but did not get the support they had expected, and their opposition eventually ceased altogether. The new hostel, café, and car park were duly completed, and opened in 1970.

During the quarter of a century since its inception, the SNPA has championed many protests, not least of which happened in 1973 when an underhand attempt was made to destroy the Cromlech boulders before anyone had an inkling of what was going on. These huge rocks, lying on the side of the road half way up the Llanberis Pass, are relics of the Ice Age and were left behind on the valley floor as the ice receded. Some local people regard them as an important part of their heritage, and to others they are landmarks of great interest; but it is the climbers who value the boulders most of all, and the most important reason for preserving them is that many of Britain's climbers made their first tentative movements on rock there.

One morning in December 1973, Harvey Lloyd, warden of the new Pen-y-pass Youth Hostel, saw two men drilling holes in the top of the boulders. They told him they had been ordered to have the holes ready for blasting by mid-morning as they were going to demolish the boulders to widen the road.

Harvey Lloyd alerted the the SNPA, which immediately went into action and after a meeting at the site a stay of execution was ordered. It had been a very close-run thing, but this was not the end of the matter. The Welsh Office became involved and massive petitions to 'Save the Boulders' were organised. For over five years the SNPA campaigned to prevent the demolition of these irreplaceable landmarks until, on 6 January 1979, it was announced the boulders would be by-passed. An intensive nationwide public protest, co-ordinated by the SNPA, had succeeded.

Between 1972 and 1983, the Central Electricity Generating Board built a massive hydro-electric station in Llanberis. This involved, amongst other things, widening and straightening existing roads and building new ones, and building a dam to enlarge a lake in full view from the valley below. The SNPA made its views known to the CEGB which accepted that the whole scheme had to be as inconspicuous as possible and any adverse impact on the environment kept to an absolute minimum. The generating station itself was built in a vast cavern hollowed out inside the mountain; the dam, high in the mountains, was superbly landscaped and is virtually invisible from the valley. Stone walls were rebuilt along the improved roads, and all the power cables from the generators to the National Grid sub-station seven miles away at Pentir were laid underground. The entire scheme has had a far less objectionable impact on the environment than most people feared, and really is a marvellous achievement.

The SNPA has intervened whenever it thought it necessary, but it has not always been easy to decide how far to go. In some cases, like the 'Battle of the Boulders', there could be no compromise, but the Society accepts that some change is necessary and inevitable. It is their aim to ensure that any changes are made with the least possible disturbance to the environment. There are, of course, some people who oppose what they see as unjustified interference in the development of communications and industry, but in spite of this there have been many notable successes. The SNPA has not always had its own way, and the lost battle of Cwm Dyli pipeline was one of its few failures. For over eighty years there had been two large black pipes running side by side from the eastern end of Llyn Llydaw, across Cwm Dyli and down to the small power station in the Gwynant valley below. The CEGB wished to replace the old turbines and increase the flow of water by replacing the two pipes with one large pipe. The Society saw a golden opportunity to remove the hideous scar which had defaced one of the best-loved landscapes in Britain for over 90 years, and requested the CEGB to bury the new pipe underground. They refused to bury the pipe, but promised to make it as inconspicuous as they could. However the new pipeline, with huge supporting concrete blocks spaced along its entire length, is even more hideous and obtrusive than the old one, and the proof is there for all to see. Had it not been for the continuing vigilance and campaigning by the SNPA, a large petrol service station and cafe which had been planned would almost certainly now be a feature of the landscape opposite the *Pen-y-gwryd Hotel*, as would an extensive picnic site and carpark between the Mymbyr Lakes at the other end of the valley. Both of these developments would have despoiled this outstandingly beautiful area for the tens of thousands people who come to Snowdonia for its wildness and uncontaminated scenery. Wire fences would have replaced old stone walls in the picturesque Lledr valley and, in many other areas, road improvement schemes would have spoilt much of the finest scenery in Snowdonia. The SNPA has indeed made an enormous contribution to the preservation of so much that is beautiful and irreplaceable, and continues to do so.

22: Schoolboys Tragedy on Clogwyn Goch

In 1963, the Mountain Leadership Certificate was introduced amid growing concern for the safety of young people being taken on the hill as part of their education. Coroners in mountain areas showed little sympathy towards adults who, with little experience, took other peoples' children into potentially dangerous situations.

When the MLC was introduced it did not cover the different requirements of winter conditions but there were people who nevertheless thought they had learned enough to tackle ice, snow and 'Arctic' weather conditions, sometimes with tragic results.

A typical case of over-confidence, coupled with a lack of adequate appreciation of walking on snow and ice, happened on Sunday 20 February 1972, when a party of 15 boys and four masters from Dulwich College, all of whom were members of the school Venture Scout group, were walking round the Snowdon Horseshoe in a clockwise direction and had reached the summit of Snowdon. Here they found the ground conditions to be very dangerous, with a covering of hard-packed snow and ice. The leader decided to retreat down the railway track to Llanberis, as he knew that normally this is the safest and easiest route. But without experience of traversing high ground in severe winter conditions, he did not perceive that Alpine techniques are demanded and that both ice-axes and crampons are essential equipment.

For the most part the track from Bwlch Glas to the bend before Clogwyn Station should not have presented this party with any difficulty. It is fairly wide and they could walk down on the right of the railway line, well away from the steep edge. Midway along Clogwyn Coch, however, is the notorious 'Killer Convex'. The minimum equipment necessary as you walk on to the ice at that point is an ice-axe in your hand, and the knowledge of how to use it to arrest a slide. Today the railway track is 'out of bounds' and there are warning notices at both ends of this particular stretch directing walkers on to the Llanberis path which is parallel to, and above, the railway line.

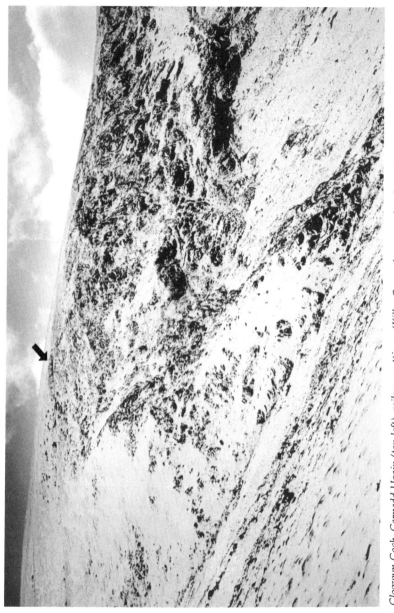

Clogwyn Goch. Carnedd Ugain (top left), railway cutting—'Killer Convex'—arrowed and 700 ft cliff to Cwm Du'r Arddu (bottom right).

The party set off down the railway track and found the going slippery, but at first it did not present any difficulty. None of the adult leaders was aware of the 'Killer Convex', and the leading boys walked straight on to the dangerous narrow stretch of track. The ice was rock-hard, and it would have been difficult to arrest a slide even with an ice-axe at the ready, but there were only two axes between the party, none of them had crampons, and although the leader had a rope, it remained in his rucksack. The three leading boys slid over the edge one after the other and disappeared down the cliff into Cwm Du'r Arddu. Having seen what happened the fourth boy stopped, only inches before the treacherous ice. The remainder of the party then safely negotiated the narrow stretch by keeping close into the back wall of the cutting. Near Clogwyn Station, they traversed to the bottom of the cliff where their three friends were found. Their injuries were frightful, and all would have been killed instantly.

This tragedy, coming so soon after a disastrous expedition on the Cairngorm plateau during which six schoolchildren from Edinburgh died in a blizzard, shook the whole mountaineering community and caused special concern among all outdoor activity organisations. Locally there appeared to be some difference of opinion about the tragedy of Clogwyn Coch, and one well-known mountaineer was reported as saying that, 'it was sheer bad luck; conditions on the ground were favourable and I was very surprised when I heard it had changed on top'. Another view was expressed by Harvey Lloyd, warden of the Pen-y-pass Youth Hostel, who stated, 'it was obviously dangerous on the mountain today at that height. There was a lot of snow and ice,' he said, and added that while conditions had not looked difficult at Pen-y-pass, 'the situation changes as you move up from our 356m above sea level'. It is evident that there was no snow and ice at lower levels, and that it was a clear and crisp morning when the party set out.

It was reported in the *Daily Mail* that the leader of the Dulwich College party had insisted on waterproof clothing and strong boots. He did not consider that ice-axes, crampons or ropes were necessary, though he carried a rope in his rucksack in case of emergency. He told the reporter, 'I know these mountains well enough to be confident that what we were doing was quite reasonable'. But quite clearly not reasonable enough.

Many well-known mountaineers made their views known to the Press, and the one point on which there was complete agreement was that in winter, if there is any chance of there being snow or ice on the routes, then an ice-axe is a must, and crampons should always be carried in case they are needed. One opinion was that the leader should have consulted the National Park Wardens, or Harvey Lloyd at the Youth Hostel, about conditions on the route they intended to follow. Many Youth Hostel wardens in mountainous country will know enough about local conditions to be able to give advice if asked.

The wealth of comment by experts following the deaths of the three boys led the press to imply in their coverage of the accident that similar incidents are bound to happen from time to time.

But other mountaineers, some of whom had been involved in the recovery of the three bodies from Cwm Du'r Arddu and who had carefully considered and discussed all the facts, did not agree that it was simply a case of bad luck or that further similar accidents were inevitable. The principals of ten outdoor activity centres in Snowdonia were far from happy about the adverse publicity and the effect it might have on their centres if the matter was not put into proper context. Three days after the event these ten met to discuss what they felt was incorrect and misleading conjecture. They issued a statement which was published in an article by Chris Bonington in the *Daily Telegraph*, and which stated that they 'did not accept the implications that a certain number of such accidents are inevitable'. They emphasised their belief that properly equipped and conducted parties should be able to move safely in British mountains in winter conditions. In addition to the normal equipment carried by a walking party, any group going on the hills during the winter months must be equipped with an ice-axe for each member, and ropes in relation to the number in the party.

The possession of items of equipment is not in itself sufficient to ensure safety, and the party must be instructed and practised in its use. Furthermore, party leaders should be experienced and qualified mountaineers. Finally, they insisted that the minimum qualification for a leader in this sort of situation would be the Winter MLC. The British Mountaineering Council and the Mountain Leadership Training Board together recommended that every organisation sending groups of young people into mountain or moorland country should make it obligatory that they be accompanied by the holder of the relevant summer or winter certificate.

The MLC had never been intended to be anything more than a minimum qualification for leading walking groups in summer: it does not cover either rock-climbing or snow and ice conditions, for which separate courses are run and further certificates awarded. Aspiring leaders for the winter certificate are required to do a week's initial course followed by at least a year's experience and then a final week's assessment course, all of which means commitment, hard work, and determination.

Chris Bonington ended, 'People must realise that mountains are dangerous places and there will always be an element of risk, and therefore there must be some accidents'. But if the advice of the 'ten wise men' is heeded, the occurrence

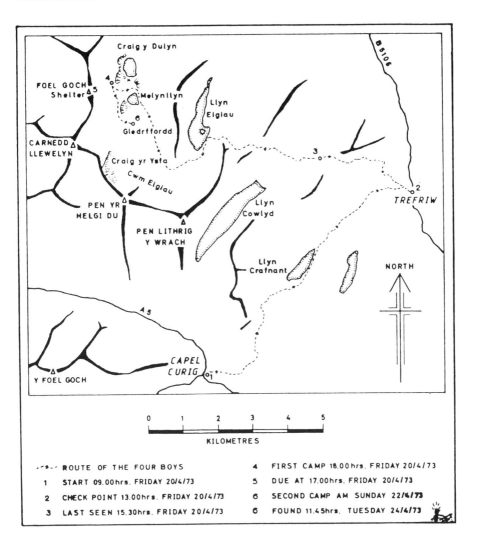

KILOMETRES

```
--•--  ROUTE OF THE FOUR BOYS
  1    START 09.00hrs. FRIDAY 20/4/73
  2    CHECK POINT 13.00hrs. FRIDAY 20/4/73
  3    LAST SEEN 15.30hrs. FRIDAY 20/4/73
```

```
  4    FIRST CAMP 18.00hrs. FRIDAY 20/4/73
  5    DUE AT 17.00hrs. FRIDAY 20/4/73
  6    SECOND CAMP AM SUNDAY 22/4/73
  6    FOUND 11.45hrs. TUESDAY 24/4/73
```

of needless accidents will be reduced to the minimum, both in numbers and in the degree of severity. It boils down to leadership and experience, and adult leaders who exceed their capabilities carry an awesome responsibility.

23: Good Friday, 1973

After months of training for their Duke of Edinburgh Gold Award, four boys from the John Warner Comprehensive School in Hoddesdon, Hertfordshire, arrived in North Wales for the Easter weekend, 1973, in the charge of 29-year-old Roger Baldwin, Youth Officer for South East Herts, assisted by other instructors who were to act as assessors during the expedition which was scheduled to last four days and cover 50 miles. The boys, who were very well equipped, were Christopher Dell (15), Stephen Attwood (16), Terry Hankin (16), and Graham Brown (16).

Roger Baldwin listened to a BBC general weather forecast at 2am on Good Friday, and went to sleep happy that reasonable weather seemed to be assured for most of the weekend. What he didn't hear, however, was a later forecast issued by Manchester Meteorological Office which predicted very different conditions for Friday, with the temperature in the mountains of North Wales down to 2 degrees with cold rain and hill fog lasting all day.

Good Friday dawned as predicted in the 2am forecast, and in the words of Christopher Dell, when they set out from Capel Curig at 9am 'it was quite fine'. One who had heard the later forecast was Dr Tony Jones, who was shortly to take over as leader of the OVMRO from Ron James. He later expressed his views forcibly that "the boys should never have been out in that weather. I did not go out that day - it was cold, wet, and horrible, and when you are only 15 or 16 you do not have much in the way of reserves, either mentally or physically, if things go wrong".

It was not long before the predicted deterioration in the weather set in. The first leg of the expedition was from Capel Curig, along the old drovers' route to the track junction and down to Llyn Crafnant and Trefriew in the Conwy Valley, a distance of five miles of easy walking. The boys arrived at the check point in Trefriew at about 1pm with no problems and all in good heart. The next leg was almost due west, and ascended steadily to Llyn Eigiau, then steeply to the next check point at the mountain refuge on Foel Goch, where they were to meet up with two of the assessors. As they toiled upwards the weather worsened; they were now heading into strengthening wind and driving rain as the temperature dropped. The boys made much slower progress than planned and they were last seen by other walkers by the side of a stream, at a height of 450m at 3.30pm, and heading in the direction of the refuge. At this point they had covered only about half of the 16-mile route planned for this day, and the steepest section up to Foel Goch still lay ahead. About half an hour after leaving the stream, Chris Dell began to show signs of hypothermia. His legs went wobbly and 'I felt terrible', he said. They struggled on, but soon after passing Llyn Dulyn, they found the going more difficult with rocky outcrops and deep gullies. Hill fog had come down, the rain turned to sleet and then snow, and visibility was reduced to a few metres. There was no appointed leader, but the four boys were at one in realising the danger of pressing on in such atrocious weather, and being to all intents and purposes lost, they stopped and put up their small tent in the vicinity of Craig Dulyn. It was now 6.00pm, one hour after the time they should have checked in at the refuge on Foel Goch, which was then only 1km away in a horizontal plane, but some 440m higher. In view of Chris Dell's deteriorating condition and of the other adverse factors weighing against them, their decision to camp was correct and was the result of the thorough training they had been given by their instructors. The boys settled down in their tent to eat the last of the day's supply of solid food — sausages, peas and potatoes. They now had only emergency rations consisting of mint cake, chocolate, glucose, soup and condensed milk. When they woke next morning, there was a blanket of snow six inches deep, it was foggy and freezing, and visibility was no more than a few yards. The outlook was not good, and the boys decided to ration their food, eating a little of each item for breakfast. They then agreed to stay where they were in view of fierce wind and limited visibility.

Baldwin was by now concerned for the safety of the boys, and he and the assessors, who had been waiting for them at the refuge, checked the route during the morning and into the afternoon, but they told no one that the boys had missed their checkpoint the previous evening and were overdue. Saturday night came and went, but on Sunday morning the weather had eased a little, and after eating some more chocolate the boys felt that they should try to carry on. It was still misty and cold and they knew they were off-course, but they kept hoping that the weather would improve so that they could continue the expedition as planned. They made an attempt to retrace their steps to safer, lower ground, but after they had gone about two miles, they found themselves once again in difficult craggy ground. Wisdom prevailed as they remembered what had been drummed into them on many training expeditions, that if they got into difficulties they should stay put until help came. So they pitched their tent again on Sunday afternoon at Gledrffordd, and decided to conserve their body warmth and energy, and sit it out. Since they first pitched the tent on Friday evening, their only means of passing the time was sleeping, listening to the small transistor radio which Stephen Attwood had taken with him, and singing hymns such as the old favourite, 'Guide me, Oh Thou Great Redeemer, Pilgrim through this barren land'. The words were so apt that it did much to help keep their spirits up as Sunday passed into Monday, their third night out on the mountain.

Throughout Saturday the expedition leader and assessors had tried unsuccessfully to locate the group, but although they were confident that the boys would do the right things, they couldn't be sure that an accident or illness had not overtaken them. Early on Sunday morning they made another attempt to find the party and continued to check the route the boys should have taken. By mid-afternoon they had failed to find any trace, and at 3.45pm Roger Baldwin reported the situation to Ogwen Cottage MR Post. Only then were the rescue services made aware of the drama beginning to unfold high up on the Carneddau. The staff at Ogwen Cottage immediately informed the police and told the duty radio operator at Bryn Poeth, and he set the rescue routine in motion. Later there was adverse comment as to why a delay of 36 hours had elapsed before the rescue teams were called out, but Tony Jones explained that 'it is up to each individual group or organisation to make the decision when to call in the rescue services'. There was very little to be done so late in the day, but a low-level search involving members of Ogwen Valley and RAF Valley MR teams and police officers was begun at 4.30pm and continued until darkness fell. A large-scale search was planned to begin at first light the next morning, with Tony Jones and Ron James as search co-ordinators. The voluntary civilian MRTs, with SARDA handlers and their dogs, Royal Air Force MRTs, helicopters from C Flight, and the North Wales Police were all involved. An informal 'Search Panel', which included the search co-ordinators and representatives of all the organisations taking part, was set up on the second day to plan the most effective use of all the resources available. This was one of the early occasions when a Search Panel was used in North Wales, and the experience gained in this extensive operation was useful in the setting up of a formal Search Panel by the NWMRA in November 1973.

On Monday, 50 people searched the Carneddau in very poor weather conditions, and later in the day search dogs and a helicopter were used, but the latter's use was restricted due to low cloud. Alistair Haveron, an RAF Valley party leader, reported by radio at 10.20am that the weather was "just about a white out" and considered that conditions on the easterly slopes leading up to the refuge on Foel Grach were too bad to operate a line search.

News of the search had been broadcast on the BBC 1pm news bulletin and almost immediately local volunteers began to arrive at Ogwen Cottage to offer help. During the afternoon of Easter Monday, the number of searchers steadily increased as climbers and hill-walkers from all over North Wales converged on Ogwen Cottage, and a Police mobile canteen was set up to cater for their needs when they returned to base at the end of their searches. As they arrived, each group or individual was asked to report to a command centre manned by the police where details of their experience, age, fitness, home address and so on were recorded, and each group of 12 people was briefed by Tony Jones to carry out a detailed search of a given area. The search area was gradually being expanded to cover the possibility that the boys had travelled further than had been thought. After a day's searching the search parties returned to base perplexed that they had found no trace of the boys. Every news bulletin from then on carried up-to-date information about the progress of the search operation, and at 6am on Tuesday morning, Stephen Attwood's father, who knew that his son had his small transistor radio with him, broadcast a message telling the lads that there was an extensive search going on and they must carry out their survival procedures and wait for help to arrive. The message was heard inside the tiny tent; it gave young Stephen quite a jolt to hear his father's voice, but it cheered them up to know that a lot of people were out looking for them. Any thoughts of making another attempt to rescue themselves were forgotten and knowing that it could not be long before they were found, they just sat and waited.

Later that morning, searchers gathered at Ogwen Cottage for briefing at 7am and by 8am, the first parties were on their way to their allotted areas. This large force now consisted of 438 people, plus five SARDA dogs and handlers, and an RAF helicopter. It was said at the time to be the biggest search ever mounted in Snowdonia, but it did not compare to the scene in 1846, when it was reported that over 900 people spent many days looking for Rev Henry Wellington Starr on and around Snowdon.

The weather forecast for Tuesday was more hopeful, but the cloud base was still very low, which restricted the helicopter from searching the higher levels.

By mid-morning the fog began to thin and the helicopter was able to start over-flying the area where the boys were most likely to be; as the cloud lifted, it progressively flew higher up the mountainside. At about mid-morning the four boys, whose tent was still enveloped in mist, heard the noise of the helicopter getting closer, and hoped that their ordeal was nearly over. Stephen Attwood left the others in the mist-shrouded tent and headed down towards the sound of the helicopter. He had gone almost 600 yards when he emerged from the mist, and seeing the helicopter hovering some distance away from him, he waved his yellow anorak. At this stage the helicopter pilot, Flight-Lieutenant Gordon Mitchell, his navigator Flight-Lieutenant Stan Burt and the winchman, Master-Aircrewman Stanley Ormston, displayed skill and courage by flying through a low corridor, only 20 feet high, between the snow-covered ground and the base of the mist. As soon as the crew saw Stephen, they picked him up, and he was able to tell them the approximate direction of the tent. Gordon Mitchell manoeuvred the aircraft towards the area and found the tent a mile away at Gledrffordd. The three boys were picked up and flown to Ogwen Cottage, reaching there at 11.45am, They were all cold and exhausted, but soon recovered after drinking cups of hot soup provided by the Police mobile canteen.

The search parties on the mountain, many of them several hours walking time away, were recalled to base and everyone was off the hill by 3.30pm.

'Was it all necessary?' That was the question being asked across the Nation at the time, and a number of experienced mountaineers were quick to give their views to the media. With hindsight the two mistakes were firstly, the failure of the expedition leader to get an up to date weather forecast before the group set out from Capel Curig. He should have been aware how quickly the weather can change in the mountains of Snowdonia, especially at that time of year, and to rely on a forecast already seven hours stale when the boys started their expedition was an error of judgement. Furthermore he should have obtained a fresh forecast after the group had set out so that if the weather was expected to deteriorate they could have been stopped when they reached the checkpoint at Trefriew four hours later.

The second, and probably more serious, mistake was the choice of area and route for the 50-mile trek. The rules for the Duke of Edinburgh's Gold Award expedition state that it has to be a genuine 50-mile trek, but to choose some of the highest mountains in Wales in the spring, when the weather is often unreliable, was not a wise decision.

Once the alarm was raised, and the search operation was started, it was described as 'a classic of its kind'. All concerned, from the search panel to the leaders and members of the parties on the mountain, the helicopter crew, the police — not forgetting their life-restoring hot soup always ready for those coming in off the mountain — and not least the boys themselves for keeping cool heads and carrying out their survival routine, deserved the highest praise.

24: Search for Peter Edris Dimond — Ogwen Valley, November 1973

The search for the four schoolboys on the Carneddau in April 1973 involved 438 people on the fourth day. It was to prove a trial run for a longer and even more extensive search only seven months later.

The 39-year-old, head pharmacist from Pankridge Hospital in Timperley, a bachelor named Peter Edris Dimond, left his home on Thursday 15 November telling friends that he was going for a day's hill-walking either in the Lake District or North Wales. When he hadn't returned by Friday evening, his friends informed the Police and then drove to the Lake District on Saturday where they spent that day and Sunday looking for his car. A description of the car and Dimond had been sent to the North Wales Police and the rescue services were asked to keep a watch for them. Late on Sunday his bronze-coloured Singer Vogue was observed by a police patrol in the car park between Ogwen Cottage and Tryfan. OVMRO and RAF Valley MRT[1] were called out by the Police at 10.30pm and a search for Dimond was immediately started in the Ogwen Valley area. A description of Dimond was obtained from his friends who indicated that he tended to be a 'loner', that he had between ten and 15 years' mountaineering experience, and that his standard equipment was sufficient for a day's walk on the mountains. Suggestions were put forward as to routes he might have taken, the predominant one being that although his car had been found in the car park on the A5 road — with a consequent road walk of 1 km in order to round Llyn Ogwen — he would most likely have chosen a route on the Carneddau. However, there were only five established facts : Dimond was missing from his home; his car had been found in the Ogwen Valley; he was a loner; he was experienced; he was well equipped. The main possibilities of his whereabouts were:

   a) on the Idwal skyline, that is Tryfan, The Glyders and Y Garn;
   b) on the Carneddau.

During the early hours of Monday, Tony Jones, K C Gordon and Has Oldham began to plan a search covering these two routes to begin at first light. Since Friday the weather had been consistently dry and calm, but extremely cold, and

1. RAF Valley MRT had a police radio installed in their signals truck.

although Dimond was said to be an experienced hill-walker, there was growing concern for his welfare. The main worry was that if he was lying injured somewhere, he would be suffering from shock, and the freezing temperature would reduce his chances of survival rapidly: he had now been missing for four days and nights. It was felt that if he had managed to find some shelter, he might survive for another 24 hours, but not much more.

The civilian MRT responsible for that part of Snowdonia was once again the OVMRO, and the search co-ordinator, as in April, was Tony Jones. The Ogwen team was supported by RAF Valley MRT and a helicopter making a total of about 50 searchers available at the start of the day. The two teams were divided into eight search parties which started at 8am, while the helicopter joined the search shortly afterwards, and continued flying until dusk, making several sorties with various rescue personnel as observers. During the afternoon the Llanberis team, with staff and students from Ogwen Cottage and the Llanrug OAC joined the search, but there was no sign of the missing man.

Tony Jones and his colleagues were faced with a series of decisions as there was simply no indication as to where Dimond might have gone. With their available resources they had chosen to concentrate on Tryfan and the Glyders and the southern part of the Carneddau. This was an area of approximately 50 square miles, but the rough and rocky terrain and the relatively small number of personnel made it a difficult area to search effectively.

During the day more volunteers arrived at Ogwen Cottage as news spread that a man was missing, and when the day's search ended at dusk, the original 50 searchers had grown to over 100, including several policemen. By the time they came down to search base in the carpark at Ogwen Cottage, the Search Panel was already being set up. The Police had brought in their Incident Caravan during the afternoon to serve as search headquarters, and their invaluable Mobile Canteen was also on site ready to dispense hot drinks and soup to the tired and hungry team members.

The Search Panel met at 7pm that evening. Under the chairmanship of Brian Gray, the following responsibilities were apportioned: Search Controller — Has Oldham; Team Controller — Tony Jones; Radio Controller — John Ellis Roberts; Police — Jack Bunting; Members — John Mills and Arthur Clark; Medical Advisor — Ieuan Jones; Transport — Steve Farrow. The Panel took over the running of the search and further help was requested from South Wales, the Peak District and other areas ready for an extension of the operation on Tuesday. From then on there was a rapid build-up of civilian and service personnel , and when the operation was restarted at dawn there were 417 experienced walkers and climbers organised into teams, each with a specific area to cover. On that day the following organisations were in action: RAF MRTs from Valley, St Athan and Stafford; helicopter from 'C' Flight; Dyfed-Powys Constabulary MRT; Ogwen Valley, Llanberis, Llandudno and Rhinog MRTs from Wales; Edale, Buxton, Kinder and Glossop MRTs from the Peak District; five SARDA handlers and their dogs; 11 Outdoor Activity Centres from North Wales; St Helen's Mountaineering Club; four Service units, one RAF; one Royal Navy; two Army.

The whole area had been subdivided into 42 sectors, plus one or two specialist areas such as the east face of Tryfan, and all but two had been covered by dusk. Although weather conditions were ideal with clear visibility, daytime temperatures at sea level remained about three degrees below freezing and progress high up was slower and more hazardous due to a coating of ice on the ground. Towards dusk the last searchers on the mountain were re-called to base for the night and were safely off the hill by 6.30 pm. Apart from the discovery of a few items of equipment, none of which could be positively identified as belonging to Dimond, the day's search proved fruitless.

More volunteers had arrived during the day, but the Search Panel wished to extend the search on Wednesday on the Carneddau range (northwards and eastwards from Pen yr Ole Wen and Carnedd Dafydd), and further assistance was requested from the Peak District MRO and from the Mid-Pennine Mountain Accident Panel. The search recommenced at 7.30am and continued until dusk and on this day the police had signed in 560 people when the search began. This made it the largest recorded operation of its kind in Britain since 1846, and the total number of volunteers who took part at some time or another during those three days exceeded 1,100. Now the search was extended beyond OVMRO's area, mainly to the south into the Llanberis MRT domain. It was estimated that over 200 sq miles of mountain were covered.

This new area was subdivided into 31 sectors, and there were still the two sectors on the north side of the Glyders which had not been properly covered on Tuesday and were to be searched by a larger party. In addition, small parties searched the main cliff areas of the Carneddau and four outlying areas. It was all to no avail. By the end of the day there was still no sign of the missing man and the search panel decided to continue the operation for the fourth consecutive day on Thursday, but on a much reduced scale. Official MRTs were to be withdrawn, and the search continued on a limited basis with small parties. There were some areas which, in the opinion of the panel members, demanded more detailed investigation and parties were sent out but again found nothing. It had been an intensive effort which had not yielded a single clue, and many people were inclined to the view that Dimond had deliberately disappeared, possibly to escape from some personal problem.

Tony Jones and the OVMRO were not entirely satisfied and continued to look for the man, mainly at weekends with a few search dogs and occasional volunteers. This went on for several more weeks, but eventually organised searching, even in a low key, was dropped; even then there were still plenty of weekend hill-walkers, and in addition outdoor centres and RAF Valley MRT continued to keep a lookout when out on the hill. The OVMRO asked all mountaineers in the general area to keep a lookout for what was by then probably a dead body.

On 10 April 1974, almost five months after he went missing, Peter Dimond's body was found by a hill-walker, George Bridge from Sale in Cheshire, who had been looking for a cave at Quartz Pinnacle — SH 638594 — east-south-east of the summit of Y Garn. He reported that a body was in a sitting position under a large boulder in a recess in the rocks. Members of the OVMRO, accompanied by a police officer, went to the spot to recover the body, and found that it was in a bivi-bag and well sheltered from the wind and weather.

Dimond was completely hidden from view, and from a distance the colour of his equipment and clothing was such that it blended with the surrounding rocks. In short, he was perfectly camouflaged. After recovery, the body was removed to the mortuary in Bangor where it was formally identified as Peter Dimond. In post-mortem examination the pathologist found a massive quantity of barbiturates in the body which he declared had caused his death. At the inquest, Bridge told the coroner that the immediate area was more like a series of crevasses than a cave, and that the opening went down about 20 feet.

There was no doubt in the coroner's mind when he said that the amount of barbiturates was so excessive that 'one can only come to the conclusion that it was taken with one object in view' and accordingly he recorded a verdict of suicide.

25: Unnecessary Rescue

It is not unknown for climbers or walkers, usually with somewhat limited experience, to get into difficulties, allow themselves to be rescued and then, as though to white-wash themselves before even a word of criticism has been levelled at them, announce to the world in general, and the media in particular, that they had been in no danger and their 'rescue' had been totally unnecessary.

On 29 November 1973, 27-year-old Liam Kennedy from North Wales was assisted off the north-east face of Lliwedd with his climbing companion, and was reported by the Press as saying that he had 'nothing but admiration and praise for the Llanberis MRT. Their techniques and expertise are first class', and he added, 'They agreed that we were in no danger and that our equipment was more than adequate for the night in the open'. Mr Kennedy also took it upon himself to 'issue a warning to anyone going to the mountains this winter...to stay away from them until the summer if you don't have enough experience and adequate survival equipment'.

Kennedy had set out on that Thursday with 26-year-old Mrs Cynthia Mary Hughes, from Rhyl. He was reported as being a member of Denbighshire Mountaineering Club, with five years' climbing experience in Wales, Norway and Ireland, but his companion had 'only recently started mountaineering'. Their own account to the Press stated that they left Pen-y-pass at about 10am, allowing plenty of time to complete their planned climb on the north-east face of Lliwedd. The route they were attempting was on West Buttress in the vicinity of Slanting Gully. 'We moved extremely quickly and smoothly up the first section of the climb and then began to encounter ice in patches which covered many of the holds. This meant that we had to clear them with ice-axes, and of course we were slowed down enormously. The ice was not unexpected, but there was no way anyone could know it was so bad. We negotiated this tricky section safely and in the gathering darkness moved speedily up the final, easier, section of the climb. However, by this time total darkness finally set in and we were about 80 feet from the summit. Although the remainder of the climbing was relatively easy, it would have been foolhardy in the extreme to attempt it in pitch darkness.' Kennedy continued, 'We were in a good sheltered position and carrying all the necessary emergency equipment for an overnight stop. The night was perfectly clear and wind-free, and with the equipment we had we knew we were in no danger even if the weather did change. It was simply a matter of waiting the night out and completing the climb in the morning'. Kennedy added that they had put on their spare woollen jumpers, worked out a time-table for their emergency high-protein food, and wrapped themselves in space blankets. They even had bivi bags[1] which they would have used if the weather conditions had deteriorated, 'and of course we were wearing windproof climbing jackets and over-trousers'.

The couple did some static exercises to improve their circulation to maintain body heat with minimum loss of energy. Consequently during the eleven hours spent on the ledge they were, he said, 'sheltered, warm and safe. At no time was

---

1. Polythene bags large enough for an adult to get into to protect him from the elements; short for bivouac bag.

there the slightest danger of us freezing, falling or of perishing in any way whatsoever. I am much too experienced and we were both very well equipped.' Of Mrs Hughes, Kennedy said she was 'really brave at all times. Some people might tend to panic, but she was incredibly calm and rational throughout'. According to Kennedy there had been no snow storms but, 'apparently someone on the road saw our lights on the mountainside and alerted the MRT, but when they got to us we were concerned only about getting a message to Cynthia's parents and husband to say we were all right, and we told the rescuers that we didn't need their help. However, two members of the team climbed down to us[1] reaching our position at about 5am, and although we would have been climbing off ourselves in two hours anyway, we climbed up the rope with them. There was no dragging, hoisting or winching involved'. They were taken down to Pen-y-pass Youth Hostel where they said all they needed was a cup of tea, after which they split up and returned to their respective homes.

To anyone with real experience, this story must read like a fairy story about the little boy who did everything right and could do nothing wrong. What did the real experts make of it?

The first discrepancy between Kennedy's story and the report of the incident by John Ellis Roberts is that the couple had been seen in a climbing equipment shop five miles away at Capel Curig sometime after the alleged 10am start. Secondly, snow was clearly visible that morning on the north-east face of Lliwedd, and any one with a modicum of experience of winter mountaineering would expect that at 700m asl there would be some ice, especially on an exposed face. In spite of this, neither of the climbers had an ice-axe when they were brought to the top of the cliff, in contradiction to Kennedy's statement that they had to clear ice from many of the hand-holds with ice-axes. Normally mountaineers carry a head torch so that if they are still climbing in the dark, their hands are left free to climb, but neither had one, and they had only one hand-held torch between them.

There was also discrepancy between the description of the weather conditions in Kennedy's story and what they were actually like. As darkness fell, the weather was at first clear with temperatures around freezing. The position of the couple was pin-pointed well before midnight and twenty minutes later it started snowing. Kennedy and Mrs Hughes were rescued at 5.30am, but it continued to snow until 7.30am, and by then the snow was lying right down to the road level in Nant Gwynant which is only 68m asl. The whole of Lliwedd, rising to 898m, was completely covered and progress on foot was difficult and slow.

---

1. Park Wardens John Ellis Roberts and Sam Roberts.

It had been some time after dark that Cynthia's husband reported to the police that his wife had not returned from a mountaineering expedition, and this information was received at almost the same time as information from a motorist driving from *Pen-y-gwryd* towards Nant Gwynant, whose passenger had seen a light flashing two and a half miles distant inside the Snowdon Horseshoe. This report was confirmed by a police patrol. Quite clearly then, the flashing light had been seen, and subsequently enabled the rescue team to pinpoint the position of the crag-fast climbers. There had been no mention of flashing his torch in Kennedy's story, but during his evacuation from the cliff face, he told his rescuers he had been flashing it to try to attract attention since 6.30pm and that he was glad to be off the cliff because of the deteriorating weather.

As regards their equipment, there was much criticism. Whilst it was said to be adequate for a day's climbing under normal (summer) conditions, it was definitely not so for a long rock-climb under winter conditions. For an overnight stay on such an exposed rock face their equipment was insufficient, and in particular neither of them wore a crash helmet , which is considered essential on Lliwedd because of falling stones.

All the points mentioned above were included in a letter written by the leader of the rescue operation, John Ellis Roberts, to the Free Press Association on 19 December 1973, in order to present the true story of what actually happened. It left little doubt that Kennedy's version of events was misleading, since the writer of the letter was a first-hand witness of the incident and had been present throughout the long night. In conclusion, John Ellis Roberts stressed that civilian MRTs are made up of volunteers who are all local mountaineers, and 'do not go looking for all-night incidents for something to do'. This had been the fourth all-night rescue the Llanberis MRT had dealt with in the previous four weeks. Each time the incident had involved people who had miscalculated the severity of the climb under prevailing conditions and the level of their experience to undertake such expeditions, and lacked the judgement to turn back well before becoming benighted. The only plausible part of this incident was Kennedy's belated advice to would-be climbers to stay away from the mountains until the summer, unless 'one has the necessary equipment and experience'. But coming from one who, in the light of events, clearly did not have either, such advice has a somewhat hollow ring.

26: Cader Idris

Cader Idris, meaning the 'Chair of Idris', is a mountain range seven miles long running in an east-north-east direction from the coast between Barmouth and Aberdyfi. Its highest point is the summit of Pen-y-gadair, 877m, which stands proudly as the southern sentinel of Snowdonia. There are two other principal peaks, — Tyrrau Mawr, 780m, 2 miles to the south-west, and Mynnyd Moel, 840m, $1^1/2$ miles to the north-east. On the north side between these two peaks there is a $3^1/2$ mile stretch of sheer rock face, and near the summit of Pen-y-gadair a vast amphitheatre of rock, 300m high, embraces many fine climbing routes. Running towards the south are rocky ridges and wild, splendid crags and a number of llynniau (lakes) before the aspect changes to one of steep grassy slopes of little interest to rock-climbers. Cader Idris has long been a popular venue for climbers and walkers alike, and records show that during the second half of the 19th century some of the best-known alpine climbers of their time used the mountain as an alternative to the northerly parts of Snowdonia. But the number of mountaineers who came here was small in comparison with those who visited Snowdon.

The first recorded misadventure on Cader Idris occurred in September 1864 when a man named Smith, who was 'Mr Colborne's clerk in Newport', was lost on the mountain. He was on a walking tour in North Wales and had arrived at Machynlleth where he tried to hire a guide to take him over Cader Idris. The guide refused, and advised Mr Smith not to attempt the ascent on his own that evening as it would soon be dark and the weather was bad. However, he relented slightly and went with Smith just far enough to put him on the right track before turning back. Nothing was seen or heard of Smith after that, and six weeks later his brother came to North Wales and made enquiries of him in Machynlleth, Tywyn and Dolgellau. No one had any idea what might have happened to him, other than the guide who had warned him not to go and had subsequently pointed out the way. The mountain was searched without result, but in the following May a man out on the mountain top with his terrier dog heard the dog bark, and looking over a precipice saw the remains of a man's body lying at the foot of the crag.

Foxes and crows had made short work of the man's remains, but from the injuries to his skeleton it was clear that he had fallen from a great height and that he must have been killed outright. Lying not far away was a knapsack containing some money and papers bearing Smith's name and address; his stick and hat were found nearby. The local guide from Dolgellau thought that he had probably tried to find a short route down to the village, but had fallen over the precipice in the growing darkness and mist.

*

The next recorded incident happened in May 1891, when three friends, S. A. Thorn, H Hope and S Black, after spending a few days together hill-walking in the Snowdon area, decided to tackle Cader Idris. They booked in at The Cross Foxes Hotel which is about three miles from Dolgellau on the cross roads where the Machynlleth road turns south off the Dolgellau–Dinas Mawddwy road. They set out from there rather late at 4pm in the afternoon to begin the ascent of the imposing mountain, little dreaming of the adventures they would have before the following morning. There is no record of which path they used to ascend the mountain, but the obvious one is from the roadside at SH 730114. This would mean a walk along the road of just over 4 miles before starting to climb, which would have been at about 5.30pm. Long before they reached the Saddle above Llyn y Gadair between the summit and Cyfrwy, they were, in their own words, 'fairly knocked up', having started the ascent after a heavy day`s walking, and too much tea. After a prolonged struggle, and just as the sun disappeared over the horizon, they reached the summit and thought it sensible to have a rest before starting the descent. Having recovered their wind and jerked their weary legs into action again, they began to trot down towards the hotel but after a short time they realised that they had lost the path and try as they might, they were unable to find it. This in itself would be alarming, but to add to their troubles the mist began to roll up the slopes on all sides as if to engulf them, and in a very few minutes they could see nothing below them except a sea of clouds all 'jockeying for position' as it were. Anyone having a written guarantee that in a reasonable time they would safely reach the bottom would, no doubt, have enjoyed the striking view presented by the banks of cloud rolling at their feet. For those who realised that they were lost, there was very little enjoyment at the sight. They were determined not to spend the night on the mountain unless it was absolutely necessary, so for 3 hours they felt their way cautiously down, again and again having to retrace their footsteps owing to a steep gully or a precipice blocking their way, and eventually they found themselves in exactly the same place from which they had started.

By now they were fearfully cold and hungry but felt that the only course open to them was to make the best of a bad job, and wait for daylight. The only gear they were carrying with them in their rucksacks was their nightshirts which they

Cader Idris from the North.   [SNP]

now put on hoping to get some extra warmth. Perhaps it was the nightshirts which suggested the idea of attempting to get a bit of sleep, so they sought shelter behind some large boulders and tried to find comfortable positions to lie down. But it was in vain, for never did a bed of stones feel as hard as those on which they lay. After trying to sleep, once more they started slowly descending. Like three phantoms they moved silently and carefully through the mist and any belated traveller seeing these wraith-like figures in white would immediately have taken fright.

Daylight eventually came and the three men were able at last to see their route and get safely down. It was just after 6am when three bedraggled travellers presented themselves at the hotel where their beds remained unslept in, and it was not until they had had a good wash and clean up that the hotel staff were able to recognise them. After a good breakfast they retired to bed for a few hours and then returned to the *Pen-y-gwryd Hotel* where the three of them, much the wiser, sat down and wrote an account of their adventure on Cader Idris in the visitors' book. At the end of the story they added a rider — 'The moral is don`t attempt to cross mountains without compass and ordnance maps'.

Over a century ago, adventures like this got very little publicity unless they ended in death or serious injury. The lessons to be learned from such incidents would probably be appreciated only by the friends of those involved to whom they told their story. Nobody else, other than a few guests who might read the account in the hotel visitors' book, would hear about it and realise how easily the expedition could have come to a dreadful end.

*

In September 1900, 22-year-old Wilfred McInnes was on a cycling holiday in North Wales. He had never climbed a mountain, but when he arrived in Dolgellau on 13 September, he found out that many visitors made an ascent of Cader Idris. Accordingly he decided to set off early the following morning, climb the mountain, and arrive at Barmouth in the evening as previously planned. He cycled as far as the *Gwernan Lake Hotel* at the start of the Fox's Path and although he found it very difficult to walk up the rough track in un-nailed shoes, he eventually reached the summit. There he decided not to descend by the same route, but to try another way. Stretching away to the west from Pen-y-gadair, is a mile-long ridge with a precipice on the north side, some 200m high to start with, tapering to nothing at the far end, and below the precipice is a scree slope running the whole length of the ridge. McInnes set off along the ridge, hoping to find a way down to the easier slopes where he could traverse back to re-join the Fox's Path. After about 1/4 mile he thought he could see a way down. He walked down the grassy slope towards the edge of the precipice, but the grass was dry and the smooth soles of his shoes gave him no grip whatsoever. McInnes went as far down as he could, but decided that it had become too steep. He tried to re-trace his steps but was unable to climb back up. As he looked around he saw a place where he thought he might be able to climb down, not knowing that there was a precipice immediately below him. He took off his shoes and socks hoping to get a better grip in bare feet, and then, in trying to get past a rocky outcrop, he found himself sitting astride a piece of rock. That was all he could remember when he regained consciousness about six hours later at 6pm to find himself lying in scrub below the scree. He had lost his glasses, shoes and cap in the fall and his search for them was unsuccessful. Soon it was dark, and McInnes dragged himself into the lee of a large stone where he lay all night and in spite of a heavy hoar frost, he slept reasonably well, and at no time felt particularly cold. He thought it was about 7am next morning when he started to walk barefoot in the general direction of Dolgellau. He was very weak and fainted several times on the way, but eventually, having crossed three streams and passed through a gate in a mountain wall, he heard dogs barking and followed their sound until he arrived at a farm house. He had covered between two and three miles from where he had spent the night. McInnes was tended carefully by the farmer and his wife and taken down to Dolgellau, three miles away, in a cart with no springs. He was examined by a doctor and the District Nurse, and his injuries were found to be severe, the worst of which were a fractured skull and compression of the brain, long deep cuts and bruising all over his body, including the soles of his bare feet, together with loss of use of his right arm. Although at first he was feverish, the symptoms soon disappeared, he was considered to be out of danger, and after several months' rest he eventually recovered.

A report published by another climber, Fred W Jackson, who went to the scene of the fall to try to work out what had happened, said that McInnes must have fallen at least 80 feet, and this was agreed by a shepherd and a mountain guide who had also gone to the scene. McInnes had not been killed because of two main factors. The precipice over which he had slipped was so sheer that probably he would have been thrown outwards and not touched the rock before he hit the ground. Then the place where he landed was entirely free from rocks and was covered with thick coarse grasses, ferns and bilberry bushes, which absorbed some of the momentum of his fall. This patch of greenery was on a very steep slope, so that McInnes would have struck a glancing blow and rolled down to where he finally came to rest. It was a remarkable escape.

*

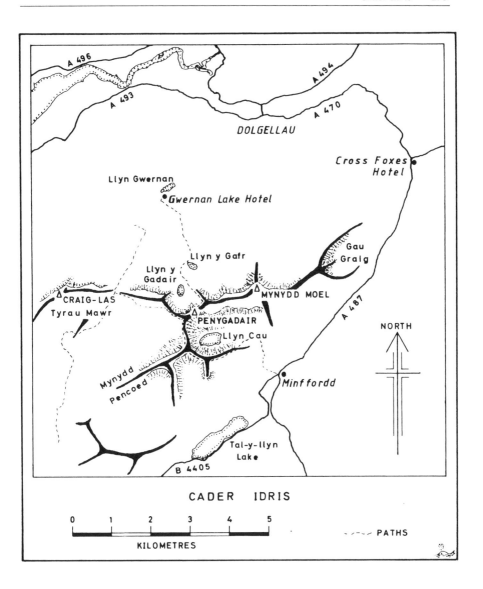

CADER IDRIS

Arnold Lunn, in his book *The Mountains of Youth*, first published in 1925, describes how in 1909 he spent some days climbing on Cader Idris with his friend, C Scott Lindsay. The day after they had climbed Great Gully in Cwm Eigiau accompanied by two other friends, one of whom, named Warren, was a surgeon on the staff of the London Hospital, Lindsay decided to take a day off as he was feeling rather tired. Warren and his friend went out together, and Lunn went off alone and climbed the east ridge of Cyfrwy which he found interesting but not very difficult. On 28 August he and Lindsay were again climbing together, and at the summit of Pen-y-gadair, Lindsay decided to 'sit the next one out' as he was not feeling too fit. Lunn left his friend where he was and started to descend the east ridge of Cyfrwy, intending to climb up the north ridge. The day was perfect; it was warm and sunny with the most wonderful views across the lower hills to the 'burnished silver of the sea' and he describes it as 'one of those days when to be alive is 'very heaven'. 'I was glad to be alone,' he wrote, 'I revelled in the freedom from the restraints of the rope ... I have never enjoyed rock climbing more. I have never enjoyed rock climbing since'.

While Arnold Lunn was so enjoying himself, Lindsay was basking in the sunshine and also enjoying the splendid views all around him. Suddenly he was startled by the thunder of a stone avalanche coming from the direction of Cyfrwy and, seeing a lone walker approaching, he shouted to him to follow, and dashed off towards the Cyfrwy ridge.

Arnold Lunn had just lowered himself from the edge of what is known as 'The Table' when, without any warning, the mountain seemed to sway and shake as in an earthquake. He hung on, pressing himself hard against the face of the cliff, when suddenly a huge block, about ten feet high and several feet thick, came away from the cliff and swept him with it into space. He somersaulted and struck the cliff some way below, then after bouncing off and crashing into the cliff two or three times, he came to rest on a sloping ledge about seven feet wide. He heard the thunder of the rocks as they continued to fall another 150 feet, and realised how narrow his escape had been. Lindsay later estimated that Lunn had fallen 100 feet, and whilst his leg was severely damaged he had somehow escaped any other injury. When he saw his leg, Lunn was horrified, for the lower part was bent almost at right angles, and was shattered and crushed. He shouted for help, but at first heard no response and wondered if Lindsay had become bored and started to descend to the hotel. He shouted again and again, wondering in between times if he had climbed his last mountain. Then suddenly there was an answering cry from Lindsay, and Lunn sobbed with heartfelt relief. Lindsay was preceded by an old man who was the keeper of the hut on Cader Idris, and after looking at Lunn's damaged leg he reprimanded him for straying off the path on to 'rough places' where even the natives did not venture! It was now after 4pm, and the problem was how to get Lunn down to safety. Lindsay, who had turned green at the sight of the shattered leg, suggested to the ancient hut-keeper that they should go down a bit and get a gate from one of the mountain walls and carry Lunn down on it. The old man, however, opted for using sacks but Lunn felt that whilst sacks might be appropriate for a corpse, he preferred something more comfortable. Lindsay left Lunn in the care of the old man, and went down to raise the alarm and try to find their companion of two days ago, the surgeon Warren. Shortly after he had left, the old man decided to go down to the valley to tell his wife what he was doing. By then Lunn's condition was starting to deteriorate as it got much colder, and the pain became worse, but the hut keeper returned with some warm tea for which Lunn was extremely grateful. The time was now 7.45pm and there was still no sign of help but at 8.15pm the local policeman arrived with a hastily assembled rescue party and a makeshift stretcher. Descent from the ledge on which he lay ran conveniently on to an easy slope, but it was not until midnight, eight hours after his fall, that Lunn was carried into the Angel Hotel in Dolgellau where Warren attended to his injuries.

Arnold Lunn's leg was broken (a compound fracture) and crushed, and twice during the following days he was on the verge of having it amputated, only to be saved each time by a providential drop in his blood pressure. At the end of a week he was taken home and for four months he lay on his back, before starting to walk again with the help of a splint. His damaged right leg was slightly crooked and two inches shorter than the left leg, but Warren's skill had left him with a reasonably serviceable right leg for which he was truly grateful. Fifteen months after his fall, Arnold Lunn started to ski again, and in another nine months he actually climbed the Dent Blanche in the Alps, although the effort exhausted him and caused considerable pain. His nerve had been damaged by his awful experience, and much of the enjoyment of rock-climbing had clearly gone out of his life for ever, but Arnold was not finished, and he went on to have outstanding skiing and literary achievements.

*

On Saturday, 13 July 1974, Peter Hall, landlord of the *Lake Gwernan Hotel*, reported that a car had been in his carpark since Thursday 11 July. Police enquiries revealed that it belonged to Miss Alisa Elizabeth Morrell who was on a walking holiday in the Tywyn area, and this was the first indication that she was missing. Mrs Hall, the licensee's wife, said that she had served Miss Morrell one drink in the bar, and she had then watched her set off up the Fox's Path opposite the hotel at about 1pm on 11 July.

On Sunday morning, Tony Mills from the Outward Bound School Aberdyfi MRT had organised preliminary searches of the base of the northern crags from Llyn Aran in the east to Craig Las in the west, and the tops of the crags to the summit of Pen-y-gadair. The searches were carried out by 24 students and six staff from the OBS, Aberdyfi, and during the afternoon of the same day, a further 24 students and four staff joined the search and covered the southern cwms, whilst the Rhinog MRT searched the area to the west of Gau Craig.

Following a national radio and television news broadcast during the day, a sighting of Miss Morrell on the Fox's Path heading up towards the summit beyond Llyn Gafr, early in the afternoon of 11 July, was confirmed by the leader of a group which had followed her up as far as the llyn. The police also discovered a tent in a campsite at Ynys Maengwyn, Tywyn, which was confirmed as belonging to the missing woman and the Search Panel was convened at Dolgellau Police Station at 9pm that evening. Tony Mills became Team Controller, and Tony Jones took over as Search Controller. Has Oldham took on the role of Radio Controller. Also present at this meeting was Sergeant Maurice Morrell of the Merseyside Constabulary, Miss Morrell's brother, who gave the Panel a concise word picture of his sister which was valuable information. The information he gave included a description of what she was wearing and her experience as a walker: she was intelligent and level-headed; she was an enthusiastic but not an ambitious walker, and it would be out of character for her to do any actual climbing or scrambling; she was not in any way emotionally disturbed when she left home; she had a brochure from the local tourist office, but possibly no map.

In view of the length of time that she had been missing, all the civilian teams in North Wales and the RAF teams from Valley and Stafford had been called out, and assistance sought from individual volunteers.

The mountain was divided into search areas and acting on Maurice Morrell's advice that his sister would not do anything ambitious, it was felt that she would most probably be found in a low-lying area, especially near the quarry in grid square SH 7014.

The search started at first light on Monday, while the Search Panel set up the search base in team vehicles in the carpark at SH 697152 at 5.30am. Before mid-morning the police had brought in their incident caravan and mobile canteen, and the GPO laid two outside telephone lines to the incident caravan. Throughout the morning the weather was so bad, with mist and heavy rain and a gale force wind, that the SAR helicopter could not fly. At about 8am, information was received by the police that Miss Morrell had been seen at 3.30pm on 11 July at the top of the scree about 300 yards from the summit of Pen-y-gadair. This gave a different perspective, and priority was changed to the cwms around and below the summit. There was confirmation of this information at 12.30pm by another walker who had seen Miss Morrell on 11 July, at the top of the scree at about 4pm. All the sightings agreed, and the overriding feeling was that she must be close to the base of Pen-y-gadair. Whilst plans were being drawn up to send a party of rescuers to search the gullies on Tuesday, two members of the RAF Valley Team, Tom Walkington and 'Dickie' Bird, were searching the head wall to the south of Llyn y Gadair, and found Miss Morrell's body lying on a ledge approximately 50 feet above the screes. She appeared to have fallen about 500 feet from the summit of Pen-y-gadair.

27: Off The Beaten Track

Throughout the years many accidents have been caused by walkers getting off the beaten track and following sheep tracks or water courses in mistake for paths. In October 1976 there was a major incident on Clogwyn y Garnedd on the east face of Snowdon which happily ended with the people involved living to tell the tale.

A party of 15 Americans aged between 14 and 17 and three adult teachers from the United States Air Force Base school at Woodbridge in Suffolk had booked four nights at *Jesse James' Bunkhouse*, a privately owned outdoor activity centre in Penisa'rwaun, near Llanberis. They had asked Jesse, who was a member of the Llanberis MRT, to take them for mountain walks on the first and second days of their stay. At the end of the second day the leader of the party, Mr Elwood Carter, told him that he and his colleagues thought they had enough mountain know-how to be able to take their young charges safely up Snowdon the following day. They decided to go up the Pyg track, but before they started out Jesse gave them a thorough briefing, telling them specifically not to stray off the well-trodden path up the Zigzags. Once they had reached the marker stone at the top of the path, all they had to do was to turn left, drop down to the railway line and then follow it to the summit building followed by a short scramble to the summit cairn. He also warned them that extra care should be taken on the return when descending the Zigzags, as there was a thin covering of crisp snow on the paths and it could be slippery. All the students were equipped with good clothing and Vibram-soled boots, but they had no ice-axes though they did have a length of rope with them. They were also carrying a map and compass. The party set out from Pen-y-pass at 10.45am, and Jesse James had no qualms about their ability to follow his briefing and return safely to the *Bunkhouse*. It was 28 October, and the weather, although misty with restricted visibility, was reasonably calm.

Back at the *Bunkhouse* the evening meal was scheduled for 5.00pm, but there was no sign of the American party. It is usual to allow about two hours if a party or individual does not return at the expected time, and that is what Jesse did on this occasion. At 7.30pm, he and a friend who was staying in the Bunkhouse - a master at St Paul's School named David May — left to do a preliminary search. They went up to Pen-y-pass where they found the Americans' vehicle in the carpark, which suggested to Jesse James that some misfortune may have befallen them. He telephoned John Ellis Roberts, who had just returned from the rescue of a 13-year-old boy with a broken right leg near the base of Clogwyn Coch. John first of all grabbed something to eat before setting off for the Miners' track in his Park Land Rover. Meantime Jesse James and David May set off on foot in the dark along the Pyg track and just beyond the junction of the Pyg and Miners' tracks above Glaslyn, Jesse got a fleeting glimpse through a break in the mist of a light high up on the east face of Snowdon. He shouted loud and slowly, 'Are–you–all–right?' and they both heard a distinct reply, 'Yes'.

David May went down to Glaslyn to meet John Roberts and give him the possible location of the missing party, and Jesse carried on alone to the summit of Snowdon. He had with him 108 feet of 9mm rope which he always carried in his rucksack, and which he belayed to an old iron stake just below the summit cairn. He then climbed down the face as far as the rope would allow, using the rope as a handrail rather than trying to abseil. He was now at the end of the rope, and estimated that he was somewhere at the top of the northern Trinity gully, and he tried to make verbal contact with the group. There was no reply, but once again he saw lights through the mist and he reckoned they were some way lower than he had previously thought. He climbed back to the summit where he met John Roberts and a number of the Llanberis team who were all competent climbers and who had already been involved in the earlier incident below Clogwyn Coch. They had with them two 250 foot ropes. They belayed one of the ropes to the iron spike, and John, followed by Jesse with the other rope, abseiled down to the full length of the rope. But it was not enough, and they were still not able to establish voice contact. They tied the second rope to the first and John abseiled down again. At the end of the rope he made verbal contact with an American who said, 'We are OK, no injuries, just cold butts'; to which John replied, 'Stay where you are. We'll get you off at first light'. By this time it had become clear that an attempt to rescue such a large party up the icy slope in the dark would be unjustifiably hazardous. John then climbed back to where Jesse

James was waiting, the two of them rejoined the other Llanberis team members by the summit building and John announced his decision to do nothing more until daylight. The whole party stayed up there for the rest of the night, bivouacing in the shelter of the summit building which had already been closed for the winter. John radioed the rescue base which had been set up at Pen-y-pass to give them an update on what had so far happened and what the plans were for the next morning.

Just before dawn it was decided that in view of the weather, the location of the party, and their condition, the evacuation should be made from the base of the cliff. John asked the police for assistance from 'C' Flight subject to suitable flying conditions. Soon after first light a second party from the Llanberis team set out to attempt to contact the American party from below by climbing up some very rough ground between the Trinity Gullies and Ladies' Gully. The summit party went down the Zigzags as far as the small pool near the copper mines, and then traversed across to where the missing youngsters had by then been located by the second party from the Llanberis MRT, and where the evacuation by helicopter was already beginning. In Jesse's own words, 'the ground they had to cross to reach the Americans was really evil — steep, rough and extremely slippery' — and he could not imagine how the party had managed it without some one coming to grief, nor why they pushed on when it must have been obvious that they could not be on the Zigzag path. They still had flasks of hot coffee they had carried up the night before to warm up the crag-fast youngsters, but to the surprise of those who heard it, one girl, on being offered a cup of coffee, replied, 'Gee, haven't you got any tea?'.

Altogether 19 team members, eight students from the Llanrug Outdoor Pursuits Centre, three police officers from Llanberis, and the helicopter crew, were involved in the incident, which was not declared closed until 11am that morning.

As Jesse James approached the Pen-y-pass carpark, he spotted a 'wall' of press reporters, and remembering that attack is the best form of defence, he told them in no uncertain terms that although the Americans were staying at his Bunkhouse, and he had guided them on the mountains on the two days preceding this expedition, the only part he had played in it was in an advisory capacity before they set out. He told them that if any of them suggested that he was in any way to blame it would have disastrous consequences for his business, and he would personally burn down the newspaper offices responsible! The reporters took note and no mention was made of his Bunkhouse in their reports of the incident.

Back at the *Bunkhouse*, Jesse took the three adults to task. Their story was that on their way up they had taken longer than expected and 'it suddenly got dark'. Becoming disorientated in the mist, they took a compass bearing, but unfortunately made a mistake and found themselves heading straight for the summit. They finished up at a point of no-return — likewise of no-going-forward either — and found themselves on a steeply sloping grassy ledge. No suitable rock was found to which to belay themselves and they spent the night grabbing each other as they tended to slide down the slope.

In retrospect one can only think that they were incredibly lucky that only a fewof them were flown to hospital with mild hypothermia, and that no one was detained. The adult leaders seem to have had poor mountain sense and they failed to follow the detailed briefing Jesse James had given them.

*

On 5 July the previous year (1975) a 43-year-old American physics professor from Seattle, Washington, who was staying with his wife in a cottage in Betws Garmon, went for an evening stroll up the steep south-westerly slopes of the Moel Eilio ridge, immediately behind the village. It was about 11.30pm when he headed back for the cottage, and in his hurry, he fell and severely injured himself. When he had not returned by midnight, his wife raised the alarm and he was soon found by members of the Llanberis MRT. The team carried him on a stretcher more than 500 feet down the scree to a waiting ambulance. In hospital, X-rays showed that Mr Baker's injury was a cracked pelvis. He was in a distressed condition, and to add to his misery, he found that his wallet containing £60 and $200 was missing. Next day local police and others searched for it without success, but the following day John Ellis Roberts went back to look for the wallet. He found it wedged in a crack in a rock, and returned it to the professor, who said it was a 'real pick-me-up'. His comments are worth recording here, for he said, 'I thought that the chances of finding the wallet were less than one in a hundred, but the fact that the search was made and persisted in, shows an amazing goodwill and something I could never have expected. I feel that although I have suffered a lot of pain from the injury to my pelvis, I have almost been compensated by the fact that I have met so many pleasant, dedicated, unselfish and sincere people in this country'.

A week after the rescue of the American party on Snowdon in October 1976, John Roberts received a copy of the *Seattle Times* in which there was a detailed report of the rescue. It had been posted to him by Professor Marshall Baker whom John and the team had rescued 15 months earlier.

28: Technical Rescues

There are no hard and fast rules for what are sometimes called technical rescues. Every situation has to be dealt with as a new and separate problem in the light of the current factors — the location, access to the accident site, evacuation route, the nature of the injuries, daylight or darkness, weather conditions, and the number of experienced rescue personnel and type of equipment available. There is no one-off solution and it is for the team leader to adapt practised techniques and the resources on hand to the situation confronting him.

The technical development of crag rescues has kept pace with the technical development of mountaineering itself, and what might have been considered an exceptionally difficult rescue 30 years ago could well be regarded as a fairly normal operation today. The OVMRO, RAF Valley MRT and the staff at Plas-y-Brenin have been involved in the development of sophisticated equipment and devices, and in the constant improvement of techniques to evacuate casualties from places of difficult access. Successful technical rescues have been recorded in various books such as *Whensoever*, but there are two stories well worth repeating here.

Since last century, the beauty spot at Aber Falls on the northern edge of the Carneddau, which is approached from the A55 trunk road along the east bank of the Afon Rhaeadr Fawr, has seen more than its fair share of tragic accidents, mainly to walkers coming down from the Carneddau. Most of these accidents have been caused by walkers slipping on a smooth slab of wet, greasy rock which lies right across the path just above the head of the waterfall. On 13 April 1873, a barrister named F T Payne, whose sight was very poor, slipped there and was killed. It is likely that his defective eyesight was largely to blame for this tragic accident. A little over three years later, in the summer of 1876, a young walker named Empson, who was staying in Llanfairfechan, was killed at exactly the same place when descending to the road. Then in April 1885, an experienced Alpinist named Maitland Wills, who was walking with two friends from Capel Curig to Aber, slipped off the path at the same spot and fell to his death. In August the same year, a Police Magistrate from Hammersmith in London, Paget by name, fell at the same place and was severely injured. The toll was mounting, but these are only a few examples of the long list of accidents at Aber Falls, which at that time was probably second to Snowdon itself in the table of misadventures.

*

Tying two or more ropes together to make one long rope for a specific purpose might seem to be a common-sense thing to do, but it is not necessarily quite as simple as that, as the first of the 'Technical Rescue' stories shows. Soon after dark on 1 December 1957, the RAF Valley MRT led by Flight-Sergeant J R (Johnnie) Lees was called out to rescue a student who had fallen whilst climbing the 300 foot cliff at Aber Falls. By the light of flares the young man could be seen lying on a ledge about 100 feet up from the foot of the cliff and about 15 feet to the right of the waterfall. Police and firemen had tried to reach him without success, and Lees decided that a long lower from above was the only way to deal with the problem. The team climbed round to the top of the cliff with their ropes and found a sound tree to use as the belay. It turned out that the tree was not directly above the casualty, but about 12 feet to his right.

One of the team members was Corporal Technician S R G (Vic) Bray who was wearing nailed boots, and Lees suggested that Vic Bray be lowered to the casualty. Lees then climbed down to a position just above the almost vertical part of the cliff where he found a small but secure ledge from where he could relay messages to the lowerers above him.

The longest ropes available at that time were only 120 feet, and the team tied three of them together. Vic Bray was lowered down with Johnnie Lees providing a link between Bray and the lowerers. Bray reached a point level with the casualty but then had to traverse to his left to reach the ledge where the injured man was lying and clip him to the rope. He then reversed the traverse he had just done by penduluming back with the injured man. The student was successfully taken off, and. Bray was later awarded the Bronze Medal of The Royal Humane Society for his part in this rescue.

*

Just five weeks after the Aber Falls rescue, Johnny Lees and his team were in action on Craig-yr-ysfa, high up in the Carneddau. Four members of the Army Mountaineering Association — Colonel Gerry Finch (who was accompanied by his two sons), Major Hugh Robertson, Lieutenant Roger Eagle and Army Padre Fred Jenkins — were climbing the Amphitheatre Buttress in three parties of two climbers. The first rope — consisting of Fred Jenkins and one of the boys — had reached the top of the crag, and Gerry Finch and his other son were making good progress not far behind them. Major Robertson was leading the third rope and was negotiating an icy pitch when he slipped and fell about 30 feet, landing on a ledge about 200 feet from the start of the climb. Roger Eagle climbed down and secured Robertson, who appeared to have serious head injuries, and shouted to Colonel Finch who was just arriving at the top of the climb. The Colonel instructed Jenkins to explore a possible evacuation route and then made all speed with his sons down to Ogwen Cottage to raise the alarm. A scratch rescue team was hastily assembled, but as it looked as though it was going to be a difficult job, the RAF Valley team was called out. The time was then 4.30pm. Colonel Finch left his sons at the Cottage, and returned with the team to the top of Craig-yr-ysfa where Lees with the RAF team arrived almost simultaneously. They had driven from Valley via Betws-y-coed and Trefriw to the road-head in Cwm Eigiau then walked to the top of Craig-yr-ysfa in just under three hours from receipt of the call-out message.

Lees took the Colonel and two of his own men, Paddy Andrews and Vic Bray, 750 feet down the Buttress to the ledge where Robertson and Eagle were located. Immediately below them were 200 feet of vertical rock with occasional overhangs, and even in daylight and with benign weather conditions it would present a difficult problem. Robertson, whose skull was fractured, was delirious and thrashing about, it was dark and the rockface was icy, and to Lees there appeared to be no alternative to climbing down the vertical face.

Immediately after the Aber Falls lower, when it had been necessary to tie three ropes together to get the required length, Lees's foresight and representations to the Air Ministry resulted in 500-foot ropes being supplied to his team 'to cater for exceptionally long stretcher or casualty lowers' and they had arrived in time for this incident on Amphitheatre Buttress. It had been apparent the moment they arrived that the ropes were very heavy, and no time had been wasted in devising a plywood reel which enabled a man to carry one of them on his back.[1]

By the time Lees and his group had reached the ledge, Roger Eagle had been there for seven hours, trying to restrain Robertson, who had become more and more difficult to control, and both men were extremely cold and in danger of getting frost-bite. Lees instructed the others to make a rope carrying-seat, put Robertson into it, and lash him to his back. Then, with Robertson still struggling to free himself, Lees abseiled down with a supporting top-rope being fed out by Andrews and Bray. He reached the bottom safely where other team members were waiting with a stretcher. The combined weight of Lees and Robertson was 28 stone, and Lees was somewhat concerned about the breaking strain of nylon!

---

1. The modern method is to have the rope 'stuffed' into a rucksack. It is possible to abseil and pay out the rope from the rucksack.

It did not go unnoticed that even after the tremendous strain, both physical and mental, of this epic descent, Lees insisted on taking his turn carrying the stretcher to the ambulance down in Cwm Eigiau.

Robertson eventually recovered and at once went to see Johnnie Lees and his team to thank them. He asked what equipment they most needed, and Lees replied, 'a Tragsitz harness'. This is a device specially designed to replace the rope carrying-seat which they had had to prepare to get Robertson down from the ledge. In due course Robertson brought a Tragsitz back from Austria, where it had been developed. Since then it has become a standard piece of equipment in most MRTs.

For his performance that night on Amphitheatre Buttress, Johnnie Lees was awarded the George Medal, and he was subsequently awarded the British Empire Medal for his services to MR in the 1962 New Year's Honours List.

From the mid-1960s the increasing use of helicopters, which can sometimes complete a rescue whilst an MRT is still on the way to the accident, has markedly reduced the number of technical rescues carried out by MRTs. The crews of RAF Whirlwind helicopters, which were later replaced by the Wessex, often with one or two skilled rescuers on board, have been able to carry out rescues on many occasions which otherwise would have required a team to carry out a very time-consuming technical operation. The usual practice is for the helicopter to be manoeuvred into a hover position and the winchman and/or MRT member lowered to the casualty. After being given first-aid treatment the injured person is winched up on a stretcher accompanied by the rescuer, and flown direct to hospital. Many helicopter winchmen and some members of MRTs have done dramatic things at the end of a thin wire cable, often in remote areas far from the gaze of onlookers. But sometimes they have done it in the full glare of publicity. On one such occasion the pilot had to hover below the top of a crag in full view of drivers in the Llanberis Pass, and so that his winchman could get near enough to the casualty, he had to manoeuvre close to the rock face. Shortly before the casualty was on board, an anorak fell from the top of the cliff, and struck the tip of one of the rotor blades. For the pilot it had suddenly become a technical rescue in a different sense. The vibration which developed told the pilot that his rotor was out of balance, and he had to fight to keep the aircraft under control. He remained airborne, finished the winching, and flew the casualty to the hospital in Bangor where he landed safely. On inspecting the damaged rotor he realised that he wouldn't be able to take off again and a new rotor-blade had to be brought to Bangor from RAF Valley.

Helicopter crag rescues demand the highest degree of co-ordination between the helicopter crew and rescue team personnel, and the success of the operation

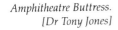

Amphitheatre Buttress.
[Dr Tony Jones]

depends a lot on the exceptional skill of the pilot and his crew in manoeuvring the helicopter. On 16 February 1975, 24-year-old Roentgen Sethan, from Leicester, was climbing on Clogwyn y Grochan on the first pitch of Nea when he fell and landed on a ledge 40 feet down the face. John Ellis Roberts and two other members of the Llanberis MRT, Gwynfor Williams and John Williams, were called to the scene and climbed up to the ledge where they diagnosed a suspected broken shoulder. To winch the injured man into a helicopter was a feasible option even though there was very little space to move on the ledge, but to try to lower Sethan down could well result in causing further damage to his shoulder. A request for a helicopter from RAF Valley was made to Police HQ in Colwyn Bay.

Piloted by Flight-Lieutenant John Garnons-Williams, the helicopter came in and hovered close to where John Roberts and his two companions were crouching on the ledge. The helicopter hovered almost directly above the casualty and the rescuers on the ledge, but high enough above them so that the down draught from the rotors would not imperil them. The winchman, Keith Edwards, with a Neil Robertson stretcher, was then lowered on the winching cable until he was level with John Roberts and about 20 feet out from the cliff face. He then had to set up a pendulum swing until he was close enough for John to grab him and pull him on to the ledge. The operation demanded exceptional skill by John Garnons-Williams to maintain the precise hover position, since the pilot cannot see what is happening below the helicopter, and has to rely on the winch operator for information and guidance. It also demanded courage and skill by Keith Edwards; it was vital that he swung in exactly the right direction for one slight deviation by the helicopter could have caused him to crash into the rock face. The pendulum swing was done with supreme accuracy, and Keith came close enough for John Roberts, who was safely belayed, to lean out and pull him on to the ledge. Sethan was strapped into the stretcher and he and Keith Edwards were winched up into the helicopter which then flew the injured man to hospital.

Co-operation between 'C' Flight and local civilian MRTs has been developing steadily over the past quarter of a century, but occasionally there are disagreements. MRTs have a wealth of local knowledge and experience which can be invaluable to the helicopter crew. Sometimes the rescuer, who for example may be on a narrow ledge with a seriously injured casualty, will request the assistance of a helicopter and will tell the pilot by radio as he approaches, how he wishes him to proceed. On rare occasions, after the pilot has agreed to do what the rescuer has asked, he or his crew may have a change of heart, perhaps because it isn't safe to do it. MRT personnel, the patient and the helicopter crew are at considerable risk during a rescue operation, especially one involving a hover close to a rock face; the captain of the aircraft is primarily responsible for his helicopter and his crew. Confusion during such incidents is bound to arise now and then, but can be avoided by teams and helicopter crews training together and discussing potential problems so that they know each others' difficulties and build up a good working relationship.

*

On 15 October 1972, Surgeon Commander Charles Chapman, stationed at the Royal Naval Hospital in Plymouth, was climbing with a party on the West Peak of Lliwedd, and when 300 feet from the top he slipped and fell 100 feet on to a narrow ledge where he came to rest with a sheer drop of 600 feet immediately below him. His friends realised that they did not have the expertise to help him,

OVMRO demonstrating stretcher lower, Tremadoc, 1967.   [Neil Adam]

so they first had to finish the climb before they could go down to raise the alarm at Pen-y-pass. Before they left the casualty they had run out an 11mm diameter climbing rope joined to one of 9mm diameter to make one length of about 300 feet, and belayed near the top of the climb, so that the loose end ran to the ledge where Commander Chapman lay. This was going to be an excellent marker for the rescue team as it would be dark when they reached the spot. As soon as the alarm was raised at Pen-y-pass, John Ellis Roberts called out the Llanberis and Ogwen Valley MRTs, and he and Llanberis team members made their way to the summit of Lliwedd where they found the rope. John abseiled down to the ledge where Commander Chapman lay, and the difference in diameter of the two lengths of rope gave the impression that he was on the end of a piece of elastic. The Commander was a big, heavy man, and had by then been lying there for over eight hours; he was in a lot of pain, with a broken lower leg. One of the Ogwen Valley party abseiled down to join John on the ledge, and they prepared an ampoule of Fortrol to relieve the pain.[1]

John asked the Commander if, being a surgeon, he would prefer to administer it himself, but he replied that he would rather not! It was already dark, and by the light of torches John injected the Fortrol and set the broken leg with an inflatable splint. He then got into the Tragsitz and with great difficulty they got the Commander strapped into it on John's back. At the top, Tony Jones, assisted by Neil Adam and other rescuers, had set up the OVMRO Mariner wire-winch system with which they slowly lifted the heavy load of John and his patient up the rock face. It was an epic struggle, and John was utterly exhausted when they finally reached the top of the cliff.

The injured man was transferred to a stretcher and carried down by the two civilian teams and the RAF Valley and RAF St Athan MRTs who had joined in the rescue operation. He was soon in the C & A Hospital in Bangor where he was reported to be 'comfortable'. The following day he was given VIP treatment when an RN Sea King helicopter arrived at Bangor to airlift him back to the Royal Naval Hospital in Plymouth.

For his efforts in this rescue, John Roberts was given a tankard as a personal 'Thank you' from the grateful Surgeon Commander.

*

1. Fortrol was introduced as an alternative to Morphia. At the time it was not classified as a Dangerous Drug, and its advantages were that it was a powerful pain reliever; it has no hypnotic effect; it is non-addictive; its effect lasts for three hours; it is available either in tablet or ampoule form. There was however, a chance that it might cause vomiting and it could not, therefore, be used with neck or spinal injuries. Fortrol was later re-classified as a Controlled Drug and is no longer issued to MRTs.

Three years after this rescue John was involved in another crag incident when on 23 November 1975, two climbers got into difficulties on the Main Wall of Gyrn Las in Cwm Glas. The two men had been delayed in their climb by a slow party in front of them, and before they reached the bottom of the last pitch it was dark. They chose to attempt to finish the route rather than try to climb down in complete darkness, but as they tackled the ascending traverse up to the left, the second, Alan Bertrand, aged 44, fell off and swung away from the rock face. Michael Cuthbert, aged 30, was belayed on a 2 foot wide ledge and he managed to hold Bertrand. He couldn't lower him to a ledge as he had no idea in the dark what was below them and as the two climbers were not conversant with self-rescue techniques, Alan was unable to extricate himself from his predicament.

The party which had delayed them had finished their climb and disappeared, and the two men remained crag-fast unable to attract any attention. After a time the other party's torches were seen below as they made their way down the cwm, and Cuthbert shouted to them to go and get help. When the two raised the alarm, Llanberis MRT members – John Ellis Roberts, Mike Muldoon, Harvey Lloyd, Chris Wharmby, Cledwyn Jones and Gwynfor Williams – were called out. They assembled at Blaen Nant at the start of the path leading up into Cwm Glas. There had been no contact with the party that raised the alarm and, thinking that perhaps it had been a hoax call, John and the others were about to go home when they thought they saw a light high up in the cwm. What had happened was that the other party had gone back up into Cwm Glas to help and were in dead ground when the rescuers arrived, their torch lights being invisible at Blaen Nant. The rescuers then climbed up to the slopes immediately below Main Wall where they met the other party who indicated where the two men were cragfast. They went up to the start of the climb and were able to make voice contact but couldn't see them. Appreciating that it would be very difficult to climb up to the two men in the dark, the rescuers made their way on to the top of Gyrn Las and arrived at the finish of Main Wall. It now started to rain heavily, which made things even more difficult and unpleasant, but John was able to abseil 150 feet to Michael Cuthbert, who by then was very cold and tired, but unhurt. He was lifted up the cliff by means of an improvised pulley system which the team on top had set up. John then abseiled as far as he could, but not far enough to reach Bertrand who was some way below him, still hanging free on the end of the rope. John had now reached a ledge and he was able to find the rope attached to Bertrand, and set up a second pulley system which enabled him to winch the uninjured Bertrand up to his ledge. A rope was lowered and Bertrand was then hauled to the top. Bertrand was wearing a Whillans sit-harness which had enabled him to switch his weight from one buttock to the other throughout the hours he had been hanging free, and this relieved the pressure and maintained his blood circulation. Had he been using a waist belt only — at that time a common practice — he could have died within a few minutes from asphyxia.

It was still raining very hard as the rescue party and the two erstwhile cragfast climbers made their way down to the valley which they reached as dawn was breaking. On their way they found that the small stream the rescuers had crossed on their way up had become a raging torrent.

29: Animal Rescues

It might be thought out of place to include a chapter about the rescue of animals, but even before the turn of the century, there were animal rights activists no less amongst mountaineers than elsewhere in the community as the following entry in the *Pen-y-gwryd* visitors' book shows. This unusual plea was entered by 'F F, Wimbledon' on 29 June 1897:

I desire to call the attention of Alpine climbers who visit Snowdon during the winter with axe and rope to what is locally known as the Gaol, on the precipitous face of Snowdon above the copper mines. There is a narrow ledge on to which one sheep at a time is attracted by the herbage, but from which there is no return. The sheep lives as long as any grass is within reach, but then starves, and falls a thousand feet into the lake. Another instantly takes its place. It would be an act of kindness if some climber would block up the access to this fatal ledge, or better still, blow it down with a charge of dynamite.

It seems that little if any notice was taken and by the start of the 1939-45 war the sheep-trap was still there.

In 1915, George Leigh Mallory accompanied by Hugh Heber-Percy and a 'congenial stranger', climbed the South Buttress of Tryfan and rescued a small lamb which Mallory carried to safety in his rucksack — the precursor of the animal rescue bags which have been widely used since the early 1960s.

Animal rescues really started towards the end of the 1940s when shepherds and farmers asked the RAF MRT, if they happened to be in the area, to help them to rescue their cragfast sheep. Prior to this, the loss of a sheep in the mountains was considered to be one of the hazards of their trade and unless some kindly climber happened to be in the right place at the right time, the animal would eventually starve and fall to its death. At the end of the 1950s and beginning of the 1960s, Johnnie Lees and Paddy Andrews of the RAF Valley MRT developed a small lifting harness to make life easier when helping farmers rescue sheep; the design is now used when winching search dogs into and out of a helicopter. Since 1966, John Ellis Roberts, has been closely involved in the rescue of 480 climbers/walkers, and 689 animals, made up of 565 sheep, 73 lambs, 33 Feral goats, 16 dogs, 1 horse and 1 cow.

Animal rescues have been carried out in areas other than the immediate neighbourhood of Snowdon, and these have been done by Wardens when they happened to be available, or by one or other of the MRTs when Wardens were not able to deal with the farmer's request. Today the loss of a ewe or lamb is a serious financial loss for a sheep farmer, and when one of his animals is brought down safely, he is duly grateful. For both Wardens and MRTs it is important to build up and maintain the goodwill of local farmers, who on many occasions have turned out to help in mountain rescues.

It is not only farmers who are grateful for animal rescues, and the Royal Society for the Prevention of Cruelty to Animals has frequently expressed its gratitude to those people, such as RAF Valley and the civilian MRTs, who have rescued animals stuck on the mountains; in particular to John Roberts by making the following awards: one Silver medal, four Bronze medals, 13 Bars to Bronze medal, 12 Certificates of Merit, the 1988 Elsie M J Evans Award for 1988 and one Certificate of Commendation.

The rescue of large animals cannot be compared with the cragfast rescue of a sheep, but nevertheless such an operation presents its own problems. Two such incidents have occurred on Snowdon, and both involved a co-operative effort by the farmer, National Park wardens, a veterinary surgeon and a helicopter. One incident occurred on the slopes above Nant Gwynant where a horse was happily grazing. It reached over a high-tensile wire fence to grab some rather lush grass and tipped itself over the fence and almost rolled down into a gully the other side. It caught one of its rear legs in the top of the wire and was stuck there for two days until the farmer found it in a somewhat distressed state. By the time he had contacted the wardens, he and his men had managed to move the horse a few feet on to higher ground where it was inspected by the Vet. There was no possible access for a tractor and the horse was lying directly underneath electricity cables. There was a possibility that a helicopter could be used, but the horse would have to be moved manually a considerable distance away from the overhead cables. When the wardens arrived, they brought a heavy-duty tarpaulin, some ply-wood boards, and the hand-winch which they normally used for moving boulders on the mountain. The horse was manoeuvred on to the tarpaulins which had been placed over the ply-wood boards, and was successfully winched 200 yards clear of the overhead cables. There a helicopter lifting net was spread out and the horse was tranquillised and rolled on to it; the helicopter gently lifted the horse a little above the ground and flew it down to the farmstead in Nant Gwynant. The rescue of a cow was somewhat similar and happened on very rough ground to the north-west of Beddgelert where the animal, which was due to calve, was seen to be in difficulty. The farmer, a vet and two Wardens were airlifted to the cow where the vet tranquillised her and the procedure was repeated as with the horse. Once the cow was in the net, she was flown to the farm where she proceeded to calve without further problems.

With a large animal it is usually an easy matter for the vet to tranquillise it, but that is difficult when a smaller animal is stuck on a rock face or down a quarry hole. It is unlikely that anyone will be able to get near enough to administer the dose, because the animal tends to back away from a helping hand. Yet most small-animal rescues happen because the animals are stuck on rocks or, as occurs more frequently with dogs, stuck down holes or old mine-shafts.

One established method that has been developed for dealing with crag rescues is for two climbers to go to the top of the cliff and find a belay. They then abseil down on either side of the animal to a level slightly below it and effect a pincer movement so that between them they catch the animal and get it into their 'bag'. In the early days John Roberts found that the harness developed by Lees and Andrews at RAF Valley was not ideal, and allowed the animal too much freedom to struggle. Soon after he had become a Warden, John was asked to rescue a wild goat on Clogwyn y Grochan in the Llanberis Pass. He borrowed an old coal bag from his coalman, and although it had a small tear in it to start with, the hole was very much bigger by the time the goat had been lowered to the ground. The idea was sound, and on the basis of that trial, he designed a large canvas, bucket-shaped bag with four straps and a draw cord. Once inside that, in almost complete darkness, the animal would be immobilised and thereafter the lower would be comparatively easy. Colin Pibworth, an RAF mountain rescuer, made a prototype for him, and once it had proved itself in action, there was no problem in getting replacement bags made when required. Such is their strength and durability that the RSPCA have adopted the same pattern for use elsewhere.

Once the animal is in the bag, one of the rescuers abseils to the base of the cliff with it, whilst the other man goes back to the top to release the belay. It is a bonus when, occasionally, RN or RAF rescue helicopters are exercising in the area and offer to help by winching the rescue bag off the crag and flying the animal down, leaving the two rescuers to recover their equipment.

*

John Ellis Roberts approaching a crag-fast goat.   *[Steve Peak]*

A tragic incident involving an animal occurred on 26 November 1977, when 26-year-old Isobel Lindsay, a member of the OVMRO, and wife of John Lindsay, a member of the same team, was killed in a mountaineering accident in Cwm Lloer, above the eastern end of Llyn Ogwen. There was a considerable depth of snow that morning, and following a night of sub-zero temperatures there was plenty of ice. Isobel was out walking with her pet dog and in Cwm Lloer she met up with four other members of the Ogwen Valley team. They joined forces and began to climb to the ridge between Pen yr Ole Wen and Carnedd Dafydd. All were wearing crampons and carrying ice-axes and, finding two gullies in excellent condition, they split into two parties; Isobel, Jon Robinson and Barry Pinion to climb one gully and Robert Owen and Meirion Jones to tackle a second gully about 30 yards to the right. They did not rope up, and in fine crisp weather with very little wind they made good progress up straightforward climbs. When Isobel's group was about 100 feet from the top of the gully they came to a rock 'island' which they had to work their way round, and Isobel put her dog on a 10 foot lead which she looped to her wrist. Jon saw that her progress was being impeded by the dog, which was refusing to follow her, and he asked if she would like a top rope, to which she replied, "No, I'll be all right; the dog can manage". A lone climber, Peter Evan Butler, who had climbed the gully and was resting near the top, saw Isobel cutting large steps in the snow which he assumed were to enable the dog to get up the slope. As he continued to watch, he saw her give a couple of tugs on the lead, but still the dog refused to move. She then gave it a hefty tug and as she did so, her feet shot from under her and she fell past where her dog was standing. The lead went tight, the dog was pulled off its stance, and collided with her just as she appeared to be controlling her slide with her ice-axe. Isobel at once lost control and she and the dog fell 500 feet to the bottom of the gully. Robert Owen and Meirion Jones in the right-hand gully did not see what was happening, but alerted by the dog's yelp, they stopped climbing and saw Isobel and the dog sliding down the slope to the bottom of the gully. They immediately started to descend and 15 minutes later reached the spot where she lay. There was nothing they could do for her. She had suffered very severe head injuries and also had a deep lower abdominal wound caused by her ice-axe cutting the femoral artery. The dog was lying nearby with a fractured leg. OVMRO base at Bryn Poeth was informed of the accident by radio, and a helicopter from 'C' Flight arrived soon afterwards to airlift Isobel to Ysbyty Gwynedd where she was pronounced dead on arrival. Her death caused a deep sense of shock amongst Isobel's colleagues in the OVMRO, 'C' Flight and in the RAF Valley MRT which was exercising that day in the area.

30: A Sad Farewell

The stories in this book demonstrate that accidents can happen to all sorts of people for all sorts of reasons. Contrary to what the media might say, the annual toll of life on our mountains is not due entirely to casual walkers who are unaware of the dangers to be faced. Even coroners have sometimes made that misjudgement, as was the case after Black Easter when it was said that 'these mountains were invaded by an army of what I call novices ...'. Some of those who died that weekend were experienced alpinists, and as Lord Hunt has stated, 'accidents also happen to those of us who have enjoyed a life-time of experience as mountaineers', which is born out by the final story in this saga of mountain misadventures.

Sir Anthony Keith Rawlinson, KCB, aged 59, was a senior civil servant, and a very enthusiastic and experienced climber. He was the President of the Alpine Club, and had come to spend the weekend of 21–23 February 1986, at the *Pen-y-gwryd Hotel*. He was to be the guest speaker at the Annual Dinner of the Climbers' Club at the *Royal Victoria Hotel* in Llanberis on the Saturday evening. After having a chat with Chris Briggs he left the *Pen-y-gwryd* at 9.30am on Saturday, 22 February to walk, on his own, round the Snowdon Horseshoe. Soon after noon Sir Anthony left the summit of Crib Goch and walked along the ridge towards Snowdon. He was still walking alone, but there were a number of people both in front of him and following. It was a fine sunny day with no wind, ideal for walking, and the warmth of the sun had started to melt the snow which overlay ice; for the most part, however, there was a good deal of bare rock along the ridge. Nevertheless, Sir Anthony was wearing crampons.

Peter G E Ashman and Bryan Harley had walked up into Cwm Glas Uchaf from Blaen Nant in the Llanberis Pass, and had stopped for a rest by the side of Llyn Glas. They were looking up towards Crib Goch when they saw something which looked like a body fall from a point about half way along Crib Goch ridge, and land on the scree 1,000 feet below. Fearing the worst, Peter and Bryan made their way across to investigate. It took them 20 minutes to cover the $1/2$ mile from the lake to where the object had come to rest, and to their horror they saw what they had suspected — a body. The severity of the damage to his head left them in no doubt that he had been killed outright, and that there was absolutely nothing to be done for him. Another walker who had come up from Blaen Nant came across to join Peter and Bryan, and volunteered to return to the road and raise the alarm. Above on the ridge, few people realised what had happened and they could be seen making their way across, unaware of the tragedy which had occurred. One mountaineer on the ridge who had seen Sir Anthony falling was Ian Savage, an instructor at the Kent Mountain Centre in Llanberis, and he immediately went down to Pen-y-pass, where he raised the alarm.

At about 1pm, Sir Anthony's body was airlifted to Ysbyty Gwynedd in Bangor by a helicopter of 'C' Flight, which had picked up Dr H P Nicholson from the hospital on its way to Cwm Glas. On arrival at the accident site, Dr Nicholson examined the body and stated that Sir Anthony had suffered very severe fractures of the skull consistent with a fall from a great height, and that he was dead beyond any doubt. The body was examined in the casualty department at the hospital and Sir Anthony Rawlinson was pronounced 'dead on arrival' at 1.50pm.

Of all the people who were on the ridge when Sir Anthony fell, no one came forward who may have seen exactly what happened. The only evidence which might have been relevant was given at the inquest by D Wilson who had just left the summit of Crib Goch to traverse the ridge when he saw someone fall off the ridge about 200 yards in front of him. He did not see what had caused the man to fall, but in his opinion conditions underfoot were bad with soft melting snow on ice, and, 'in some parts there were snow cornices on the ridge. Instances occurred when people had to walk on these which was obviously dangerous, but the only way to progress along the ridge'.

Sir Anthony Rawlinson was the only President of the Alpine Club to die whilst holding office, and he was also the first President to die in a mountain accident.

*

The following story is included here as it illustrates that unsuitable footwear can easily result in tragedy. On 22 February 1988, 52-year-old John Henry Guinness from Dublin was walking with his wife Jennifer, his son Ian, and other friends. They had come over for a weekend-break and were staying at the *Imperial Hotel* in Llandudno. It was a relatively calm but overcast day with little or no wind, and the cloud base was about 2,500 feet. Above 2,300 feet there was an accumulation of snow and ice, some of which was extremely hard in places, calling for crampons and ice-axes. Conditions underfoot were described as hazardous, and although every one in the party was well-dressed for winter hill-walking, none of them had either crampons or an ice axe. John Guinness was wearing walking boots, but they were not suitable for walking in snow and ice conditions. They were very flexible which made it difficult to kick footholds in the snow. He was carrying a walking stick.

It was 10.45am when they set out along the Miners' Path from the Pen-y-pass car park, and they reached the summit of Snowdon at 12.45pm. Soon afterwards they started their descent down the zigzags, with one of the friends, John Gore-Grimes, in front. John Guinness was last but one, and his son Ian brought up the rear. It was 1.05pm when John Guinness, who had gone no more than 15 paces from the ridge, lost his footing on the icy path and was seen to slide, gathering speed as he did so, strike a rock, and then disappear into the mist about 45 feet down the slope. John Gore-Grimes continued down and reached John Guinness at 1.20pm. Other walkers who were nearby went down to Pen-y-pass to raise the alarm, while the rest of the party returned to the Bwlch Glas ridge and made their way off the mountain down the railway track to Llanberis. At 2.05pm, a helicopter from 'C' Flight picked up two members of the Llanberis MRT and at 2.15pm these two and the winchman were lowered close to where John Guinness lay. He had fallen some 700 feet and had sustained very severe head injuries; there was very little they could do for him. He was winched into the helicopter on a stretcher and flown to Ysbyty Gwynedd in Bangor where he was certified to be dead on arrival.

31: Leading Lights

Many people have played significant parts in the development of the MR service in Snowdonia, and in the course of this book I have tried to acknowledge their various contributions. There are others, such as chairmen and members of committees, whose work has gone almost unnoticed, yet is no less important for being unobtrusive. At the other end of the scale there are a few whose exploits shine like beacons in the ongoing story — men like A S Pigott who was instrumental in getting the MR Committee established, and Wilson Hey who fought his long campaign to get approval for the use of Morphia by MRTs. But it is the men 'at the sharp end' whose names are more likely to be etched in history, men like Flight-Lieutenant George Graham, the master of initiative and improvisation who in 1943 formed the first RAF MRT in North Wales with no official encouragement, funding or equipment from the Air Ministry. Then, in 1948, Chris Briggs came on the scene and began a personal commitment to help his fellow mountaineers in peril on the mountains, which lasted almost 30 years

Crib Goch from Crib-y-ddisgl.   [SNP]

until he retired from the NWMRA in September 1977.

The part played by Dr Ieuan Jones in the field of first-aid, and his innovative method of teaching this complex subject by means of tapes and slides, had a profound effect on the quality of casualty care throughout Britain and elsewhere, but sadly his contribution has not had the recognition it deserves.

In 1974, a young police officer called Clive Swombow, who was stationed at North Wales Police Headquarters at Colwyn Bay and has recently retired as a Detective Chief Inspector, was appointed Liaison Officer between the MR service and the North Wales Police. There was a meeting of minds between Tony Jones, who was secretary of the NWMRA, and Clive Swombow, and from the outset they worked closely together, especially in the sphere of radio communications, operational support and latterly Search Management. Clive has assisted Tony on lecture tours and courses in Iceland, the USA, and in Britain, and in 1980, he became Liaison Officer between North Wales Police and 'C' Flight. During the next 15 years he spent more than 500 hours flying in helicopters on training exercises or search and rescue operations. As the use of SAR helicopters increased, thereby considerably changing the scope and work of MRTs, much of the success in implementing the changes has been due to the close rapport and mutual co-operation between the NWMRA, North Wales Police, and 'C' Flight, and in this respect Clive Swombow's great enthusiasm and dedication to MR has played a very important part.

There are two other men each of whose commitment to MR exceeds 30 years, and one or other of them played leading roles in the incidents described in chapters 23–28. Both men began their involvement in rescue work in Snowdonia at much the same time in the 1960s. There are many people enjoying their lives today who owe everything to the qualities of compassion, skill and courage of one or other of these two men. Dr Anthony Stewart Gervais Jones, MBE, and John Ellis Roberts MBE need no introduction to any one who lives in, or frequently comes to, Snowdonia. However, they may not know the backgrounds of these two people who have been so closely involved in the voluntary MR scene for virtually all their working lives.

Although Tony Jones was born at Kasauli in India as a citizen of the United Kingdom on 20 July 1938, he was educated at 'Bishops' in Cape Town where he started MR work with the Cape Town section of the Mountain Club of South Africa at the age of 16 and later became a member of the 'Advanced Party' of the MRT. He obtained his BSc degree in 1961, and from 1963 to 1968 did a post-graduate course in Marine Sciences at the University College of Wales, Aberystwyth, where he obtained his PhD. While he was there, he started making regular visits to Ogwen Cottage where he assisted Ron James and his rescue team, joining the OVMRO when it was formed in 1965. In 1966 he was elected to the Committee of the OVMRO and the following year he was made a team leader. Later that year he was elected Chairman, a position he held until a break in 1990 — a stint of over a quarter of a century.

During this time, Tony became involved in the organisational and administrative side of MR in North Wales as well as developing and building up his own organisation in the Ogwen Valley. From 1975 to 1977 he was Treasurer of the NWMRA and represented the OVMRO on the Association until 1988. He also took on responsibilities for radio communications and helicopters, in which work he was greatly assisted by Clive Swombow. In 1977, he relinquished his position as Treasurer of the NWMRA and was elected Secretary - an appointment he still holds. His work did not end with the NWMRA, for in 1977 he was elected to membership of the MRC. He was Chairman of the Radio Sub-Committee from 1978 to 1988 and a member of the Medical Sub-Committee from 1983 to 1991. In 1988 Tony was elected vice-chairman of the MRC, a position he still held in 1995.

The list of courses and conferences Tony has attended, and certificates he has been awarded in connection with MR is a long and varied one and extends to South Africa, the USA, Eire and Ukraine (Crimea). Altogether he has been involved in over 760 search and rescue operations in South Africa, the UK, Norway, Austria, New Mexico and Washington State (USA).

He was elected President of SARDA (Wales) in 1991. He is a member of The Mountain Club of South Africa, The Climbers' Club and The Alpine Club. In 1993, Tony was the subject of the Television programme *This is Your Life*, a special honour in view of the fact that only a very small proportion of the people whose lives are put under the microscope on this programme are chosen from outside the entertainment profession. He was awarded the MBE in 1995 for services to MR. All he has achieved must be seen against an early setback in his life for, as a toddler, Tony contracted polio, and was unable to walk until he was 6 years old.

John Ellis Roberts was born in Chester on 6 August 1943, but his family home was in Blaenau Ffestiniog. His interest in mountaineering began when he was a member of his school Rambling Club. He joined the Air Training Corps and in 1959, the year he left school, he started working for the Duke of Edinburgh's Award. It was then that he first came into contact with the RAF Valley MRT, who gave him great encouragement and help. John chose MR as his Public Service commitment for the Award, and he took part in actual rescues with the Valley Team. In January 1961, whilst still only 17, he was assessed in MR for the Silver Award by Squadron Leader J R Sims, MBE, who was the Inspector of MR at the Air Ministry. In his report Sims wrote, 'I think he would be competent to take a leading part in a real rescue. I would not feel worried if he were to direct a rescue in which I was the casualty'. The following year John was assessed for the Gold Award and he was given charge of the RAF Valley MRT during a stretcher-lowering exercise on the Moelwyn Mountains. His assessor wrote, "the result was first class with Roberts handling both men and awkward situations with ease". He obtained both the Silver and Gold Awards.

In 1959, John obtained his first job as a draughtsman/site engineer with a large construction company engaged mainly with the Nuclear Power station at Trawsfynnydd. Then, in April 1966, he was appointed Engineering Assistant with Meirioneth Water Board based at Barmouth and in December of that year he joined The Snowdonia National Park as Head Warden of the Caernarfonshire and Denbighshire section of the Park, which covered 280 sq miles.

In 1961 John was a founder member and first Honorary Secretary of the Moelwyn Mountaineering Club, and he was also appointed Honorary Supervisor of Rescue Post No 43 at Blaenau Ffestiniog. The following year he was elected an Honorary member of the University College of North Wales

Clive Swombow   [C Swombow]

Mountaineering Club and in 1965 he joined The Climbers' Club and also the OVMRO. In 1966 he was awarded the British Mountain Guides Certificate by the BMC.

When Hamish McInnes established The Search and Rescue Dog Association in Scotland, John attended the second training course for handlers in Glencoe in January 1967, and he returned to Wales with two German Shepherd Dog pups from McInnes's SAR dogs — Rangi and Tiki. He became a committed SARDA handler, and when in 1971 the parent body was divided into autonomous associations in Scotland, Wales and England, John was the first Hon. Secretary of SARDA (Wales), a position he held until 1975. He represented the Association on the NWMRA from 1972–76.

In 1970 John resigned from the OVMRO to direct his energies into the formation and development of the Llanberis MRT of which he was a founder member. He has been the Honorary Equipment Officer of the team from its inception in 1971 and he has twice been Hon. Chairman, from 1976–79, and from 1981–83.

John was elected Secretary of the NWMRA in March 1973 at the same meeting of the Association at which Tony Jones was proposed as Treasurer. He held the position until March 1977 when he handed over to Tony. He has been a member

John Ellis Roberts   *[Nigel Hughes]*

of the MLTB for Wales since 1983, and in that year he was appointed a member of The Prince of Wales Committee.

John was awarded the MBE in 1988, for services to The Snowdonia National Park, which included his work as a warden and his participation in searches and rescues during the course of his work on the mountains over 27 years.

The combined knowledge and MR skill of Tony Jones and John Roberts is immense, and although they have not always taken the same view about controversial matters, and there has always been some rivalry between the two teams, they are inspired by the same purpose which is to save life and minimise pain and suffering to those who have had the misfortune to have an accident on the mountain.

Leaders without inspired and well-trained teams can achieve little, and tribute must be paid to the countless civilian volunteers who have committed themselves to the MR service in Snowdonia over so many years. To their number must be added the members of the North Wales Police who have manned the stations, notably in Bethesda and Llanberis and who have always been ready to go out with their local teams.

It remains to mention once again the tremendous part RAF Valley has played in the evolution of MR in Snowdonia. Not only was the first MRT in Snowdonia an RAF one, but since the end of the war, generations of volunteer members of

RAF Valley MRT have built up a fine reputation for selfless devotion to duty on the mountains by finding and rescuing many civilian victims of mountain accidents. It is true that operations to search for and rescue real casualties provide valuable training for the principal role of RAF MRTs, which is to find and rescue crashed aircrew, and that applies equally to the SAR helicopter crews.

The search and rescue work carried out by the Valley team over half a century has resulted in countless lives being saved both directly and indirectly - indirectly because of the invaluable advice and help given so readily to civilian MRTs, which enabled them to achieve such a high standard of efficiency. A succession of team leaders, many of them mentioned in this book, each holding the appointment for a three-year tour of duty, have played major parts in the narrative because of their enthusiastic help and co-operation with the civilian organisation. Sadly, in the Autumn of 1996, the RAF Valley MRT was disbanded due to Service economies, and all requests for assistance from the RAF are now made direct to the ARRC, Kinloss, who will direct the appropriate MRT to attend the incident. However, the burden of carrying out extensive searches and rescues without recourse to Valley, particularly in the OVMRO and Llanberis MRT areas, now falls on the civilian MRTs. They will rise to the challenge.

Dr A S G Jones   [Tony Jones]

32: Epilogue

When I was researching the stories for this book, a Brussels bureaucrat declared that 'There are no mountains in Britain', and I wondered if his navigation had failed him and he had somehow placed the British Isles in the Netherlands or Denmark. With so many of the foregoing stories still fresh in my mind, I thought I might send him a copy of *A Perilous Playground* when it was published, but on reflection I realised that it would be an empty gesture, and it is for the reader to decide whether the Brussels bureaucrat was right or not.

The real question is, where is the dividing line between a hill and a mountain? There is no clearly laid down height, although it is widely considered that anything over 2,000 feet is a mountain. However, if one is looking at it objectively there are other considerations such as climate. On the basis of height alone, there are many parts of the British Isles which are mountainous, though in good summer weather even the most inexperienced walkers can safely ascend them providing they keep to the well-beaten tracks. But since the majority of our mountains, including those of Snowdonia, are on the western sea-board and are therefore subject to sudden and severe changes in the weather, good summer days are the exception, and a fine, warm day may suddenly become cold, wet and windy with hill fog blotting out visibility. Looked at in the geomorphical sense, none of the mountainous land in Britain is strictly speaking composed of mountains, as are the Alps, so one has to look at it from a comparative point of view.

These stories of misadventures in Snowdonia clearly spell out how essential it is to possess basic mountain knowledge and to have the necessary equipment and adequate clothing for the time of year. It is also vital that a group, of whatever size, is properly led by someone with experience. To walk on high hills in bad weather if inexperienced is foolhardy and may well result in you putting not only your own life at risk, but also those of members of the search and rescue teams.

All who love mountains must learn to respect them and must learn the skills of mountain craft from the beginning. To be lost, injured, or even killed because of your incompetence or ignorance is an affront to human dignity; and in the event of death it is those who are left behind who pay the penalty.

One answer to a frequent question—- 'Why do you climb a mountain?' is, 'Because it's a challenge, and because of the physical and mental recreation it affords'. As Jack Longland, veteran Everest climber, once said,

> The walker or climber with experience and knowledge can stretch his powers to the full on a mountain day — not by silly notions of conquering a mountain whatever the condition of your own state of fitness — but by accurately gauging all you know against the task you have set yourself to do. And though you may hoodwink a tired referee at football when you are really offside, you can't cheat twenty degrees of frost at night on a windy mountain in a pair of shorts and with too few sweaters; and on steep snow and ice and rock you can't cheat the law of gravitation either.

Which just about sums it all up.

Bibliography

In collating the many stories and incidents in this book, I have explored and investigated many diverse sources of information. These include conversations with local historians and others with particular interest in, and knowledge of, Snowdonia, such as mountaineers who have at some time been involved in the mountain rescue scene since the end of the 1939–45 War. They are all listed under 'Acknowledgements'.

Much of my information, especially about events before the 1939–45 War has been obtained from books, journals, and newspapers which are listed below.

Abraham, George	*Rock Climbing in North Wales*, G P Abraham, 1906.
Abraham, A & Ashley, G D	*On Alpine Heights and British Crags*, Methuen & Co Ltd, 1919.
Alpine Club, The	*The Alpine Journal*, Longmans Green, various issues.
Angell, Shirley	*Pinnacle Club*, The Pinnacle Club, 1988.
Ashton, Steve	*Scrambles in Snowdonia*, Cicerone Press, 1980.
Benson, Claude E	*British Mountaineering*, George Routledge, 1909.
Birkett, Bill & Peascod, Bill	*Women Climbing*, A & C Black, 1989.
Borrow, George	*Wild Wales*, Collins, 1962.
BMC, The	*Mountaineering*, The BMC to 1956, 1947.
The Carnarvon and Denbigh Herald newspaper reports from the 19th century.	
Card, Frank	*Whensoever — 50 years of the RAF Mountain Rescue Service 1943-1993*, The Ernest Press, 1993.

Carr, H R C &   The Mountains of Snowdonia, Crosby Lockwood, 1948.
   Lister G A
Chamber's Journal, 7 May 1887.
Clark, R W &   Mountaineering in Britain, Phoenix House, 1957.
   Pyatt, E C
Climbers Club,   The Climbers Club Journal, The Climbers Club, 1898 et seq.
Condry, William   The Snowdonia National Park, Wm Collins & Co Sons, 1966.
Dean, Steve   Hands of a Climber, The Ernest Press, 1993.
Greene, Dr Raymond   Moments of Being, Heinemann, 1974.
Hankinson, Alan   The Mountain Men, Heinemann, 1977.
Hankinson, Alan   Geoffrey Winthrop Young, Hodder & Stoughton, 1995.
Hill, Vernon   A Scrapbook of Snowdonia, 1982.
Hoare, D L F   Snowdon — That Most Celebrated Hill, The Author, 1987.
Hunt, John   Everest, Hodder, 1953.
James, Ron   Rock Climbing in Wales, Constable & Co, 1970.
Johnson, Thomas   The Itinerary of a Botanist (Translation), 1907.
Jones, Dewi   'The Old Snowdon Guides', Transations, Caernarvonshire
                                Historical Society, late 1980s.
Lunn, Arnold   The Mountains of Youth, Eyre & Spottiswood, 1925.
Lunn, Arnold   Mountain Jubilee, Eyre & Spottiswood, 1943.
McKee, Alexander   The Golden Wreck, New English Library, 1977.
Maslen-Jones, Bob   Countdown to Rescue, The Ernest Press, 1993.
Moffat, Gwen   Space Below My Feet, Hodder & Stoughton, 1961.
Moffat, Gwen   Two Star Red, Hodder & Stoughton, 1964.
MRC, The   Mountain & Cave Rescue, The MRC, 1947.
MRC, The   Rescue, The MRC, et seq.
Ogwen Valley MRO   Silver Jubilee Newsletter, OVMRO, 1990.
Pen-y-gwryd Hotel   The Locked Book Visitors 1850s et seq.
Perrin, Jim   Menlove, The Ernest Press, 1993.
Pilley, Dorothy   Climbing Days, G Bell & Sons, 1935.
Poucher, W A   The Welsh Peaks, Constable & Co, 1983.
Rucksack Club, The   The Rucksack Club Journal, Rucksack Club Committee, 1907 et seq.
Smith, W P   Haskett   Climbing in the British Isles (facsimile reprint), The Ernest Press, 1986.
Smythe, Frank   Over Welsh Hills, Black, 1941.
Thomson, J M Archer   Climbing in the Ogwen District, Edward Arnold, 1910.
Williams, Rol   Three Stops to the Summit, Cyhoeddiadau Mai, 1990.
Wilson, Claude   Mountaineering, George Bell & Sons, 1893.
Wray, Fitzwater   The Visitors' Book, J M Dent & Sons, 1937.
Young, Geoffrey   Mountain Craft, Methuen & Co, 1920.
Winthrop Young, G W   Snowdon Biography, J M Dent & Sons, 1957.
   et al.